Contemporary Issues in Food Supply Chain Management

Jane Eastham, Luis Kluwe Aguiar

and Simon Thelwell

(G) Goodfellow Publishers Ltd

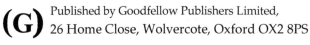 Published by Goodfellow Publishers Limited,
26 Home Close, Wolvercote, Oxford OX2 8PS

http://www.goodfellowpublishers.com

British Library Cataloguing in Publication Data: a catalogue record for this title is available from the British Library.

Library of Congress Catalog Card Number: on file.

ISBN: 978-1-911396-09-3

Copyright © Goodfellow Publishing Ltd, 2017

 Design and typesetting by P.K. McBride, www.macbride.org.uk

Cover design by Cylinder

Printed by Baker and Taylor, www.baker-taylor.com

Contents

Part 3: Case studies and new areas of research

List of tables

List of figures

List of authors

Luis Kluwe Aguiar, Agri-marketing, Harper Adams University Newport, UK.

Edward Andrew, Our Cow Molly, Cliffe House Farm, Dungworth, Sheffield.

Marcia De Barcellos, Universidade Federal do Rio Grande do Sul Porto Alegre, Rio Grande do Sul, Brazil

Andrew Beecham, Fresh produce production, Post-harvest technology; Horticultural production systems, Harper Adams University Newport, UK.

Jonathan C. Cooper, Sustainable Development and Environmental Science, Harper Adams University Newport, UK.

Anne Eastham, archaeologist, Welsh Royal Commission, retired. Freelance researcher, Pembrokeshire, Wales.

Jane Eastham, Supply chain management, Harper Adams University Newport, UK.

Lucy Gilbert, Harper Adams University Newport, UK.

Philippa Griffiths, Harper Adams University Newport, UK.

Renato Grillo,Center of Natural and Human Sciences - Federal University of ABC, Santo André, SP, Brazil.

Hao Liang, State Key laboratory of Chemical Resource Engineering, Beijing University of Chemical Technology, Beijing, P.R. China

Louise Manning, Food Integrity, Safety and Governance, Harper Adams University Newport, Shropshire, UK

Jim M Monaghan, Fresh produce production; Post harvest technology; Horticultural production systems Harper Adams University Newport, UK.

Gabrielle Parkes, Economics and Tourism, Harper Adams University Newport, UK

Natalia Rohenkohl do Canto, Universidade Federal do Rio Grande do Sul Porto Alegre, Rio Grande do Sul, Brazil

Andy Swinscoe, Courtyard Dairy Unit 2, Settle, Newport, UK.

Simon Thelwell, Supply chain management, Harper Adams University,Newport, UK.

Frank VrieseKoop, Food Science, Harper Adams University, Newport, UK.

Yongqin Wei, State Key laboratory of Chemical Resource Engineering, Beijing University of Chemical Technology, Beijing, P.R. China

Preface

We live in a globalised world, however much the Brexiteers and Trump voters wish it were not so. Though that's hard to see on the food front as we concentrate on the daily job of feeding ourselves and our families—trying to eat healthily, safely and with pleasure. Yet every day we eat this globalised complexity. The most modestly stocked food cupboard and fridge will have foods that come from the four corners of the earth and will have passed through the hands of the giant corporations at the apex of the industrialised food system—the few companies (fewer and more gigantic by the year) who have near total control over the trading of seeds and grains, bioengineering reseach and the production of meat, grains, oils, etc. They're there in our kitchens: the ready meals and ready to pour sauces, as well as the staples: sugar, corn and wheat flour, vegetable oil, potatoes, salt, beans, tuna, ketchup, cola, curry powder...

In my early days as a food journalist I wrote a column called Food Biz for an American food magazine. I monitored all the business media for stories about the food industry in the *Economist, FT, Business Week, Wall St Journal, Forbes*, etc, etc. That was at the urging of my financial journalist husband, sceptical of me making food the focus of my journalism. If you're going to do it, he said, then follow the money. It was good advice and my Food Biz years were an education. Writing the column gave living, day-by-day substance to what I'd seen in my early research into why the pesticide aldicarb (now banned in the EU and USA) was being used on the potatoes I was feeding my baby and why it was getting into the water supply where I was living. It showed me the power of industrial food production as a money-making enterprise first and last.

Over the past thirty-five years the increasingly concentrated industrialized food system has not only become immensely profitable but has also influenced what we eat by pushing to the margins the reality of food as health, food as culture, food as social glue, food as pleasure. But we need to have those discussions because food is not just another commodity. How it's produced, traded, shopped for, cooked and eaten shapes our world... and us. As this book so brilliantly illustrates.

Sheila Dillon, presenter of BBC Radio 4's The Food Programme

Part 1
The supply chain – problems and dilemmas

1 Defining Food and the Implications for Food Supply Chains

Jane Eastham

Introduction

The objective of this book is to offer students and academics food for thought. It is designed to examine issues facing the food supply chain, including food supply and security. It considers supply security in terms of food availability, traceability, the delivery of a sustainable diet, technological changes and the impact of current governance structures. The text revolves around the central theme of supply chains and the management of supply, but notes that a safe, effective food supply system is fraught with complexities, dichotomies and paradoxes.

For instance, the need to attain and deliver safe food may have implications in terms of food waste. Food waste may be an input to ensure sustainable sources of energy, but there is also a paradox between the supply of fuel and the supply of food, where there is increasing competition between the uses of land resources – resources that are equally important for the productivity of other industrial sectors. Within this book, we examine but some of these issues and attempt to highlight to the reader the level of interconnectivity and tensions in the delivery of food security and economic, social and environmental sustainability and the provision of safe and nutritious diets.

The major issue is how one manages food supply when faced with a product which is highly perishable and consequently has a high potential of wastage, and where there are long lead times between the decision to produce the product and delivery to market. Food integrity is also at risk, where the relatively low margins of the sector may encourage stakeholders to practice opportunistic and sometimes malevolent action.

This chapter broadly considers the complexity of the issues affecting food and food availability and how the emergent governance of the supply chain has impacted upon the distribution of net margins; a consequence of the distribution of power within the supply chain.

Food glorious food: Why is food different ?

Those involved in the distribution of sufficient safe nutritious food to populations are faced with greater levels of risk and less control over the volumes they produce in relation to demand than other industrial sectors. Risks experienced by the food supply sectors are both natural and contrived. Climate, weather and other natural phenomena can have a major impact on the volume of production, whilst the perishability of products may result in a lack of availability between harvests. Volumes produced may also be inflated or depressed as a consequence of speculation, both by farmers and other businesses either within or without the food sector, and/or by government intervention.

Whilst many influences will have a negative impact on margins within the food supply chain, it is also worth noting that nutritious food is central to human endeavour. The failure to deliver a nutritious diet can have enduring impact on the wider economy and the performance of other industry sectors.

■ Delivering the food

Food is grown in extensive and intensive farming systems, in domestic gardens, hedgerows and with limited or no human intervention at all. Yet the availability of sufficient quantities of food to feed a population is subject to the variability in conditions apposite for food production, as well as to the effective delivery to consumers. The challenge for the sustainable supply chain revolves around the management of supply and demand. In practice, for the farmer, this requires the balancing of volume and price; ensuring safe practice in the growing of products, whilst at the same time optimising value. For the distribution sector, the challenge is to ensure that food reaches food retailers in the condition in which nutritious safe food can be sold to the consumer.

The assurance of safe, nutritious food requires the monitoring of practices throughout the supply; a challenge exacerbated in the context of commodities with a short shelf-life and low margins. This requires that all practices in all tiers within the supply chain be monitored. In order to ensure that such monitoring occurs, food has become one of the most heavily regulated sectors; the legal responsibility in the UK for which, so-called 'due diligence', is in the hands of retailers. The need for regulation and inspections is made more critical with the growth of ready and quick fix meal solutions and the growing criticality of temperature controlled storage and transportation. Additional processing and the costs of maintaining chilled or frozen supply chains temperatures have constrained margins still further.

The most critical aspect of managing temperature is to ensure against the contamination by micro-organisms, which can be pathogenic and/or result in food spoilage and reduce shelf life. However, other micro-organic contamination, such as Bovine Spongiform Encephalopathy (BSC), are zoonotic and have resulted in variant Creutzfeldt-Jakob Disease (vCJD) and as a consequence are damaging to farm incomes, and consumers' health. Even non-zoonotic diseases such as foot and mouth, particularly when addressed through mass slaughtering policy, undermine financial returns of farmers. The challenges of managing and monitoring micro-organic contamination are exacerbated in the context of extended food supply chains.

The emergence of extended and complex elongated supply chains means that consumers are no longer aware of provenance, and furthermore there are greater issues of traceability, greater potential for opportunistic and malevolent behaviour and malpractice, and thus a greater need to monitor the supply chain, to ensure nutritional food safety and avoid adverse economic consequences. For some it is not simply the issue of the risk in elongated supply chains, it is also an issue of diet (see Griffiths in Chapter 15). Through the disconnection of the consumer from the producer, consumers lack understanding of how food is produced and processed. In conjunction with the purported decline in culinary expertise in western countries, the consumer has become unable to influence the food they consume, in terms of cost, variety in diet and nutritional value.

■ Back to beginnings

For many millennia, humans were hunters and gatherers, served through a short supply chain with generally a diverse diet that supplied adequate nutrition (Lindeberg, 2012). Consumption was not simply immediate, which reduced the potential for pathogenic contamination of food products, but also offered greater nutritious balance and fueled further collection of food. When pastoral and agricultural communities emerged some 7-10 thousand years ago, increased yields facilitated the development of more complex, static societal infrastructures. However, in nutritional terms, the greater reliance on grain resulted in poorer diet with a degeneration of human health (Pollard, 2008) as measured by the smaller stature of early agriculturalists as compared with hunter-gatherers (Larsen, 2015). The fixed nature of the agricultural populations and, to a lesser extent pastoral communities, presented a challenge of assuring continuity of supply in the context of seasonality and the need to develop storage and preservation techniques.

Controlled intervention in the production of food might feed a larger population, but ensuring year-long availability and protecting against wastage and nutrient loss through bacterial and enzyme activity, presented a challenge.

The problem was exacerbated where yields varied considerably from year to year. Access to early written documentation found in religious texts shows the need to grow excess produce to ensure continual availability. Preservation techniques were developed, and some of the early techniques included drying and fermentation to allow easy storage. We note in Genesis 41 v 1-53, an early example of managing supply and demand in this vein, where Joseph is put in charge of ensuring sufficient storage of grain to feed Egypt during the seven lean years.

Whilst the Pharaoh had advance notice as to future availability of food supply, normally farmers are not so divinely informed and their ability to match demand and supply to ensure sufficient food and the maximisation of returns is dependent upon a whole series of interconnecting factors beyond their control. Weather conditions, pests and disease can have an impact on the total volume produced, and thus the price paid to farmers, and can vary across regions, countries and continents. How much food should be produced and indeed the amount of land to put over to the production of a crop is not only determined by local but regional, continent and global conditions. The balancing of food production to ensure farm prices and food availability is thus a complex activity. Unlike other commodities, identifying the volume that is required involves planning in advance, based on imperfect information on demand. This is a function of respective lead-times for food commodities; from the time of sowing or insemination through to consumption. For wheat, the lead-time from sowing averages at around 9 months, whilst pork, with current state of the art genetic interventions, will be ready for market in around 4.5 months, and so on. Were demand or climatic conditions to change, there must be a delay before the farmer can respond. In pig farming, for instance, this has a name – the 'cobweb effect'.

■ The distinctiveness of food as a financial commodity

The problem of ensuring sufficient stock without deflating price has exercised economists and engineers over time (Eastham, 1939; Carter and Revoredo-Giha, 2009). In modern commodity markets the situation is distinctive from the biblical illustration above.

In capitalist economies there is a distinction between stocks kept to ensure availability and those stocks used in a speculative capacity, i.e. the commoditisation of the primary food product. The discrimination between stocks as, what has been described as 'working capital'. that is stocks to ensure that food is available for consumption and stocks as 'liquid capital', which are food stocks in excess of demand between harvests, leads us to recognise that whilst storage does much to stabilise supply and price, food is also used in a speculative capacity (Eastham, 1939:105; Carter and Revoredo-Giha, 2009:4). Where there are significant levels of liquid capital through speculation, price inflations can occur that are unrelated to the issue of demand and supply. Index type investments and significant flows of money into commodity futures signal to speculators that others have insider knowledge with respect to potential demand or supply, and this signal results in their revision of the future value of the commodity and drives the price upwards (Irwin *et al.*, 2009). Index type investments are investments which are linked to the underlying market index of the food commodity.

These types of investment have been seen by some to contribute to the advent of price bubbles, as seen in the inflated food prices in 2008 to 2013. Price inflations are followed by price deflation (Carter and Revoredo-Giha, 2009). This is by no means the only explanation of commodity price increases, although whatever the cause there is a net impact on the consumption of a healthy diet by the poorer members of the society. Alternative causes are said to range from the bio-fuels policy, jumps in input costs due to energy price shocks, reduced farm subsidies in Europe, exchange rate movements, growth in demand in developing countries, the impact of global warming, climatic changes on crop production and indeed the dominance and opportunistic behaviour of downstream players, e.g. UK multiple retailers (Sumner, 2009), but these tend to relate more to explanations of price rises rather than bubbles.

While bubbles have an impact on the access to affordable food by poorer consumers, over the longer term there can be a negative impact on farm income. Where farmers respond to initial price rises by investing, with a view to expand production and profit from price increases, they risk financial loss where prices subsequently deflate. As such this may have an impact on both the sustainability of farm prices and indeed food security. The introduction of market led pricing and the removal of government financial support of farming activity, under the current WTO policy of market liberalisation, makes farmers more vulnerable to price shocks. It places a question mark over the current policy of market liberalisation, in contrast to government interventions that are designed to manage both the price paid to farmers and retail prices.

■ Competition for land and food resources

Challenges to ensure food security are also affected by fossil fuel depletion and the growing competition over land resources. Agricultural land resources are now being deployed for the production of bio-fuel from corn, soy, rape, sugar cane, palm oil, and jatropha; the deployment of which is incentivized by policy makers across the developed world and by transnational corporations seeking cash crops. Such measures may exacerbate this issue of food poverty, particularly in the context of population growth with the predicted 9.6 billion people by 2050, but it does offer farmers alternative buyers and the possibility of higher prices.

Alternative uses of agricultural land have heightened the perceived inadequacy of food resources, although this is a contested position with counterclaims that current levels of production are sufficient for the delivery of a nutritious diet to current population levels. The problem is held to be rather on of effective distribution (Tomlinson, 2013).

■ Food as a status symbol and the impact on the management of supply

Food not only fuels human health and economic productivity, it has also a symbolic identity, demonstrating affluence, status and roles in society. With growing affluence in BRIC countries (Brazil, Russia, India and China) and in MINT countries (Mexico, Indonesia, Nigeria and Turkey), there is increased pressure on land resources and food production systems as a consequence of a growing middle class and the switch to more affluent diets (Weinzettel *et al.*, 2013).

In societies where there is little social stratification, food is about availability and the elaboration of common staples. In societies with institutionalised forms of social ranking, the attribution of specific status to food evolves as well (Van de Veen, 2003). The issue of the social standing of food is by no means new, and what is of interest is that unlike many symbols of status, the status attributed to a food product can vary over time.

Take for instance the humble oyster, which has had a checkered history. A treasured inclusion to any Roman table and banquet, (Gunther, 1987) they later became a food for the poor, and were used to eke out other protein sources, as found in dishes such as oyster and beef pie, before reaching a more elevated status in more recent European societies (Miracle and Milner, 2002).

Others such as Levi-Strauss have explored the issue of the relative status of how food was cooked, for instance in the case of meat, whether it was stewed, braised, or roasted had implications on the both the social standing of the consumer and the poignancy of the occasion (Levi-Strauss, 1964). In terms of supply and balance of carcass, it is important to note that cuts of meat appropriate for roasting form a smaller proportion of the carcass that those for a prolonged cooking process as found in stews. The growing affluence of societies can increase demand for more tender cuts of meat, requires increased production of livestock, a greater demand for land and a greater impact on the environment.

Thus food is distinctive from other products as a consequence of issues of perishability, shelf life and the need for continual supply, both in terms of the balancing of supply and demand, due to pre-and post-harvest conditions. For the consumer, it is important both for health and social standing. It also, along with fuel, is an important factor in the creation of healthy economies. Increased and changing demand for food, coupled with the emergent non-fossil fuel industry, creates both increasing pressure on land resources as well as challenges for the supply chain. In this next section, we will be primarily examining the supply chain, with the view to understanding the structure, but also how some of the dynamics of the relationships have implicatio ns for food security and the sustainability of food supply.

Supply chain implications: Mapping out the UK supply chain

So, what is the current infrastructure, can this deliver a sustainable food supply chain, and what are the management challenges?

The first stop is the farmer and, in this instance, the UK farmer. The globalisation of the food supply chain is on the one hand a threat to UK farm income, with consequences for the availability of nutritious safe food and sustainable food sources. The increasing globalisation of the market. as promoted through the direct influence of the Uruguay round of General Agreement of Tariff and Trade (GATT) talks, has forced down food prices and wrought. or at least contributed to. the decline in the number of UK farmers. This is a consequence of greater number of alternative suppliers from around the world, which presents retail buyers with more bargaining power and greater leverage over indigenous food producers. Following the results of the 2016 USA presidential election, and the results of the UK referendum with respect to EU membership, circumstances may change.

Access to global sources has been enabled through foreign direct investment by transnational corporations(TNCs), who have been an important source of external private capital for less developed countries (Kurtish-Kastrati, 2013). This, with a particular emphasis on investment in cash crops, had enabled economic development through the introduction of jobs, technology etc. On the other hand, it has been suggested that the major beneficiaries are the TNCs who have enhanced their profitability through a process known as transfer pricing (Arezki *et al.*,2013) a mechanism that allows for tax avoidance in host countries. This is particularly so where TNCs operate their head office functions in developed countries such as those in the EU. Seventy three percent of all TNCs are based in economic regions such as EU, Japan and the US (Dobb *et al.*, 2013).

The growth of TNCs has increased the levels of concentration throughout the supply chain. Figures given by the Oxford Farming Conference (2012) suggested that there was considerable concentration within the sector: four companies account for 75% of global grain trade, 10 companies over 40% of global retail, seven companies control virtually all the fertilizer supply, five companies 68% of agrochemicals, four companies control over 54% of the farm machinery sector, and four companies control over 50% of propriety seeds, circumstances which have been exacerbated through transfer pricing.

High levels of concentration have implications for the availability of products and the revenues of farmers, who have few opportunities to switch suppliers or buyers (Eastham, 2014). The persistent problem of pre- and post-harvest perishability offers buyers and sellers the occasion for opportunistic behaviour, in that they take advantage of the dependency of suppliers in their negotiations of terms, conditions and price.

In the UK, the four top retailers hold over 70% of market share, and consequently are able to influence and control prices paid to farmers and processors, a problem exacerbated, as on the global stage, by the fragmented nature of farming. This means that farmers are heavily dependent upon the nationally based agents of the transnational agrochemical and other farm input companies and on the retail buyers. The problem is increased where farmers have, in productionist or indeed post-productionist farming systems, invested extensively in equipment and facilities.

Farming by its nature requires considerable investment, but problems are augmented, as indeed are the costs of production, where farmers are required to invest in new procedures to retain their buyer's business. Consistently, with the policy drive to attain more from land, input costs have increased with hybrid seeds, increased mechanisation and animal genetics, potentially increasing their dependency on suppliers, an aspect by no means mitigated by the introduction of alternative technologies, such as precision farming and mechatronics, as promoted in initiatives such as the Agri-Tech strategy (Burton and Wilson, 2012).

The examination of market power within food supply chains has been represented by the image in Figure 1.1, which depicts a large number of farmers who supply into a diminishing number of buyers who supply to a large number of end consumers. Market power can be defined as the ability to affect prices – to set customer prices above competitive levels (seller power) and/or to set supplier prices below competitive levels (buyer power). The ability to affect prices is seen to be a consequence of the respective level of control that each exchange party holds over the resources critical to the other (Cox et al., 2001). Relative criticality is measured through facets such as strategic and operational importance, that is to say, the respective contribution to core competence and inimitability, search costs information impactedness, availability of substitutes and alternative suppliers, and levels of contestation within their respective market places. With many suppliers, and here we have only identified EU farmers, the reality is that retail buyers are able to switch and draw upon suppliers globally. Fear of delisting makes them still more vulnerable to further attrition of power and prices.

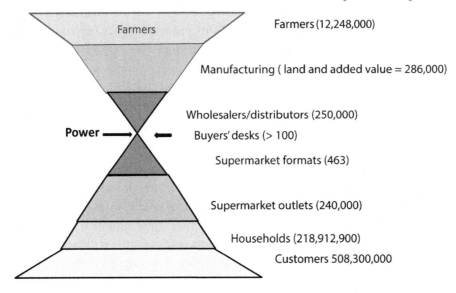

Figure 1.1 : European levels of concentration throughout the food supply chain

Figure 1.2 shows that similar power imbalances are seen in the UK and not are only there uneven levels of concentration of businesses throughout the supply chain but also the unevenness in the distribution of gross value added. GVA gained by retailers stands at over £26 bn, some three times greater than that generated in the farming community.

■ The UK farming sector

In the UK, the term agriculture includes: horticulture, including fruit, vegetable and flower production; cereals and oil seeds; dairy; livestock; and arable each of which have suffered as a consequence of the globalisation of food supply. The farming industry experienced a 50% decline in numbers of farms between 2003 and 2015. This is a function of low succession levels, business failures and consolidation within the sector (Vidal, 2003; DEFRA, 2016). The sector remains one of the most fragmented within the UK food supply chain with 212,000 farms by 2015 (DEFRA, 2016). Nevertheless, agriculture remains an important economic activity with a gross added value of £8.8bn, supporting circa 478,000 farmers/employees in 2015. Yet an examination of data published by the Department of Environment Food and Rural Affairs (DEFRA) over the last decade shows a long term overall decline in those who draw their income from farming activities.

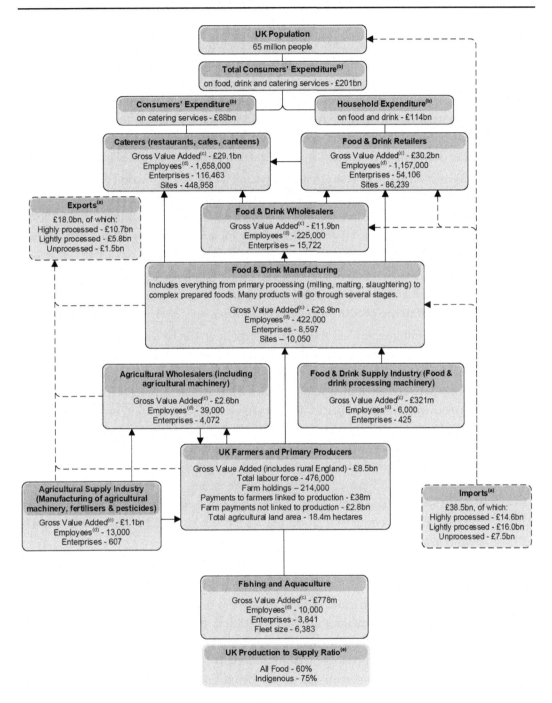

Figure 1.2: DEFRA, 2016 UK supply structure, adapted with permission from DEFRA, 2016

It is notable that GVA was up from £5.115 billion in 2006, when average net farm incomes were around £20,600. Average net farm incomes have risen also during the interim period to £30,900, in 2011, although a 12% drop in the Single Farm Payment had reduced the sum received in 2013. There is little evidence that the replacement of the Single Farm Payment with the Basic Payment Scheme will in any real way halt or stem this trend. Some of the highest incomes have been those of cereal farmers, and although farm gate prices have risen as consequence of the deflation of the pound in 2016, the real impact of Brexit is as yet unknown.

Whilst farm prices rose after 2008, perhaps as much a function of poor weather conditions as the shift towards index linked investments following the financial crisis of 2008, and prices for wheat continued to rise up until 2012/2013 (Piesse and Thirtle, 2009), recent predictions show incomes returning to pre-2011 figures (DEFRA, 2014).

There are suggestions that returns on livestock may be more sustainable, where alternative markets for both poultry and pig meat develop as a consequence of the growing affluence of BRIC and MINT countries.

One farming sector has been particularly hit in the UK, that of the dairy sector, where average incomes have fallen from £76,375 in 2013/14 to an estimated £45,500 in 2016. Much of this can be ascribed to declines in farm prices, which have frequently between attributed to price wars within the retail sector (Eastham, 2014). Coupled with low farm prices, farmers have experienced significant increases in costs of production related to their reliance on composite feed, and labour saving technologies, which has resulted in many exiting the sector, and a shift towards larger scale dairy units. Prices did rise steadily between 2009 and 2013, with a peak average of 31.7 pence per litre, but more recently the market has seen a rapid descent in farm gate milk prices, where the price per litre was often lower than the cost of production; a situation that can also be linked to the removal of milk quotas in the EU.

■ Changes to the agricultural sector

Whether the financial vulnerability of farmers presents a risk to food security is in debate. UK policy makers are concerned that future food security is contingent upon self-sufficiency and much of their policy is now driven by the need to increase efficiency and food production both nationally, international and globally. This agenda is feared by some to be to the benefit of mainstream agribusinesses in whose interest it is to expand production volume, albeit using less petrochemical inputs, with little consideration in the nutritious value of the food produced (Griffiths, 2016). This is the same discourse that drove the 'green revolution', a strategy supported by state intervention in the UK and elsewhere from the 1960s.

In this era, increases in food production, were driven by the applications of petro-chemicals in the form of pesticides and fertilisers, coupled with plant breeding and water management (Gardner, 1996). The emphasis on 'productionist' methods continued, supported in Europe through the Common Agricultural policy, until into the late 1980s when there was a call for more environmentally friendly production methods and a greater emphasis on extensification (Muirhead and Almas, 2012). By the end of the 1980s, agriculture in the productionist form was seen as environmentally degrading and unsustainable.

New alternative technologies have been introduced to reduce the use of petro-chemicals in farming sectors, and in an era described as 'neo-productionist'(Evans *et al.*, 2002), these have been promoted through such strategies as the Food Strategy for Wales (2010) and the Agri-Tech strategy in England. Policy makers are, however, uneasy as to the limited adoption of agri-tech initiatives. Suggestions are that farmers are reluctant to invest in new technologies where they perceive little of evidence of sufficient financial returns to cover their inputs, and where the increased investment results in a greater lock-in to buyers or supplier (Gebrezgabher *et al.*, 2015; Howley *et al.*, 2015); a particular risk when faced with the imbalanced power dynamics within the supply chain.

The UK retail and food service sectors

The two sectors, retail and food service, hold a significant proportion of the gross value of the food supply chain with a combined gross value of £59.3 bn in 2015 (see Figure 1.2), which is up 20% from £51.3 bn. in 2012. The number of enterprises across the two sectors amounts to 170,569, with approximately two-thirds of the total operating in the catering sector.

■ Mainstream retail stores

Whilst the catering sector is relatively highly fragmented, food retail is characterised by a number of very large key players such as Tesco, Asda, Sainsburys' and Morrison's, and a large range of smaller specialist operators in permanent sites, markets or online. In retail, these four key players dominate the hypermarket/supermarket format holding 75% of the market, of which the largest, Tesco, holds over 30% of the market share across different formats including hyper stores, superstores, convenience stores and on line delivery (IGD, 2016). The apparent fragmentation, as suggested by the larger number of enterprises, is a consequence of the continued development of small specialised retailers, both as extensions from farm enterprises as well as stand-alone operations.

Table 1.1: Types of format in the retail sector

Type and size	Product range	Types of labels	Location	Market share %age change		
				2008	2015	2020
Superstores and hypermarkets Over 2500 sq ft	Full range of food and non food SKU, over 30,000	Manufacturers and private labels	Out of town and city centres	45.83	40.4	34.7
Small supermarkets 3000-25,000 sq ft	Less than 30,000 SKU	Manufacturers and private labels	Central towns Motorway service stations	21.83	20	17.8
Convenience Less than 3000 sq ft	Sells minimum of 7 convenience categories, e.g. milk, bread,	Manufacturers and private labels (e.g. SPAR and other symbol groups)	Towns, suburbs, forecourts Symbol	19.68	21.2	22.2
Discounters	Limited range of stock – circa 3000 SKU	Largely private and exclusive labels	Towns Outskirts of towns	3.59	7.2	11

The history of emergence of the current retail structure goes back to the removal of the recommended retail price index in the 1960s, when retail prices ceased to be set by the food manufacturer. From the 1950s, when retail chains (i.e. those of more than 10 outlets) represented 22% of the market, by 1971 the figures had risen to over 44%, and have steadily increased over subsequent years (Wrigley, 1987; Clark, 2000). Moves by consumers to weekly shops driven by emergent role of working women and the growth in car ownership, weakened the monopoly of local grocery businesses (Hollingsworth, 2004). By the end of the 1990s more than 60% of the market share was held by the top four retailers who consolidated their position through the introduction of their own channels of distribution, thereby shifting their business away from the traditional wholesale sector (Shaw and Gibbs, 1995; Fernie *et al.*, 2014). To a large extent the development of a more cost effective delivery format to the consumer was inevitable, due to the low margins associated with food. By increasing their economies of scale, major retailers were able to cut prices on key products, reducing margins further to between 2-8%, with the net effect of forcing smaller retailers out of the market. This presented a new obstacle to the access of certain communities to nutritious food. The location of out of town supermarkets resulted in what has been described as 'food deserts' for families who had limited access to transport (Lang and Caraher, 1998). This became less of an issue more recently with consumers switching away from large weekly shopping to convenience shops and discount stores and more frequent purchases, both of which are located in more central venues. This trend has been particularly notable since the downturn in the economy post 2008.

■ The larger retailers' strategies in maintaining market share

Since the downturn in the economy there have been a number of shifts in retailers' strategies. These have included the development of alternative formats, a reassessment of pricing strategies and increased new product development amongst others.

Development of new formats

Until 2008, over 67% of food sales took place through the tills of hypermarkets, super stores and supermarkets. UK shoppers tended to remain loyal to individual retailers and, more importantly, were likely to undertake one large weekly shop. Since 2008 shoppers have spread their spending across the range variety of grocery channels. IGD figures in 2014 showed that 95% of shoppers used at least two channels, and 70% of them used a combination of supermarkets and convenience stores. In Table 1.2, it becomes evident that major retailers, recognising changes in shopping trends, have sought to extend their offering across channels. Waitrose, Asda and Tesco now operate in the convenience sector, which none the less is still dominated by independents and symbol groups.

It is notable in Table 1.2 that whilst there has been limited increase in sales, market share of the seven largest retailers operating supermarkets and hypermarkets have decreased only slightly over the period from 2009 to the present day, a consequence perhaps of the success of the strategic changes made. Each of the major seven, and particularly those with most to lose, i.e. Tesco, Sainsbury's, Morrison's, and Asda, have put in place strategies to attempt to retain market share. Key strategies have included pricing/promotional strategies and increased investment in new products in the processed food categories.

Revisiting their pricing strategies

Changes wrought by the economic crisis also included retail price strategies and levels of new product launches. In the context of retail price strategies, up to the 2010 there were two distinct types EDLP (Every Day Low Pricing) and Hi-Lo (high background – low promotion). Discount retailers such as Aldi and Lidl used Every Day Low Price strategies, as whilst non discounters such as Asda, Tesco, Waitrose, M & S, Sainsbury's and Morrison's variously used a mixture of EDLP and Hi-Lo, with particular emphasis on promotional strategies such as buy one get one free (BOGOF).

In an effort to maintain their market position, it is evident that pricing strategies have tended to converge, with a clear shift towards minimising retail prices. Retailers have put pressure on prices paid to suppliers but their shift away from promotional multiple buys could, in contrast, allow suppliers to improve margins. Multiple buys are known to distort demand, which has repercussions for the prediction of demand for suppliers and each stage of the upstream supply chain.

Table 1.2: The major UK retailers. Extracted from multiple IGD sources 2016

	Turnover (mn)		Format	Turnover per format %		Number of stores		Market share total %	
	2009	2015		2009	2015	2009	2015	2009	2015
Morrison's	15,410.00	15,966.73	Superstore Convenience Online	100 (N/A) (N/A)	98.6 0.58 0.78	425 0	498 5	11.5	10.8
Sainsbury	19,963.74	23199.00	Superstore Hypermarket Convenience Food discount Online	83.38 9.6 4.46 2.6	72.73 12.12 9.97 0.4 4.98	509 28 335 N/A	523 74 707 N/A	16.3	16.3
Tesco	39,963.68	42,816.6	Superstores Hyper markets Convenience Online	2306/na	479 1600 5 dark stores	1643 634 190	2645 655 252	30.6	28.2
Asda	19,865.40	22,548.95	Superstore Hypermarket Online General Convenience	84.19 11.11 2.75 1.96 0	81.86 10.17 5.9 1.95 0.05	318 29 0 24 0	538 32 0 33 18	17.0	15.6
Waitrose	4,317.19	6,080.84	Superstore/ supermarket Hypermarket Convenience Online	95.66 180.03 6.900 0	86.80 505 189.1 307	214 5 4	278 5 62	3.8	5.2
M&S	9346.7	10.720.34	Dept store Convenience (exclu. food hall) Food Hall	66.12 33.88	58.6 41.80	383 346 294	381 384 294	3.9	3.59
Cooper-ative	10,154.37	9,253.00	Superstores Convenience Other non-grocery Drugstore and pharmacies	46.14 24.5 22.02 7.34	38.19 34 27.81 0	1017 1966 N/A 790	626 2176 N/A 0	7.7	6.3
Aldi	2150	8392.99	Discount store	100	100	410	612	2.9	6.1
Lidl	2124	4680	Discount store	100	100	500	630		4.4.

This level of unpredictability can cause suppliers at each tier to overproduce causing what is known as the 'bullwhip effect'. This describes the effect of the distortion of information transferred in the form of orders to upstream players. With limited information as to the buyers' sales strategy, their inventory levels or other facets such as their promotional activity, upstream members can be misled in their inventory and production decisions and where the variance of orders may be larger than that of sales. The distortion tends to increase as one moves upstream – a considerable problem where products are costly to store and have a relatively short shelf life (Paik and Bagchi, 2007).

Table 1.3: Retail pricing strategies

	Upto 2010	**Since 2010**
Asda	EDLP	EDLP
Tesco	Mixture of Hi-lo, discounting and EDLP	Finding ways to cut prices by reducing stock keeping units
Sainsburys	Hi-lo	Phasing out multiple buys
Morrisons	Mixture of Hi-lo, discounting and EDLP	EDLP
Waitrose	Mixture of Hi-lo, discounting and EDLP	Mixture of Hi-lo, discounting and EDLP
M&S	Mixture of Hi-lo, discounting and EDLP	Mixture of Hi-lo, discounting and EDLP
Iceland	Hi-low	Hi-Low
Aldi	EDLP	EDLP
Lidl	EDLP	ELDP

The development of new products

The use of private label products by retailers as a competitive strategy has been prevalent since the 1960s, when it was used as a mechanism to further redress the power imbalance placed on them by the recommended retail price index. Since the 1960s, total sales have risen from 10% in 1965 to 27% by 1984, (West, 1988; Harris and Ogbonna, 2001). Since 1990 the percentage has been relatively constant at circa 50% (Martin, 1999; Mintel, 2014; Nielsen, 2014). As the percentage share of private own label has grown, average operating and net margins within the food manufacturing sector have declined (Morelli, 1997).

Across the retail sectors (including foodservice) 1000s of new products are launched each quarter; these can be significant innovations or simply rebranding. Waitrose claimed to have launched 4,900 new own label products in 2014 (John Lewis Partnership, 2015). Many of their new products were home meal solutions or ready meals. Whilst this has arguably offered a growth opportunity for manufacturers, the costs of innovation would appear to be passed on largely, if not predominantly, to the manufacturer, with little security of continued returns from their investment. Retail ownership of the own label product specification means that most manufacturers risk being delisted at any time, where cheaper suppliers are found.

The development of own brands has thus added to the power imbalance between retailers and manufacturers, and average net margins for manufacturers have declined from around 12% in the 1960s to 8% in 1986, particularly for manufacturers of private brands (Collins and Preston, 1966; Strak and Morgan 1995; Ogbonna and Wilkinson, 1996).

As stated earlier, since the 2008 crisis, operating margins have declined further and are between 2-6% for both retailers and main brand manufacturers (Butler, 2014). Smaller suppliers offering private brands are reputedly under greater pressure with even smaller margins, and indeed insolvency figures for small food companies in 2014 were up 28% on the previous year. It is also notable that those who fared best were those smaller enterprises producing their own branded products with average figures of 8.5% (Scott-Thomas, 2014).

Emerging alternative retail formats amongst the independent sector

Over recent years, with consumer concerns over the carbon footprint/food miles associated with the production of food, there has been a re-emergence of interest in the provenance of food and traditional sources. Successive food scares: salmonella in eggs and listeria in soft cheese in the 1980s, BSE and vCJD in the 1990s and Foot and Mouth in 2001, drew the consumers and policy makers to consider the implications of elongated supply chains on the integrity of supply. Whilst the first farmers' market in the UK started in Bath in 1997 (Eastham, 2005) the drive for 'local food' was promoted further following the Curry report in 2002, particularly as with the closure of the countryside during the foot and mouth epidemic, consumers began to connect the playground of rural areas with the production of food. Don Curry's call for the reconnection of the producers with consumers in conjunction with the consumer movement to know their food source, did much to stimulate the development of local initiatives, and brought about both the delivery of 'local' food by mainstream retailers as well as the creation and revival of alternative supply channels. This source of supply has been of interest to the more affluent consumer seeking greater surety, either through buying directly from the producer or from local shops and markets, as well as extending the 'rural' experience for leisure seekers (Eastham, 2005). Whilst markets, both traditional and farmers' markets, farm shops, and independent specialist shops are in a period of revival, they remain a very small proportion of total food sales.

There have been over 1000 traditional markets held across the country in such towns as Market Drayton, as well as yearly events such as the continental market in Sheffield. In addition, there has been the re-emergence of farmers' markets. Since the establishment of the first UK farmers' market in Bath, many have followed suit, and there are now some 500 farmers' markets across the UK. UK farmers' markets normally draw on producers from a 30-50 mile radius. The failure rate is high, largely due lack of commitment to specific markets by producers and consumers, and markets have been seen to fold within one or two years. Numbers of markets have reduced considerably from 2012 when 750 markets were reported (Bardo and Warwicker, 2012).

Alternatively, producers may set up farm shops, a long established format, which is becoming increasingly popular. A farm shop sells fresh produce, which are normally grown, picked, reared or produced on the farm or on land close to where the shop is located. The concept of farm shops has been augmented recently from a direct marketing channel to an entertainment activity. Farm shops are increasingly offering catering facilities and other events to extend the customers' experience.

Finally there is also a revival of independent specialist shops, which are traditional retailers including bakers, fishmongers, delicatessen, greengrocer, wine merchants and butchers, who offer consumers a single product category focus. These have been in decline for many decades, but recent figures suggest that there have been an increase, as suggested by the figures in Table 1.4 below. The number of bakeries, for instance, rose by 31%. Nevertheless, despite the rise in consumer interest in markets, and farm and local shops, sales remain relatively low; they are more a statement of intent than a significant source of food. Indeed, it is suggested that whilst the purchase of 'local food' is currently at around 7% of consumer sales, it is projected that this will fall to around 5% by 2020.

Table 1.4: Growth of specialist shops

Type of independent retailer	Percentage increase from 2012 to 2013
Independent supermarket	+65%
General food store	+32%
Bakery	+31%
Fishmonger	+28%
Delicatessen	+25%
Greengrocer	+24%
Wine merchant	+10%
Butcher	+9%

On-line shopping

In contrast, it is notable that the drive for ever increasing convenience is pushing forward the demand for on-line shopping in food. This is a growing sector in the food supply chain and offers the consumer the opportunity to shop through internet sites. There are various ways of picking internet orders placed at grocers and online food specialists for home delivery and customer collection. To date the increase in sales has been smaller than expected, and current sales amount to just 5% of sales, although recent announcements by Amazon suggest that they believe that this format of sales is set to increase, despite the complexities in the management of the delivery of food products to the home. Currently, however, food retailers find few direct financial benefits from operating in this sector and evidence from company reports suggests that many of these initiatives are operating at a loss.

■ The foodservice/catering sector

A key alternate route to the consumer is that of the sales of food and drink through the UK's foodservice sector. This sector has seen a significant growth since the 1980-1990s with a considerable growth in 'share of stomach', from 25% to 34% between 1990 and 2001 with predicted share of 50% in 2025 (Eastham and Ali, 2013). From the growth in GVA of 2.3% seen in the 2015 figures, the sector would appear to have been little affected by the downturn in the economy, although sales slowed down between 2008 and 2009 when consumers tended to socialise more at home (Horizon, 2016). Much of the continued growth of the sector has stemmed from within the commercial 'popular' table service restaurants/quick serve restaurants. During recent years, consumers have become more price sensitive and sought less expensive, more frequent treats; eating out more often with lower average spends of around £14.07 per head (Euromonitor, 2016; Anon, 2016).

Foodservice remains one of the most the fragmented sectors with 116,463 registered businesses operating on 448,958 sites. The number of chains operating within the sector has grown considerably from the 1990s, a consequence of their move into the sale of ready prepared meals (Eastham, 2012; Eastham and Ali, 2013). The expansion of the sector can be attributed to the growth of the quick service/popular service brands, which sought to increase efficiency, and standardisation through the decoupling and outsourcing the food production function. Yet despite the consolidation through the development of branded chains, the sector remains dominated by independents, which hold around 60% of the market, based on numbers of transactions (Euromonitor, 2016).

In Table 1.5 some of the key segments within each of the six sectors have been identified. The sector is however extremely dynamic and with new forms of food service operations emerge overtime. In Table 1.6, distinctions are made between social food service, which include business and industry, education, prisons, health care and welfare, commercial food service, bars and pubs, nightlife and leisure, and other distribution channels, such as pop up restaurants and vending. The commercial sector is the most problematic in terms of predictability of demand, which presents challenges for food supply companies.

Table 1.5: Food service formats and segments

	Sectors and types of segments within each sector		
Sector	**Social foodservice**	**Commercial foodservice**	**Bars and pubs**
Segment	Business and industry Education Prisons Health care Welfare	Table service restaurants Self service restaurants Hotels Quick serve Transport Concessions	Cafes Snack bars Pubs Winebars
Some key business chains/brands	Sodexho Compass Armed forces	Hilton hotels Accor Holiday Inn McDonalds Burger king Whitbread Plc Domino's Pizza Inc. Nando's Pizza Express Frankie & Benny's Restaurant Group Plc, Prét a Manger Pizza Hut	JD Wetherspoon Greene King Plc Starbucks Corp Whitbread costa Enterprise Inns Punch Taverns Marston's

	Sectors and types of segments within each sector		
Sector	**Night life and leisure facilities**	**Other distribution channels**	**Vending**
Segment	Night clubs Bowling alleys Discos Casinos Cabarets etc. Sporting venues Theatres and cinemas	Bakeries Convenience stores (food to go in supermarkets) Party venues Takeaway stands Pop up restaurants	Hot beverages Cold beverages Snacks Meals
Some key business chains/brands	The Deltic group	Greggs Plc Subway	Sodexho Compass

The introduction of ready meals allowed expansion through replacing skilled workforces with lower skilled labour, and giving restaurants greater control over food waste. Food wastage is a particular issue in traditional food service kitchens; food is wasted not simply a consequence of perishability but from the difficulties in predicting both total demand and demand for specific menu items during a service/meal period. The problem of predictability of demand and thus the potential risk of food waste is an issue for both sectors, but for foodservice, particularly those not blessed with a captive market, the potential loss is greater.

Where there is a captive market, as is often the case in education, prisons, health care and welfare, demand is more predictable, particularly where cyclical menus are offered, and repeated weekly, fortnightly or monthly. The commercial sector is the most challenging, particularly where menus are changed frequently as in menu de jour and a la carte menus, resulting of very short lead times for order delivery by food service suppliers.

In commercial restaurants, there are usually static menus, i.e. menus which are fixed for some period of time, as are found in many of the popular food outlets. Managers in these establishments have greater knowledge of the potential demand for each dish, which allows for greater control over waste and margins and longer lead times for suppliers. The ability to control margins is also enhanced where ready meals replace on-site production. Yet this trend has implications for the health of the nation in much the same way as ready meals in retail, where such products are notably often high in fat, and furthermore, often present foodservice buyers with little insight into the constituent ingredients of the dishes they serve to their customers.

The distinctions between foodservice formats according to types of outlets, menu types, predictability of demand, management of food and food consumption behaviour are summarised in Table 1.6. It shows the distinctiveness of service provided, the differences in menus, the technological versus labour input distinctions between the operations and the implications in terms of the nature of the product they purchase from suppliers.

Impact of the changes to retail and catering on manufacturing and distribution

The developments in and changes to the food retail and service sector have implications for the interim tiers of the supply chain. The interim tiers in the supply chain to the sectors are those of the food manufacturing and wholesale/distribution sectors, both of which have seen significant changes as a consequence of the evolving retail and food service sectors.

Table 1.6: Food service formats and characteristics

Sector	Sub sector	Function of food service	Menu types	Food inputs	Technology /v. staff skills/production area	Style of service	Venues
Social food service	In house and contract	Secondary function can be feeding stations Leisure events etc.	Table d'hôte Cyclical A la carte	This can be operated as fine dining, as in Henley, Ascot; quick service; or casual dining	Varied according to scale of event and style of service Large scale central production kitchens	Range from fine dining, cafes, vending, self-service	Hospitals, oil rigs, universities, sporting events, e.g. Henley, workplaces
Commercial sector	Quick serve	Feeding station	Static menus	Inputs largely semi or totally prepared	Regeneration with low skills level	Counter service	Out of town
	Casual dining or popular	Feeding station Casual meals	Static menus	Inputs largely semi or totally prepared	Regeneration with low skills level – grill chef	Limited table service	In town
	Casual dining, ethnic	Feeding station Casual meals	Static menus	Seated service	National skills – or regeneration skills	Table service	Varied locations, market towns and suburbs
Fine dining		Full service Food production predominantly on site Highly trained staff	Table d'hôte A la carte	Largely fresh produce	Higher levels of skills Butchery often out-sourced, prepared vegetables may be used	Table service, may include a higher level of service skills	Varied depending on social-economic characteristics of location
Pub restaurants	Gastro-pubs	Casual dining Special events	Menu of the day	Assisted service	Higher levels of skills Butchery often out-sourced, prepared vegetables may be used	Assisted service	Residential areas and semi out of town locations
	Traditional pubs	Limited menu Feeding station	Static menus	Assisted service	Varied	Assisted service	Residential areas

■ Food manufacture

Food manufacturers fall into two categories:

- ■ **Land based processors:** the processing of raw commodities, which takes place normally close to the place of primary production and

- ■ **Added value processors:** the production of processed food), which is located normally close to the place of consumption (Regmi *et al.*, 2006).

In line with the growth in demand for ready meals and meal solutions for home consumption and prepared meals for the foodservice sector, the UK food manufacturing industry has expanded rapidly over recent years and now has some 8,597 enterprises employing 422,000 people, who generate £26.9 bn gross added value (DEFRA, 2016). The sector has seen the growth of transnational and global players, including vertically integrated corporations such as Cargill, ADMs, ConAgra, as well as corporations such as PepsiCo, Coca Cola, Unilever

and Nestlé who own a large portfolio of household brands, but also smaller scale operations. Small and medium sizes enterprises currently account for around 96% of food manufacturing businesses, by number, in the UK.

■ The food wholesale sector and its changing structure

The expansion of home meal solutions and ready meals has had similar repercussions for the distribution sector. These have affected the structure of the sector, and also the growth of multi-temperature distribution, to transport chilled and frozen produce in addition to ambient. These developments have increased costs of warehousing and transportation.

As a consequence, the sector has a key role in the management of safe nutritious food. The actual market size of the wholesale sector is difficult to calculate, but data from DEFRA, as shown in Figure 1.2, suggests that it generates in excess of £13 bn. GVA. These figures relate to both the first and second tier wholesale sectors, i.e. the connection between primary production and manufacturing, and both primary production and retail, and manufacturing and retail.

Access to market is essential in the issue of food availability. Distribution failures through lack of infrastructure not only influence the distribution of food and relative availability of food for disparate regions of the world, but also the distribution of economic value and the competitive advantage of firms (Porter, 1985; Eastham, 2014). The consolidation of the retail sector has considerably reduced the number of potential channels of distribution and altered the nature of the wholesale sector, which has shifted the distribution of power within the UK food supply chain (Fernie, 1997; Fernie, 2010).

The wholesale sectors in traditional terms could be divided into first and second tier intermediaries. The first tier are those parties who hold a bulking role, i.e. buying from farmers, and consolidating primary supply; and a second tier are those who act as intermediaries either from the processing or the consolidation tiers, and have a debulking role (see Figure 1.2).

In first tier supply, traditionally there are a series of intermediaries including auction houses, traders or wholesalers, and direct manufacturer-owned distribution. Notably the sector has increasingly moved towards direct contracted exchanges between farmers and processors, and the decline in numbers of first tier intermediaries, although figures have been distorted as a consequence of the redetermination of Standard Industrial Codes (see Figure 1.2). The numbers of livestock auction markets in the UK, for instance, have declined from 259 in 1990 to circa 120 in 2015.

Traditional channels remain important to smaller independent sectors such as butchers, but are particularly important for the exchange of livestock within the farming sector. Although direct sales are increasing, the auctions are seen to be the most effective means of selling stores and breeding stock. Various forms of sales using e-technology have been tried, but they have not proved popular; buyers like to see the stock that they are considering buying. Web site activity is beginning to link some of the more sophisticated livestock breeders and finishers together in new ways, particularly pedigree breeders, but it has so far not made the inroads into the wider commercial stratified breeding/finishing sheep system that some expected.

In the second tier, there are three distinct marketing channels who serve the independent retail and food service sectors:

1 Livestock auctions and abattoirs who supply mainly directly to butchers, wholesale markets (often offering a delivered service),

2 Food and drink wholesalers, also known as cash and carries/ buying groups,

3 Manufacturer direct deliveries, and delivered foodservice wholesale supplying small independents, symbol groups such as Nisa and food service companies.

Mainstream retailers either operate their own central distribution centres, with total temperature control and specialised transportation facilities, or outsource to third/fourth party logistics companies (e.g. Sainsbury's and DHL), in order to dissipate the high investment costs (Roorda *et al.*, 2010; Fernie and Sparks, 2014). Sparks (1998) has described such changes as 'logistical transformation' in that retailers are no longer passive recipients of products, and in greater control of the issues of product integrity.

The development of retailer controlled distribution channels has led to a considerable decline in numbers of wholesale markets for fresh produce and cash and carries, which has allowed for the emergence of the delivered foodservice companies such Booker, Bidvest (3663) and Brakes. The presence of such companies in the market has facilitated the growth of the popular food service sector. The businesses Bidvest (3363) and Brakes have expanded rapidly and hold over 30% of the market share operating at a national level, as well as a plethora of regional supply companies, e.g. Reynolds Food Service. Whilst the delivered wholesalers are critical to the food service sector, they are also supplying the independent smaller supermarkets through the vehicle of buying and symbol groups.

As we go to press there are further threats to the foodservice and independent retail sectors and their marketing channels/supply chains from the acquisition by Tesco of Booker PLC. As a major supplier to both sectors, changes to Booker products and product varieties, as suggested by the media, could greatly impact on business activities and profits.

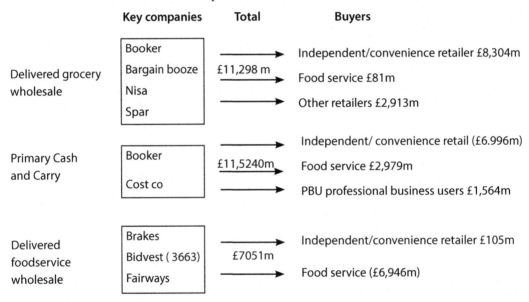

Figure 1.3: Market channels to food service and independent non mainstream retail

Future developments

It will be interesting to see what the future holds for logistics, with growing e-sales, following what has been called as the dot.com boom. Despite claims that only 6% of sales of food are either internet sales or click and collect (IGD, 2016), the growth in small domestic delivery has none the less been impressive with recent announcements by Amazon as to their shift into the grocery market. Key suggestions are that whilst there is growing demand, companies operating in the online delivery of food as part of their format portfolio are operating at a loss.

The challenge is to provide a grocery delivery service to the home at a time and in conditions convenient to the customer. Companies providing online service need to be able to pick an order of between 60 to 80 items across three temperature regimes from a total range of up to 25,000 products for delivery to customers within one to two hour time slots (Fernie, 2010). Indeed Fernie goes on to suggest that one critical factor is operating a delivery service which is cost efficient but ensures that customers are available to receive the products at the time of delivery.

Concluding remarks

This chapter is a foundation for subsequent chapters, setting out the distinctiveness of food from other commodities. As food is a highly perishable product prone to spoilage and waste, its management within the chain presents challenges for all stakeholders from farmers through to consumers. Yet the supply of food is essential to survival, an important source of income for families, societies and states, and it is also an indirect resource to the successful growth of economic activity in other industrial sectors. Sufficient safe food is thus essential for a sustained society, and this in itself can prove to be a challenge.

Matching supply to demand with products, which are normally harvested yearly, and are prone to climatic fluctuations, presents difficulties. The chapter notes that there are is also increased competition for land resources, placing constraints on the amount of food produced, and the issue of growing populations and an increase in demand for high protein animal products by an increasingly affluent consumer in MINT and BRIC countries.

Managing supply is further exacerbated by the use of food in a speculative capacity, resulting in price inflation sometimes as a consequence of inaccurate assumptions as to potential demand or supply. On the deflation of 'price bubbles' in circumstances where demand is lower than predicted, producers have incurred considerable financial losses.

These risks are exacerbated for farmers when faced with high levels of market concentration in their buyers and suppliers markets, in which they may experience high input costs and low product prices. All such complexities take place in context of the increasing need to reduce the carbon footprint in the food chain, and in particular in farming and food processing.

In following chapters, these issues will be unravelled further. Chapters 2-4 will look at issues facing businesses, including consumer trends, food safety and integrity and market dynamics. Chapters 2 and 3 can be seen to represent the differences of issues for short local supply chains versus elongated international chains. For shortened supply chains, the issue is of ensuring demand, whilst elongated chains present problems of traceability and integrity, and the need for effective information systems. Chapter 4 explores the issue of collaboration as a sustainable economic solution. It raises, in the context of information, whether information and trust present a problem for the development of sustainable governance structures. In Section 2 (Chapters 5-9) the focus is upon issues around the problem of food security, including a examination of the nutritional and ecological benefits of hunters and gathers, the impact of land grabbing, new production and processing methods and the viability of urban and peri-urban agriculture. Finally, in Section 3, the book explores a range of case studies and research based contemporary issues.

References

Anon, (2016) UK foodservice market on target for growth. www.hospitalityandcatering news.com/2016/05/uk-foodservice-market-target-growth-2016/

Arezki, R., Rota-Graziosi, G. and Senbet, L.W. (2013). Capital flight risk. *Finance and Development*, **40**(3), 27.

Bardo, M. and Warwicker, M. (2012). Does farmers' market food taste better. BBC news http://www.bbc.co.uk/news/business-18522656

Butler, S. (2014). Asda outperforms supermarket rivals with 5% boost in profits, https://www.theguardian.com/business/2014/oct/10/asda-supermarket-5-percent-profit

Burton, R. and Wilson, G. A. (2012). The rejuvenation of productionist agriculture: the case for 'cooperative neo-productivism', in Almås, R., & Campbell, H. *Rethinking Agricultural Policy Regimes: Food Security, Climate Change and the Future Resilience of Global Agriculture*. Bingley,UK: Emerald, 51-72.

Carter, C. A. and Revoredo-Giha, C. L. (2009). Eastham's commodity storage model in a modern context. Oxford Economic Papers.

Clarke, I. (2000). Retail power, competition and local consumer choice in the UK grocery sector. *European Journal of Marketing*, **34**(8), 975-1002.

Collins N. R. and Preston , L.E. (1966). Concentration and price-cost margins in food manufacturing industries, *Journal of Industrial Economics*, **14**(3), 226-242.

Cox, A., Sanderson, J. and Watson, G. (2001). Supply chains, power regimes toward and analytic framework for managing extended networks of buyer and supplier relationships, *Journal of Supply Chain Management*, **37**(2), 28-35.

DEFRA (2014) *Farm Business Survey*, HMSO.

DEFRA (2016) *Agricultural in the United Kingdom*, HMSO

Dobb, R., Remes, J., Mamnyihc, J., Woetzel, J. and Agyenin-Boaeteng, Y. (2013). Urban World: the shifting global business landscape. www.mckinsey.com/global-themes/urbanization/urban-world-the-shifting-global-business-landscape. Accessed 21/12/2016.

Eastham, J. K. (1939). Commodity stocks and prices. *Review of Economic Studies*, **6**(2), 100-110.

Eastham, J.F. (2005). Farmers market, here to stay. Proceedings of ICASS conference, Warsaw, June.

Eastham J. (2012). Challenges for procurement in the UK hospitality industry, Proceedings of EuroChrie, Lausanne, Switzerland, September.

Eastham, J. F. (2014). An analysis of the success of UK agricultural marketing cooperatives: can they effectively redress power imbalances in current market conditions? (Doctoral dissertation, University of Birmingham).

Eastham J, and Ali A. (2013). Trends in procurement in the UK Catering industry, in R.Wood (ed) *Key Concepts in Hospitality Management*, Sage.

EuroMonitor, (2016). Consumer Foodservice in the United Kingdom, May. http://www.euromonitor.com/consumer-foodservice-in-the-united-kingdom/report

Evans, N., Morris, C. and Winter, M. (2002). Conceptualizing agriculture: a critique of post-productivism as the new orthodoxy. *Progress in Human Geography*, **26**(3), 313-332.

Fernie, J. (1997). Retail change and retail logistics in the United Kingdom: past trends and future prospects. *Service Industries Journal*, **17**(3), 383-396.

Fernie, J., Sparks, L. and McKinnon, A.C. (2010). Retail logistics in the UK: past, present and future. *International Journal of Retail and Distribution Management*, **38**(11/12), 894-914.

Fernie, J. and Sparks, L. (2014). *Logistics and Retail Management: emerging issues and new challenges in the retail supply chain*, Kogan Page Publishers

Gardener, B. (1996). *European Agriculture, Policies, Production and Trade*, London: Routledge.

Gebrezgabher, S. A., Meuwissen, M. P., Kruseman, G., Lakner, D. and Lansink, A. G. O. (2015). Factors influencing adoption of manure separation technology in the Netherlands. *Journal of Environmental Management*, **150**, 1-8.

Griffiths P. (2016). UK public health in crisis: understanding stakeholder values regarding sustainable food security and its relationship with public health nutrition, MRes dissertation.

Gunther, R. T. (1987). The oyster culture of the ancient Romans. *Journal of the Marine Biological Association of the United Kingdom*, **4**, 360-365

Harris, L.C. and Ogbonna, E. (2001). Competitive advantage in the UK food retailing sector: past, present and future. *Journal of Retailing and Consumer Services*, **8**(3), 157-173

Hollingworth, A. (2004). Increasing retail concentration: evidence from the UK food retail sector, *British Food Journal*, **106**(3), 629-638.

Horizon, (2016). Foodservice market trends and data. http://www hrzns.com.

Howley, P., Buckley, C., Donoghue, C. O. and Ryan, M.(2015). Explaining the economic 'irrationality'of farmers' land use behaviour: The role of productionist attitudes and non-pecuniary benefits. *Ecological Economics* **109**, 186-193.

IGD (2016). Kantar Market shares, IGD retail analysis, November, http://retailanalysis. igd.com/Hub.aspx?id=12andtid=1andrid=24andprid=565. Accessed 15/12/2016

Irwin, S. H., Sanders, D. R. and Merrin, R. P. (2009). Devil or angel? The role of speculation in the recent commodity price boom (and bust). *Journal of Agricultural and Applied Economics*, **41**(02), 377-391.

John Lewis Partnership, (2015). Unaudited results for 53 weeks ended 31 January 2015, http://www.johnlewispartnership.co.uk/content/dam/cws/pdfs/press-releases/ john-lewis-partnership-unaudited-results-for-the-year-ended-31-january-2015.pdf. Accessed 15/12/2016

Kurtishi-Kastrati, S. (2013). The effects of foreign direct investments for host country's economy. *European Journal of Interdisciplinary Studies*, **5**(1), 26.

Lang, T. and Caraher, M. (1998). Access to healthy foods: part II. Food poverty and shopping deserts: what are the implications for health promotion policy and practice?. *Health Education Journal*, **57**(3), 202-211.

Larsen, C. S. (2015). *Bioarchaeology: Interpreting behaviour from the human skeleton* (Vol. 69). Cambridge University Press.

Levi-Straus, C. (1964) *Le cru and le cuit, Mythologiques* 1, Paris (*The Raw and the Cooked*, Johnathon Cape, 1969) English translation

Lindeberg, S., (2012) Paleolithic diets as a model for prevention and treatment of Western disease. *American Journal of Human Biology*, **24**(2), 110-115.

Martin, P.(1999). Trolley fodder, *Sunday Times magazine*, October 24-36.

Mintel (2014). The private label food consumer, UK, November.

Miracle, P. and Milner, N. (Eds.). (2002). *Consuming Passions and Patterns of Consumption*. Cambridge (Mass.), McDonald Institute for Archaeological Research,

Morelli, C. (1997). Britains's most dynamic sector? Competitive advantage in Multiple food retailing, *Business and Economic History*, **2**(2), 770-781.

Muirhead, B. and Almås, R. (2012). The evolution of Western agricultural policy since 1945. in Almås, R., & Campbell, H. *Rethinking Agricultural Policy Regimes: Food Security, Climate Change and the Future Resilience of Global Agriculture*. Bingley,UK: Emerald, 23-49.

Nielsen (2014) Cited in *Campaign*, 27th Nov, http://www.campaignlive.co.uk/ article/1324180/supermarket-own-brands-generate-half-uk-grocery-sales. Accessed 13/06/2016.

Ogbonna, S. and Wilkinson, B. (1996). Inter–organisational power relations in the UK grocery, industry: contradictions and developments, *International Review of Retail, Distribution, and Consumer research*, **6**(4), 395- 414.

Oxford Farming Conference (2012). http://www.ofc.org.uk/archive/2012/speakers

Paik, S.K. and Bagchi, P.K. (2007) Understanding the causes of the bullwhip effect in a supply chain. *International Journal of Retail and Distribution Management*, **35**(4), 308-324.

Piesse, J. and Thirtle, C. (2009). Three bubbles and a panic: An explanatory review of recentfood commodity price events. *Food Policy*, **34**(2), 119-129.

Pollard, T. M. (2008). *Western Diseases: An evolutionary perspective* (Vol. 54). Cambridge University Press.

Porter, M. (1985). *Competitive Advantage*, New York, Free Press.

Regmi, A., Gehlar, M., Wainio, J.,Vollrath, T., Johnston, P. and Nitin, K. (2006). Market Access for High-Value Foods/AER-840 Economic Research Service/USDA Thomas https://www.ers.usda.gov/webdocs/publications/aer840/30131_aer840b_002.pdf

Roorda, M. J., Cavalcante, R., McCabe, S. and Kwan, H. (2010). A conceptual framework for agent-based modelling of logistics services. *Transportation Research Part E: Logistics and Transportation Review*, **46**(1), 18-31.

Scott-Thomas, C. (2014). Supermarket price wars squeeze more food firms into bankruptcy, *Food Navigator*, 28-Nov, http://www.foodnavigator.com/Market-Trends/Supermarket-price-wars-squeeze-more-food-firms-into-bankruptcy

Shaw, S. and Gibbs, J. (1995). Retailer-supplier relationships and the evolution of marketing: two food industry case studies, *Industrial Journal of Retail Aand Distribution Management*. **23**(7), 7-16.

Sparks, L. (1998). The retail logistics transformation, in Fernie, J. and Sparks, L. (eds). *Logistics and Retail Management*, pp.1-22.

Strak J. and Morgan W. (1995), (eds.) *The UK Food and Drink Industry*, EuroPA and associates.

Sumner, D. A. (2009). Recent commodity price movements in historical perspective. *American Journal of Agricultural Economics*, **91**(5), 1250-1256.

Tomlinson, I., (2013). Doubling food production to feed the 9 billion: a critical perspective on a key discourse of food security in the UK. *Journal of Rural Studies*, **29**, 81-90.

Van der Veen, M. (2003). When is food a luxury? *World Archaeology*, **34**(3), 405-427.

Vidal, J. (2003). Farmers are dying out, *The Guardian*, 7th August.

Weinzettel, J., Hertwich, E. G., Peters, G. P., Steen-Olsen, K. and Galli, A. (2013). Affluence drives the global displacement of land use. *Global Environmental Change*, **23**(2), 433-438.

West, A. (1988). Manufacturer – retailer relationships, in A West (ed.) *Handbook of Retailing*, Aldershot: Gower, pp.250-64.

Wrigley, N. (1987). The concentration of capital in UK grocery retailing. *Environment and Planning A*, **19**(10), 1283-1288.

2 The Changing Consumer and the Emergence of Eco-consumption

Natalia Rohenkohl do Canto, Marcia de Barcellos, Jane Eastham and Luis Kluwe Aguiar

Introduction

This chapter examines the challenges facing the food industry in developing an alternative sustainable supply chain. Consideration is given to the inhibitors in the development of alternative styles of production.

In ethical sustainable production, one key requirement is that there is a shift from conventional consumption, with all the issues of health, environmental impacts from waste food, packaging, and natural resources, towards more ethical consumption. Whilst at present the consumption of high animal protein diets, processed food, ready meals and fast food represents the mainstream, the question becomes, given current technology and consumer ethics, can the food chain serve sufficient food in an ecologically ethical manner?

This critical question is given in the context an anticipated population of circa 9 billion by 2050, and a demand for increased land productivity and processing. Farmers, primary producers, processors and distributors will be expected to deliver more with less. Although at present this seems a major challenge, doing more with less may be to the financial benefit of all parties.

The chapter explores some of the implications for businesses and supply chains of developing sustainable supply chain management practices. There is a particular focus on the emerging eco-consumer and the challenges faced in developing eco-innovation projects. A case study of Econatura, a Brazillian example of an eco-innovative project, is explored to that purpose.

Consumer interests and concerns: the eco-consumer

A key consumer concern relates to the impact of consumers on the environment, from which there has emerged a particular alternative consumption model – that of the 'eco-consumer'. In addition, fuelled by a constant flow of food scares and, to some extent, issues of food security, consumers have become more aware of not only food security from the position of greenhouse gases (GHG) but also of the distinctions between organic, local and fair trade. Some of the key concerns include those of food integrity and traceability, and the issue of food adulteration and malpractice by the players within the food chain. In this section, the chapter will examine one of the areas of consumer interest and the emergence of the eco–consumer. The issue for the food supply chain is how this might be delivered.

In recent years, growing concerns about environmental issues and the need for a more sustainable means of producing food have attracted the attention of many stakeholders, including consumers, within the food chain. This has been exacerbated by the predicted growth in the global population and the problems of food loss and food waste. In this context, and since all the activities that take place along a food chain have a high impact on both the environment and society, a more sustainable approach to food production has become very topical for managers. As a result, it is important to reduce the negative externalities on people, the planet and the economy, from production, processing, retailing and post-consumption in order to make the food chain more sustainable .

Food companies have become more aware of the growing concerns consumers have about how they have exploited the natural environment, extracting often non-renewable resources. Furthermore, there is increasing recognition that in safeguarding the environment, firms are able to benefit financially through reducing the costs of production. Consequently, some food companies have attempted to counterbalance the negative externalities that could detrimentally affect their economic performance. The Carbon Trust believes that supply chains that have embedded sustainability as part of their business strategy are actually 'shaping the business models of the future'. Managers have, consequently, a key role to play in improving resilience and resource use efficiency to achieve competitive advantage. It is suggested that these could be achieved through collaborative procurement, supply chain optimization and process innovation (Carbon Trust, 2014). Thus the concept of eco-innovation has increased in significance for food managers, as it combines maximizing economic efficiency with environmental gains. The Organisation for Economic Co-operation and Development defined eco-innovation as "the development of products, processes, marketing methods, organizational structure, and new or improved institutional arrangements, which, intentionally or not, contribute to a reduction of environmental burdens in comparison with alternative practices" (OECD, 2009: 2).

In the food chain, eco-innovation can be achieved through: the use of raw materials such as organic or free range; the use of recyclable or intelligent packaging; manufacturing processes that use energy and water efficiently; and lean logistics or distribution systems that use alternative shorter channels linking end-consumers more directly and/or reduce carbon footprint by reducing empty return journeys. It can also be achieved through certification systems such as traceability or origin, eco-labels, fair and solidarity trade, ISO 14001; and processes with low carbon footprint (Bossle, 2015:82).

De Barcellos *et al.* (2015) proposed that eco-innovation represented a change in philosophy regarding how businesses are conducted. Figure 2.1 below attempts to represent how innovation and eco-innovation are promotors of change. If change is to be implemented and return positive results depends upon company's internal capabilities.

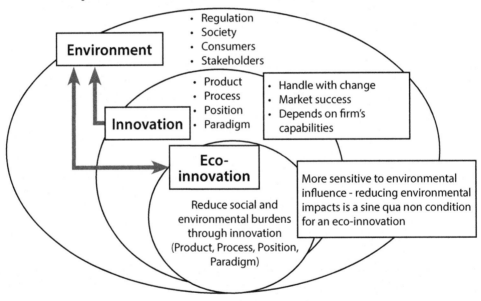

Figure 2.1: Innovation and eco-innovation. Source: De Barcellos *et al.* (2015)

To realize better results from the supply chain, companies have to be engaged with all stakeholders in an attempt to manage it more sustainably and innovatively. Seuring and Müller (2008: 1700) suggested this could only be achieved by employing sustainable supply chain management (SSCM), since it was about 'the management of materials, information and capital flows as well as co-operation among companies ultimately encompassing all three pillars of sustainability: economic, environmental and social'.

In this next section we explore how SSCM is used to aid eco-innovation practices. It directs the analysis to barriers and opportunities to eco-innovation in SSCM, in an attempt to alert stakeholders of the need to develop strategies to promote and facilitate eco-innovation. An example of a Brazilian grape juice chain where eco-innovation is embedded in its practices will be used as a case.

Eco-innovation and sustainable supply chain management

A sustainable supply chain (SSC) can be considered one which delivers positive benefits, economically, socially and environmentally. In turn, the concept of sustainable supply chain management (SSCM) emphasizes decisions or management attitudes, which enable the supply chain to be more sustainable (Pagell and Wu, 2009). Among the existing SSCM models, the models of Seuring and Müllers (2008) and Pagell and Wu (2009) offer a simplicity in their illustration of an eco-innovative process (Beske, 2012).

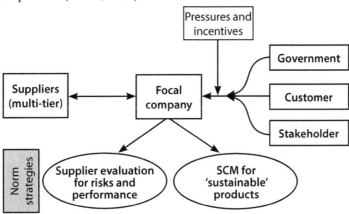

Figure 2.2: Seuring and Müller's (2008) model

Seuring and Müller's (2008) as illustrated in Figure 2.2 suggest that when focal companies, for example a bakery, offer a line of organic bread following customer demand, it can adopt an 'SSCM strategy for its sustainable products'. To do so, there is a necessity that the baker should collaborate with an organic flour miller, who in turn, would have to source the wheat from organic farmers. Alternatively, the same bakery could consider to better manage supply chain environmental risks and source its raw materials from ISO 14001 certified suppliers. In either case, buyers need to encourage suppliers to ensure the sustainable goals. The end result would be an overall increase in the chain's performance. Inherently, collaboration with suppliers is thus key to the delivery of a sustainable product under these criteria (Seuring and Müller, 2008).

Sustainable products, which are inherently ecologically innovative, offer environmental benefits, emblematic of differentiation strategies. As such they meet the demands of consumers and offer businesses competitive advantage. Pagell and Wu (2009) suggested that (as seen in Figure 2.3) innovation capability and managerial orientation would be integral to a sustainable organization and would require the re-conceptualizing of supply chain actors. These would include non-traditional stakeholders, such as non-governmental organizations (NGOs), regulatory actors, competitors and community members, and by focusing on the continuity of suppliers, ensuring that they would not only survive, but thrive.

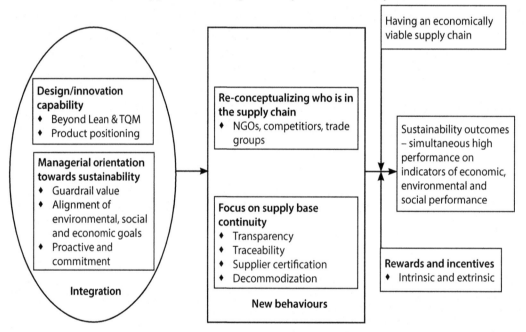

Figure 2.3: A model of sustainable supply chain management practices. Source: Pagell and Wu (2008)

Innovative capacity would be possible through practices such as decommoditisation, transparency, development of traditional and non-traditional suppliers and reduction of suppliers' risk. In their model, innovation capability was presented as one of the factors necessary for a supply chain to be sustainable. Eco-innovation could thus be considered the most suitable type of innovation to support the objectives of a SSC since it generates positive environmental results (OECD, 2009). Nonetheless, traditional performance indicators, which support a positive economic performance could not be disregarded as they also complement environmental and social performances.

The transition to sustainability is dependent not only on the consumer and consumption patterns, but it is also said to require radical changes in food production and distribution systems (Green and Foster, 2005) and a change in the entire production supply chain. This will be facilitated by the adoption and diffusion of new technologies incorporated into new economic, social, institutional and cultural relations.

This transition would therefore need to consider the interaction between different stakeholders and monitor processes, adapting strategies and leaving space for feedback and learning (Lynn *et al.*, 1996). Policies for the transition would need to combine existing tools with new approaches and methods of evaluation in order to identify the ideal combination for each circumstance (Elzen and Wieczorek, 2005).

The Case of Econatura

Econatura is a small family business that processes grapes into different value-added products. The business is located in the southernmost state of Rio Grande do Sul in Brazil. It was set up in 1979 during a crisis in the local grape and wine sector when the price paid to farmers did not cover the costs of production.

The local grape growers and wine makers were smallholders of Italian immigrant descent and to stay afloat, first cut out many of the grape crop's inputs, such as artificial fertilizers and pesticides. In the process, the farmers started to convert into a semi-organic production system, but growers were unable to attract any premium value. In 1993, to augment value and price, new methods and processes were adopted. To support these endeavours, the business received support from the local rural extension service that provided technical expertise and guidance, and as a result were able to open an organic grape juice factory in 1996. The strength of the brand was based on its single ingredient, i.e. organically produced grapes with no additives. By 2002, there was again the need to expand the business due to the increasing market share of the juice's brand.

Currently, the family-run company employs nine people and counts on 30 other local small growers to supply them with half tonne of organic grapes. All production is ECOCERT certified and the bottled juice is sold nationwide. In the process, the farmers supplying Econatura have adhered to Good Agricultural Practice standards. More recently, the company has implemented HACCP principles in all its production lines.

Aiming to make full use of the grape, the company has developed five organic products: grape juice, vinegars (red wine, balsamic and aged balsamic), grape seed oil, grape seed flour and grape peel flour. The use of all parts of the grape as raw material adds as much value as possible to its products, and is the result of extensive new product development.

Figure 2.4: Range of products. Source: Slovinscki Fotografia (2016)

Econatura has sustainability as a core value and philosophy, which is reflected in all its practices. The products are intrinsically eco-innovative; not only are the raw materials organic but the production processes also adhere to eco-principles. Econatura is a pioneer brand in the Brazilian market. In the processing of the grape, all parts of the grape are used and as a result there is zero waste. Even the stalks are composted and used as fertilizer. In addition, Econatura's products are fully traceable. All packaging is made from recycled and recyclable materials such as glass or cardboard.

Furthermore, the company has eco-innovated through being a pioneer in the use of vacuum bottling. The development and adaptation of equipment and machinery catering for a smaller scale were innovative too. The company also improved its logistics system by rationalizing routes, loads and delivery to minimize CO_2 emissions and reduce costs.

The location of the processing plant was planned by a 'bio-architect' who took into consideration the natural landscape. The so-called new eco-factory is located on a disused brickyard site amid native trees and away from sources of pollution. Most of the construction used reclaimed materials such as wood from old wine barrels and materials from demolition (wood, doors, windows and bricks). The internal furnishings and display units were also made from reused or restored old furniture. The retaining walls and the courtyard were built from both re-used concrete and stones. The fence around the perimeter is made of 250 reused galvanized pipe poles. The roof was made from approximately 320,000 tetrapack boxes. In addition, a green roof with a self-irrigation is part of a recently added extension. The new juice processing plant could be considered an eco-factory owing to its sustainable practices in all stages of production.

Furthermore, to achieve better energy efficiency, the rational use of natural resources and energy meant that solar energy, natural ventilation and lighting were integral parts of the architectural plan. To allow for natural light transparent roof tiles were made of reused glass. Rainwater is collected, treated and reused for irrigating the garden, washing pavements, vehicles and flushing the toilets.

Figure 2.5 shows a kiosk in the shape of a wine barrel. It has a multi-purpose character serving as dining room, guest house, auditorium, area for product display and tasting. The so called eco-barrel room demonstrates that it is possible to reconcile the daily needs of the business with several sustainable practices. Econatura, therefore, can be seen as being highly eco-innovative from its onset since eco-innovation has been embedded in its products, processes, facilities and general practices.

Figure 2.5: Eco-barrel building

In order to successfully develop its eco-innovative products, Econatura has had to align its supply chain to its sustainable claims. The stakeholders who participated the most in eco-innovative practices were grape producers, one organic sugar supplier (Organic), ECOCERT (the organic certifier), TrendNatural (distributor), retailers (Bendita Horta, Biopint, Sabor Ecológico and RER Divino), NGO (Slow Food Primeira Colônia), and the local Tourism and Culture authority as shown in Figure 2.6.

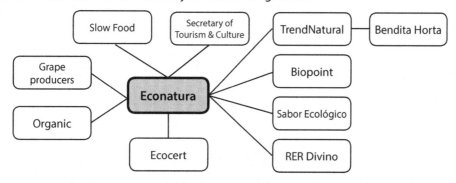

Figure 2.6: Econatura's supply chain

Barriers and opportunities to eco-innovation in Econatura's chain

Literature on eco-innovation demonstrates that there are a number of barriers to, as well as benefits or opportunities for the development of Eco-innovation initiatives. Table 2.1 depicts a range of literature in which the key barriers and opportunities have been isolated. These can be identified and categorised as technological (i.e. lack of technology), financial, skills and availability of labour, legislative/regulatory and consumer-centric. In effect, the availability of requisite technology, finances, skills and labour, appropriate legislation and regulatory frameworks and consumer interest are suggested to be important for the emergence and success of eco-innovative projects.

Despite this, it has been noted that most of the innovations that conquer the market have tended to be incremental, thus insufficient for a true transition to sustainability, since some persistent problems require radical changes to solve them (Elzen and Wieczorek, 2005). These will serve to analyse the case of Econatura and illustrate the likely barriers and opportunities to eco-innovation in the SSCM.

■ The intellectual framework applied to Econotura: Barriers

An analysis using the framework developed from the literature showed that Econotura had faced certain barriers to establishment but had been relatively free from others. All of the key barriers within the intellectual framework had been evaluated and those faced by Econotura have been identified.

Technical barriers

Technical barriers were observed throughout the supply chain, although there were particular challenges to be faced on the farm as a function of the production lead-times of vineyards and grapes, and the potential risks faced as a consequence of the climatic conditions and the market. Furthermore, organic crops return a lower yield and require more attention. The conversion from a conventional to an organic system requires adhering to specific practices set out by legislation. Some producers decided to hedge their risk by converting only half of their vineyards to organic.

Despite the prevalence of smallholdings within the Econatura supply chain, the implementation of better agricultural practices has enabled farmers to increase production capacity. This has been an advantage to the sugar supplier, Organic, who have found it difficult to source other organic product lines, which are produced more in an artisanal manner by smallholding farmers.

Barriers	Authors	Benefits/opportunities	Authors
Technical			
Development / lack of technology Lack of adequate substitute products Increased sophistication in the operation of technologies Skepticism regarding the performance of technologies Process inflexibilities Trade-off between product quality and environmental benefits Focus on unique lifecycle phases Need of a high knowledge Infrastructure requirements Technological lock-in	Ashford (1993); Dangelico & Pujari (2010); Elzen & Wieczorek (2005)	Increased efficiency in the use of resources	Dangelico & Pujari (2010)
Financial			
R&D, capital investments and infrastructure costs Risks of changes in consumer acceptance and in product quality Longer payback period of investments Price disadvantages compared to conventional products Lack of capital to investments due to a low profit margin Certification costs	Ashford (1993); Dangelico & Pujari (2010); Elzen & Wieczorek (2005)	Return of investments Increased sales Competitive advantage	Dangelico & Pujari (2010)
Labour			
Lack of qualified personnel Reluctance to hire specialized professionals Lack of team skills Employees' engagement	Ashford (1993); Dangelico & Pujari (2010)		
Regulatory frameworks			
Bureaucracy Uncertainties about the legislation Focus on traditional operations Lack of / few government incentives or risk of losing them Environmental regulations	Ashford (1993); Dangelico & Pujari (2010); Elzen & Wieczorek (2005)	Risk minimization Revenues preservation Creation of new businesses Incentive to the use and development of new products	Dangelico & Pujari (2010); Ashford (1993); Elzen & Wiecz-orek (2005); Porter (1991)
Consumer specific			
Highly specific product Risk of losing customers if product changes or is unavailable for a while Lack of consumers' awareness Lack of consumers' attitude and purchasing behaviour Preference for existing products	Ashford (1993); Dangelico & Pujari (2010); Elzen & Wieczorek (2005)	Development of new markets Improvement of the corporate image Expectation of green markets' growth and increasing gains	Dangelico & Pujari (2010)

Table 2.1: Barriers and opportunities to eco-innovation, the intellectual framework (based on the literature).

However, what constitutes organic farming varies amongst the stakeholders. The retailer Bendita Horta's interpretation of organic farming meant the negation of the use of modern technology, whilst in other countries this is not necessarily the case. As a result, Brazilian producers still face challenges to produce organically on a larger scale.

A further technical issue faced by Econatura relates to the standardization of products, particularly with reference to its use of additives to correct sugar content and improve taste. The lack of adjustment of sugar levels means that each crop produces a unique product. As a result of not using additives and preservatives, eco-nature products have a short shelf life. Both the NGO and the Tourism authority have a dystopian perception when believing that "nothing can be 100% organic since the land, water and air are contaminated". For them, the advance of GMO would result in the disappearance of traditional vine varieties.

Due to the unavailability of eco-vehicles in the region, the distribution company involved in the supply chain has to rely on conventional petrol fueled vehicles. The use of an electric bicycle was considered, but these vehicles have a limited range before recharging. Even though distribution only represents around 2% of the emissions in the food chain, any improvement to this figure will require technological development into eco-vehicles.

Financial barriers

The introduction of eco-products means that there are greater financial barriers to be faced by Econatura, related to higher investments required along the chain. The new product development cycle is longer than conventional products, a function of both the costs of producing a product with a sufficient shelf life, as well as those associated with the accreditation process. These additional costs are passed on to the consumer, and these higher prices, as indicated by the retailer Sabor Ecológico, tend to make organic products less accessible to many consumers. This is particularly the case for Econatura's organic grape seed oil, as its end price is less competitive in comparison to other traditional brands.

Labour barriers

Econatura and its supply chain stakeholders also experience difficulties in attaining labour with the appropriate knowhow and skills. One key problem relates to a lack of succession within the farming community. Farmers are not succeeded by their daughters and sons because of the more arduous labour required at the farm. Indeed there is a key impediment to the development of organic farming as there is generally a lack of specialized professionals. This is exacerbated as organic production requires more manpower than the conventional forms, and there is a general trend where younger generations are leaving rural areas. At present Econotura does not seem to be a solution for this region's rural exodus.

Additionally, there is little training and education in organic agriculture at colleges and universities in the region, inhibiting the induction of new entrants to, or the reskilling of existing professionals within, the sector. Econatura struggles to find food technologists to develop their grape oil and seed flour. Further down the supply chain, retailers experience a high turnover of staff, and despite their efforts to train and educate sales people, the company does not benefit.

Regulatory barriers

The lack of government incentives, particularly financial, also presents a barrier to the development of the Econatura supply chain. The lack of government incentives means that producers experience considerable difficulties in their attempts to become certified when faced with the highly demanding regulations and bureaucracy of the organic certification bodies. Indeed, insufficient support is provided not only as an incentive to convert but also to those undergoing the process of conversion, both in terms of funds and tax exemptions.

Consumer barriers

Furthermore, there is a level of unpredictability with respect to demand, which could lead to overproduction, but retailers have also experienced stock-out, particularly within the large supermarket chain. When demand for eco-innovative products is too high and the product specification changes or the production line is briefly interrupted there is the risk of losing customers. Consumers' uptake of eco-products has been perceived to be significant, but in general, consumers are not aware of organic products in the market and prefer the existing conventional ones. The lack of knowledge about organic products and their likely benefits was highlighted, particularly regarding more industrialised products or less known processes. One restaurant, Sabor Ecológico, practically gave up selling exclusively organic food, due to the lack of demand. In that region, although consumers tended to know more about organic fruits and vegetables, the difference between the conventional produce could not be clearly perceived. Whilst customers were receiving unique non-standardized products, the lack of standardization, and an abundance of product information, has tended, with certain product ranges, to discourage consumers from buying and put into question the intrinsic value to consumers of 'locally produced foods'.

Lack of knowledge of the certification process was also mentioned regarding its reliability and accuracy. Therefore, despite the juice having environmental certification labeling, that was not enough to make them stand out and support their more natural claims. This is alarming, since the credibility of the environmental performance is one of the vital attributes of eco-innovative products (Dangelico and Pujari, 2010). Therefore, the organic market presents barriers related to its specific characteristics, such as being a niche market with small volumes and lower demand. Companies that produce in a larger scale, such as Organic's organic sugar, end up having to sell part of the product as if it were conventional, since production outstrips demand.

Regarding less traditional products, such as grape seed flour and grape seed oil, the lack of knowledge about their gastronomic use restricts their sale. It is necessary to develop the products' demand by informing consumers of its use and create a market.

The main barriers related to raw materials refer to the limited availability of sustainable materials. Econatura could produce and sell a larger amount of products if more organic grape was available.

Additional barriers

In the analysis of Econatura, packaging was also found to be a barrier to the development of an environmentally friendly product. Econatura has found that sourcing appropriate packaging is one of the greatest difficulties when it comes to eco-innovative foods. Recycled packaging, for example, is not always suitable for storing food. Issues such as reverse logistics, the ratio of the weight of the bottle and its contents and the material used, are considered limiting to eco-innovation in packaging. For example, Econatura cannot employ recycled plastic lids on its bottles since it is a safety concern. Furthermore, packaging companies do not give much attention to the specific needs of small businesses. Hence, the company is at the mercy of the products offered by packaging suppliers, which may be discontinued or modified in accordance with the demand of larger customers.

In addition, albeit potentially a labour issue, Econatura were faced with the issue of managing suppliers' understanding of organic production. Econatura found that there are still many farmers who do not know about the harmful effects of pesticides, and prefer to keep producing grapes in conventional systems.

Management issues were also faced with downstream parties. TrendNatural pointed out that retail buyers, particularly of large retail chains, put up barriers by not including eco-innovative products in their stock. This further hindered eco-innovation diffusion. When dealing with smaller retailers, the distributor faced resistance when attempting to rationalize the delivery route. However, some shop owners disliked the change, despite offers and inducements of longer payment terms. Econatura itself might also have management barriers as they try to carry out different activities (such as processing, sales and logistics) of which they have little prior experience.

A further management issue related to imperfect competition, in that competitors, rather than working to organic principles preferred to take the less costly option of 'greenwashing', alternatively known as misleading advertising. In certain cases, this can be a consequence of diverse interpretations and lack of alignment between diverse parties of what constitutes 'organic' or 'eco-friendly'. This is frequently an issue in the case of logistics (Dangelico and Pujari, 2010), although this was not found to be so for Econatura. The chain does not always have access to sourcing raw materials and an adequate retail and logistics network. The raw materials needed are not always available in the market or may be produced in far too small quantities to influence prices. Innovation and creativity in designing products was needed. Food retailers were not fully aligned to eco-innovative philosophies and business practices. The practical absence of reverse logistics in packaging was a limitation given the limited adoption of reverse logistic strategies.

■ The intellectual framework applied to the Econotura supply chain: Opportunities

On the other hand, Econatura was able to make some key gains as a consequence of its eco-innovative status and sustainable supply chain. Based on the intellectual framework these will be discussed in more detail below.

Technological opportunities

As for the technological opportunities for eco-innovation in SSCM, Econatura sought one key advantage, that of improving the efficiency of use of resources. Farmers similarly recognized the benefits of eco-innovation and that there was a reduced need for external inputs, particularly petrochemical inputs. Organic farming allows for a more sustainable production, conserving the soil, reducing environmental impact and increasing the use of natural resources. In the long term the farm is more suited for food production.

Benefits were also attained both from the use of a smaller sweeter organic grape that produces a tastier sweeter juice with lower levels of added sugar.

Financial opportunities

The financial opportunities found were related to the return on investment, as the eco-innovative product generally has lower cost and adds value to the final product. For farmers, despite lower yields, the price premium is attractive (on average 30% more, but could even attract 200% premium according to ECOCERT). In financial terms, the return is equivalent to a conventionally produced grape. Another advantage would be the savings from the lack of need to purchase pesticides from the cost of production.

To Econatura, it is possible to obtain financial gains from eco-innovation in a well-managed supply chain. Despite the fluctuating performance of the Brazilian economy, the demand for organic products has not decreased. This might be owed to the perception of the products' superior quality, along with the appreciation of the company's philosophy. Other eco-innovative practices have increased the company's competitiveness, by reducing costs, such as transport rationalization or the use of local and seasonal products. However, the financial opportunity related to increased sales has not been perceived in all cases. Econatura could sell more if access to more organic grapes was possible.

Labour opportunities

In the case of the labour force, eco-innovation acts as a great incentive for promoting activities in the countryside. Injections of additional capital into the producers of products throughout the supply chain within the region, will generate higher levels of incomes for businesses and families, and opportunities for employment. The Econatura model offers a way in which, through high levels of linkages, there are synergies between businesses, fewer financial leakages and a sense of ownership and social embeddedness by the workforces, not only in Econatura but throughout its supply chain and the communities they serve. Thus, there is evidence that eco-innovation can increase satisfaction and employee retention.

Regulatory opportunities

Changes in the regulatory framework could be considered an opportunity, despite the uncertainty as to whether the change in legislation favouring sustainable practices minimises risks by ensuring a lower impact on the environment. ECOCERT believed that there could be also public policies aimed at supporting farmers to convert into organic production. Regulatory opportunities permeate throughout the food chain. Strict control of organic production, which preserves the reputation of companies and guarantees transparency in the certification process, would allow for opportunities for new businesses to be set up, and increased earnings. On the one hand, paying for the environmental services resulting from organic production could be considered. On the other hand, local authorities could include a compulsory clause for organic food to be part of school meals.

Consumer opportunities

Stakeholders cited many opportunities related to consumers. An appreciation of organic products and an increase in their consumption can have an impact on the chain as a whole. When Econatura was created, its owners invested in the opportunity of developing the organic grape juice market. Since then, the market demand has outrun its supply capacity. Less traditional products, such as the grape seed flour and the grape seed oil, are still under development in the market.

In tandem with the market development of eco-innovative products, the services market is also being developed. Local agro-ecological tourism has been enabled. At retail level, customer information at point of sale aids in the purchase decision – 'making the difference' being fundamental for the development of the eco-innovative food market.

The expectation of growth of the green market as a whole and the expected increase in revenue is supported by the media, which ever increasingly disseminates information about organic and healthy foods. Consumers have started to perceive organic food as being an investment in health and wellbeing, which would result in savings on medical treatments. Moreover, many initiatives tackling the negative externalities of conventional production, which favour preservation of resources for future generations, have disseminated information and philosophies related to sustainability. Hence, it is expected that consumers modify their habits in order to adopt a healthier and more conscious diet. One could also highlight the loyalty of consumers who opt for eco-innovative foods because of the perceived better taste and health benefits of the products.

Other opportunities

Packaging opportunities are regarded as relevant to the identification and positioning of the eco-innovative product, and create opportunities for positioning the product in the consumers' minds.

In the literature, the opportunity related to competitors referred to product differentiation. Respondents indicated that eco-innovation presented this opportunity not only regarding the products, but the company as a whole.

Opportunities related to SSCM impact upon all the stakeholders studied. Those companies from a same location, which were connected with relevant NGOs, tend to share information and trade amongst themselves. Potentially, these types of networks could extend their collaboration and develop shared management systems and a more integrated approach to the supply chain, allowing greater ease of accreditation as well as the monitoring and evaluating the processes within the supply chain to maintain organic status and improve the delivery of added value eco-products to consumers.

Concluding remarks

This chapter looks at a specific, at present, niche market, which given the expected growth of population and the accepted need to redress the impact of consumers on the environment, needs to become mainstream.

The major focus of this chapter is to examine a specific supply chain and the factors which may promote or inhibit the emergence of eco-innovation production and consumption. The case demonstrates the difficulties experienced in facilitating eco-initiatives in an overarching conventional system. There are opportunities and benefits for all tiers within the supply chain, but these need to be activated and encouraged through strong leadership and vision, and the cultivation of consumer interest.

Econatura's case shows how the founders' vision and leadership enabled, from the initial investment in eco-innovation, the company to develop an aligned chain. Not finding the appropriate partners, the company came up with two main strategies: they targeted (in Porter's terms) a focused market, focusing upon those eco-sensitive buyers, and put considerable effort into the development of new products.

The case examines the issues of scaling production and suggests that not only are there issues of production, but that consumers faced with choices will tend towards the known and lowest price, conventional products. The questions we leave you with are: can we scale up production, and can we roll this out to overcome conventional consumption? The next chapter discusses issues of traceability, certification and food integrity.

References

Ashford, N. A. (1993). Understanding technological responses of industrial firms to environmental problems: Implications for government policy. In *Environmental Strategies for Industry: International Perspectives in Research Needs and Policy Implications* (pp. 277–307). Washington, DC: Island Press.

Beske, P. (2012). Dynamic capabilities and sustainable supply chain management. *International Journal of Physical Distribution & Logistics Management*, **42**(4), 372-387.

Bossle, M. B. (2015). Drivers for adoption of eco-innovation and enhancement of food companies' environmental performance. Universidade Federal do Rio Grande do Sul. 146p. PhD thesis. http://hdl.handle.net/10183/131260. Accessed: 30/09/2015.

Carbon Trust (2014) Supply chains are shaping the business models of the future. https://www.carbontrust.com/news/2014/12/supply-chains-shaping-business-models-of-the-future/. Accessed: 18/07/2016.

Dangelico, R. M. and Pujari, D. (2010). Mainstreaming green product innovation: Why and how companies integrate environmental sustainability. *Journal of Business Ethics*, **95**(3), 471–486.

De Barcellos, M.D., Bossle, M.B., Perin, M.G. and Vieira, L.M. (2015) Consumption of eco-innovative food: how values and attitudes drive consumers' purchase of organics? *Revista Brasileira de Marketing*, **14**(1), 110-121.

Elzen, B. and Wieczorek, A. (2005). Transitions towards sustainability through system innovation. *Technological Forecasting and Social Change*, **72**(6), 651–661.

Green, K. and Foster, C. (2005). Give peas a chance: transformations in food consumption and production systems. *Technological Forecasting and Social Change*, **72**(6), 663-679.

Lynn, G., Morone, J. G. and Paulson, A. S. (1996). Marketing and discontinuous innovation: the probe and learn process. *California Management Review*, **38**(3), 8–37.

OECD (2009). Sustainable manufacturing and eco-innovation: towards a Green economy. Policy Brief June 2009. http://www.oecd.org/sti/42944011.pdf. Accessed 20/12/2010.

Pagell, M. and Wu, Z. (2009). Building a more complete theory of sustainable supply chain management using case studies of 10 exemplars. *Journal of Supply Chain Management*, **45**(2), 37–56.

Seuring, S. and Müller, M. (2008). From a literature review to a conceptual framework for sustainable supply chain management. *Journal of Cleaner Production*, **16**(15), 1699–1710.

2

3 Traceability: An Essential Mechanism to Underpin Food Integrity

Louise Manning

Introduction

Historically, traceability has been aligned with product identity, the origin of materials and parts, product processing history, and the distribution and location of the product after delivery (Bertolini *et al.*, 2006). Bosona and Gebresenbet (2013) argue that the driving force for the adoption of food traceability systems is unease with respect to safety, quality, economic, regulatory, technological and social factors.

Traceability has been associated with food safety procedures (Charlebois and Haratifar, 2015). It allows businesses to document production practices, through a chain of custody, demonstrate regulatory compliance, and is said to afford businesses within the supply chain the opportunity to respond to food security threats (Thakur and Hurburgh, 2009).

However, along with the ability to respond comes an onus to actually address problems if they are identified. More recently, food traceability has been seen to encompass wider notions of food integrity and authenticity (Charlebois and Haratifar, 2015), or to allow the certification of geographical origin of products, surveillance and monitoring of the chain, and to facilitate the preservation of food provenance (Pizzuti and Mirabelli, 2015). Therefore, traceability of a given food and/or its component parts provides consumers with assurance as to the source (provenance) and the safety of food. Traceability also allows for the identification of the source of contaminated or substandard product, assists in plant and animal disease control, and medicine and chemical residue monitoring, and satisfies the requirements of labelling regulations (Leat *et al.*, 1998). Drawing on current literature, this chapter aims to determine the essential requirements of a traceability system, including the underlying elements of tracking and tracing, and thus how traceability can be effectively implemented in the food supply chain. The chapter first explores the legal and market requirements, leading then to a discussion on the metrics and systems for the delivery of traceability within a supply chain. Next, intelligent packaging systems and data are assessed with respect to their value in ensuring transparency of geographic origin and traceability.

Legal and market requirements for traceability

The regulation EC/178/2002 (EU, 2002) defines traceability as the ability to trace and follow a food, feed, food-producing animal or substance intended to be, or expected to be incorporated into a food or feed, through all stages of production, processing and distribution. At the very least, unless specific provisions or market requirements exist, the prescribed level of traceability within legislation is for businesses to:

- Identify the immediate supplier of the product or food ingredient in question (trace)
- Determine the immediate subsequent recipient (track).

Whilst the regulations exempt retailers from the need to track to final consumers, traceability should deliver 'one step back-one step forward' traceability, a requirement that others have called tracking 'forward traceability' and tracing 'backward traceability' (Aung and Chang, 2014). In essence, this concept represents B2B2B (business to business to business) traceability.

In high information input supply chains such as fast moving consumer goods, the market requirements for traceability often need to exceed the legislative requirements for 'one step back-one step forward'. To ensure traceability within extended supply chains, means serving the customer with a more comprehensive 'field to fork' approach to traceability, with the extent of tracing and tracking contingent on the complexity and length of the supply chain. This market prerequisite for traceability is seen in many multi-national food service and multiple retail food supply chains. In complex multinational supply chains, tracking, as a process, records important information at relevant points in the supply chain and is delivered: "Through the analysis and elaboration of the information previously recorded by each actor involved in the chain" or product lifecycle (Pizzuti and Mirabelli, 2015:18).

Tracking and tracing material flow through handling and production operations and distribution processes requires the collation of a set of data that must be clearly linked to each specific phase of the process (Bertolini *et al.*, 2006). In order to demonstrate the variance in conceptualisation of traceability, the literature has been synthesized into three types:

■ Those which distinguish tracking as an individual construct of traceability (e.g. Thakur and Hurbugh, 2009; Bechini *et al.*, 2008)

■ Those which distinguish tracing as an individual construct of traceability (e.g. Opara, 2003: Kher *et al.* 2010); or

■ Those which integrate the requirements of both tracking and tracing (e.g. Aung and Chang, 2014; Foinas *et al*, 2006).

These types of systems underpin the value of traceability for both organisations and the wider supply chain.

The transactional value of traceability

Transactionally, traceability adds value to the product and the overall food safety and quality management system by providing first the communication linkage for identifying, verifying and isolating sources of noncompliance, and second enabling supply chain partners to determine and meet product standards and customer expectations (Pizzuti and Mirabelli, 2015). Effective traceability requires an information trail that follows the physical trail of the food item through the supply chain (Fallon, 2001; Smith *et al.*, 2005), and information sharing in supply chains "improves coordination between supply chain processes to enable the material flow and reduces inventory costs" (Li and Lin, 2006:1642). Further, Lin *et al.* (2002) assert that the higher the level of information sharing, the lower the total costs, the higher the order fulfilment rate and the shorter the order cycle time. The quality of information influences organisational and supply chain agility and the ability to be responsive, for example during a food safety outbreak (Zhou *et al.*, 2014). Thus, if a suspected outbreak of foodborne illness or a food safety incident occurs within a complex, multi-actor, low information input food supply chain, the lack of whole chain traceability makes it difficult to trace products back to source. This was demonstrated with the 2011 European *E. coli* O104 outbreak, whereby the mixing of produce ingredients in salads and buffets at food service level and the generally low information nature of food service, hindered the identification of the implicated food source (Manning and Soon, 2013).

Metrics of information quality determine the extent to which mutually shared information meets the requirements of each organisation in the supply chain (Zhou *et al.*, 2014; Petersen, 1999). Characteristics of information quality include:

accuracy, adequacy, availability, credibility, completeness, frequency, relevance, reliability and timeliness (Delone and McLean, 1992; McCormack 1998; Li *et al.*, 2005, cited by Zhou *et al.*, 2014).

Metrics of traceability: Batch, lot, traceable resource unit

A traceability system should establish and enable the identification of product lots and their relation to batches of raw materials, processing and delivery records (BS EN ISO 22000:2005). Moe (1998) defined the Traceable Resource Unit (TRU) as a unique batch that is distinguishable from other batches in terms of its innate traceability characteristics, through which each individual resource unit or lot can be identified. A lot is a group of items produced under homogeneous conditions in terms of location, e.g. production lot, processing lot or distribution lot, type and date of treatments (Pizzuti and Mirabelli, 2015). Aung and Chang (2014) suggest there are three types of TRU:

■ **Batch** (quantity going through the same process),

■ **Trade unit** (a unique unit sent from one organization to another e.g. pack, box, tray)

■ **Logistic unit** such as a pallet or a container.

Yet a batch may remain a unique unit and be recombined or added to others, as described previously with the E.coli outbreak. TRU are not static, instead they are constantly being changed and reassembled. These changes and reassemblages can include mixing, splitting, joining, aggregation of resources, segregating, transfer storage or rejection, and discarding of TRUs as new lots or batches are created (Foras *et al.*, 2015). This creates challenges when seeking to develop and implement effective food traceability systems that both track and trace food materials.

Therefore, whilst production processes can, on the one hand, be seen as a series of discrete operations, all of which can be identifiable, in some systems the process is continuous and as a result, the units of production are not then by their nature discrete. An example of this would be the continuous filling of a bulk bin with consecutive deliveries of a food ingredient (Dabbene and Gay, 2011). In this instance of continuous unit operations, the batch can only be differentiated as a result of a specific task that has taken place, e.g. bin cleaning or machine servicing. For bulk products, it is very difficult to associate any label, marker or identifier in order to directly identify the lot, instead processes of fuzzy traceability may be used, often based on the concept of dynamic simulation of the traceability associated with the process used (Dabbene *et al.*, 2014), i.e. using computer programs to model the varying behaviour of a system over time. This approach sits at odds with discrete traceability identification, which is otherwise more usually adopted within the food supply chain. The term composition-distance is used to formally establish the homogeneity of a specific lot of given raw materials that need to be tracked, i.e. that a given TRU is not 100% pure or of a consistent character, for example in the case of genetically modified (GM) material. In the European Union (EU) a product can be labelled GM free if the percentage of GM content is less than 0.9% (Dabbene *et al.*, 2014), Therefore if this approach is followed through, a batch does not have to be technically pure to be classed as 'free from', and that minor substitution of alternative product is deemed acceptable if it is below a prescribed amount. This suggests that traceability can either be considered as a technical construct or alternatively can become a political or social construct (Bertolini *et al.*, 2006) and, as such, as a characteristic, traceability is open to questions of opacity, integrity and transparency.

Traceability systems

Traceability systems can be designed to demonstrate compliance to both regulatory and market requirements, including the management of input and product flow so to improve efficiency, product differentiation and drive continuous improvement; verify country of origin labelling; assist in the investigation of food safety and product quality issues; and minimize the extent of a given product withdrawal or supply chain recall (Golan *et al.*, 2004; Smith *et al.*, 2005; Manning *et al.*, 2006; Dabbene and Gay, 2011). There are multiple benefits of an efficient and effective traceability system, including:

- Greater internal and chain efficiency;
- Greater technological use and data availability through improved integration, including linking end products directly to raw material data;
- Improvement in food supply chain management, process control and reduction of organisational and production costs;
- Competence development, including increased access to contracts and markets, and increased labour productivity;
- Precise allocation of responsibilities including labour;
- Greater control of the supply chain;
- Increased speed of intervention in case of unsafe and contaminated food and improvement in food crises management;
- Reduction of commercial risk and protection of brand names and organisational reputation;
- Protection of production and reduction of food fraud;

- Regulatory compliance reducing legal barriers to market access and avoiding penalties for non-compliance;

- Improvement in the image of companies (limited to those marketing their own brands);

- Access to more accurate and timely information;

- Increased transparency;

- Competitive advantage;

- Improving auditing processes;

- Greater capacity for loyalty of customers and customer satisfaction; access to new markets, increased sales.

   (Pizzuti and Mirabelli, 2015; Asioli *et al.*, 2014; Ringsberg, 2014; Bosona and Gebresenbet, 2013; Olsen and Borit, 2013; Bertolini *et al.*, 2006).

A traceability system can provide internal traceability within a company or production unit, or external traceability where items can be tracked and traced between companies and countries (Ringsberg, 2014). Mol and Oosterveer (2015) proposes four types of traceability systems:

- **Book and claim** (certificate based integrity system),

- **Identity preservation** (track and trace based integrity system),

- **Segregation** (separation based integrity system)

- **Mass-balance** (volume based integrity system).

   This highlights that often it is extrinsic process characteristics that are identified during traceability processes, e.g. methods of production, labour and animal welfare standards, locating batches that are in compliance with assurance standards, determining the country of origin, and so forth, rather than the intrinsic product characteristics of the food itself (Manning, 2016). Others define the properties of a two-way traceability system as groupings of materials into TRU, using unique identifiers and keys, recording product and process properties (both intrinsic and extrinsic characteristics) and directly or indirectly linking these identifiers (Olsen and Borit, 2013). Dabbene *et al.* (2014) and Golan *et al.* (2004) state that the level of traceability can be determined by four criteria namely:

- **Breadth** (number of attributes, or quantity of information connected to each traceable unit);

- **Depth** (how far upstream or downstream the traceable unit can be identified);

- **Precision** (the degree of accuracy in pinpointing a particular traceable unit's movement or characteristics);

- **Access** (the speed or timeliness with which tracking and tracing information can be communicated to supply chain members and external stakeholders, especially in the event of a product recall).

Challenges to implementing traceability include: costs, a lack in technical knowledge and skills, inappropriate infrastructure and systems, weak technology acceptance and resistance to change (Ringsberg, 2014). The costs of adopting traceability systems can be differentiated according to time and effort with regard to workforce, administration and management. Particularly in the context of the use of product recall and traceability tests, investing in equipment and data management processes, training, materials such as labels and packaging, certification and audits (Asioli *et al.*, 2014). Often, traceability systems are challenged by either the inability to link information (in documentary or other form) and/or data across the food chain, or the inaccuracy of, and errors in, documentation and which lead to an inability to access essential data (Badia-Melis *et al.*, 2015).

Thus the primary goal of a traceability system is to consistently and precisely log the history and the location of the different products and food ingredients along the supply chain, with technological advances in information communication technology (ICT) underpinning data acquisition and reducing traceability management costs (Dabbene and Gay, 2011). Traceability can only be delivered within a supply chain if there is interoperability between management information systems (Ringsberg, 2014). If a traceability system is to be efficient, then there needs to be an integrated approach to the planning, development and implementation of the product and process monitoring system (Folinas *et al.*, 2006). The authors differentiate between two types of traceability:

■ **Logistics** traceability – tracking and tracing and logging the physical movement of the product (quantity, origin, destination, dispatch date)

■ **Qualitative** traceability that links additional information to the product, e.g. pre-harvest and post-harvest techniques, storage and distribution conditions.

Thus, a traceability system can be described as "a record-keeping and task-triggering mechanism to improve consumer confidence in food consumption and to efficiently reduce the asymmetry of information across food supply chains" (Chen, 2015:70).

However, as concerns over adulteration and substitution in food products increase, consideration is being given to the need to trace innate intrinsic aspects of the food, for example through the use of isotope or DNA analysis. Indeed identity preservation (IP) is becoming an increasingly important credence or process attribute that adds economic value to a product (Dabbene *et al.*, 2014). Being able to differentiate lots such as GM from non-GM materials in a grain store, or for provenance to be assured, require IP control processes to be in place. As IP identification systems develop, this raises the potential for increased waste as non-compliant material can more readily be identified. Two contemporary issues are now explored as a focal point to this challenge: geographic origin and intelligent packaging systems and data.

Issues in traceability: Geographic origin

Peres *et al.* (2015) differentiate between techniques that can determine geographic traceability into two types: physicochemical techniques and biological techniques.

- **Physiochemical** techniques include fluorescence spectroscopy, nuclear magnetic resonance coupled with mass spectrometry of isotopic ratio (NMR/MSIR), ion exchange chromatography/atomic absorption spectrometry (AAS), site-specific natural isotope fractionation by nuclear magnetic resonance (SNIF-NMR), mid and near infrared spectroscopy (MIRS–NIRS), Fourier transform mid-infrared spectroscopy (FT-MIRS), Curie point pyrolysis coupled to mass spectrometry (Cp–PyMS), electronic nose coupled with mass spectrometry).

- **Biological** techniques encompass techniques such as denaturing gradient gel electrophoresis (DGGE) and denaturing high performance liquid chromatography (DHPLC), and the polymorphism of conformation of the single strand DNA (SSCP) or DNA chips (Peres *et al.*, 2007).

The different technologies used to collate traceability data have been drawn together from the literature (Table 3.1).

Geographic traceability rather than identifying a given lot or batch, instead tracks intrinsic elements, e.g. stable isotopes within a food, to determine its geographic source, location or origin (Dalvit *et al.*, 2007), protected designation of origin such as with olive oil (Chiocchini *et al.*, 2016; Medini *et al.*, 2015). Geographic traceability also locates wine to a specific vineyard (Petrini *et al.*, 2015) or using technology such as NMR fingerprinting, identifies the country or region of origin of commodities such as coffee (Mehari *et al.*, 2016; Arana *et al.*, 2015). Non-targeted spectrometric or spectroscopic chemical analysis followed by multivariate statistical evaluation of data of food can be used to determine geographical origin, species, or variety (Riedl *et al.*, 2015). However, whilst multivariate screening methods are increasingly being implemented for different food products, there is no worldwide, harmonised criterion for their validation, and this prevents such measures from being universally adopted (Manning, 2016; López *et al.*, 2014).

There is also a means of tracing and tracking products through genetic traceability, which involves the identification of animals, plants and food products based on their DNA (Dalvit *et al.*, 2007). DNA barcoding is an effective tool for confirming both origin and quality of raw materials, and to detect adulteration (Galimberti *et al.*, 2013). However, its use is affected by the need to have high quality reference sequences. Methods include polymerase chain reaction (PCR), short tandem repeats (STR), and single nucleotide polymorphism (SNP) that can be used to verify breed and species (Dalvit *et al.*, 2007). The use of genetic traceability tools such as those described above is gaining in ground within traceability verification techniques.

Table 3.1: Technologies of value in food, food ingredient integrity and provenance traceability (Adapted from Bosona and Gebresenbet 2013; Galimberti *et al.*, 2013; Vanderroost *et al.*, 2014; Kelepouris *et al.*, 2016; Ghaani *et al.*, 2016 citing Kerry *et al.*, 2006; Han *et al.*, 2005)

Technology	Use	Data captured
Bar Codes - 1D, 2D and QR 2D barcodes	Inventory control, stock allocation, stock movements; theft protection, anti-counterfeiting	Manufacturer ID, price, date packed
Biosensors	Identification of analytes in food, micro organisms, allergenic proteins	Authenticity data
Chemical markers, and indicators	Tracking authentic products with use of a chemical marker	Authenticity data
Chemical sensors	Monitor food quality and packaging integrity	Can measure volatile or spoilage gases, gas levels in modified packaging
Commercial traceability software	Tracking and tracing of quality assurance data and product through a supply chain	Multiple datasets can be used
DNA methods *	Identification of plant and animal cultivars, animal breeds	Authentication information
Electronic Article Surveillance (EAS) e.g. holograms, inks, micro-tags, tear labels & tapes	Anti-counterfeiting, anti-tamper and anti-theft devices	Location – activated by removal from the store or location.
Electronic Data Interchange (EDI)*	Information sharing via the internet	Information transfer
Electronic identification tags	Livestock traceability, batch management	Product identification, batch data
Extensible markup language	Information sharing via the internet	Information transfer
Freshness indicators	Identification of microbial growth or chemical changes in the food	
Geographic Information Systems	Remote collection of data, e.g. with livestock traceability	Product identification
Global Positioning Systems (GPS)	Remote collection of data, e.g. with livestock traceability, product location	Product identification, location of product during transport
Hologram	Anti-countfeiting measure used on package	Incorporates track and trace & authentication information
Inks	Thermochromatic inks that change color within a certain temperature range	Temperature control and potential for temperature abuse
Nose systems	Information on ripening, fermentation, cooking, spoilage that causes	Product integrity data
Nuclear techniques, e.g. isotopic & elemental fingerprints	Provenance and geographic source determination	Provenance checks, PDO determination
Paper records	Documents that accompany lots or batches as they move from location to location	Information transfer
Radio frequency identification (RFID)	Information sharing, temperature-time control, livestock management, theft-prevention, electronic payment, automated production systems, navigation/ inventory/ promotions management	Batch data, product identification
Remote Sensing (RS)	Remote collection of data, e.g. with livestock traceability, product location	Product identification, location during transport
Traditional sensors	Measurement of product or process characteristics	pH, light, temperature, humidity

* including Polymerase Chain Reaction (PCR) – based markers and hybridization-based markers; sequencing based systems including single nucleotide polymorphisms (SNPs) and simple sequence repeats (SSRs) and DNA barcoding

Traceability through intelligent packaging systems and data

Intelligent systems (IS) are of value in traceability, and IS in food packaging incorporate external discrete components in the final pack, such as two dimensional films or three dimensional objects (Ghaani *et al.*, 2016). IS technologies include:

1 Indicators that convey to the consumer the presence or absence or level of a substance, or a reaction that has occurred e.g. time temperature changes, gas indicators;

2 Thermochromatic inks that change colour within a certain temperature range;

3 Electronic article surveillance (EAS) anti-counterfeiting, anti-tamper and anti-theft devices such as holograms, thermochromatic inks, micro-tags, tear labels and tapes;

4 Data carriers that carry information for theft protection or counterfeit protection, e.g. 1D, 2D and QR 2D barcodes and RFID tags,

5 Sensors (chemical or biosensors) that identify analytes in food (Ghaani *et al.*, 2016, citing Kerry *et al.*, 2006; Han *et al.*, 2005).

Traceability though technical advancements in information management systems and real-time technology such as electronic data interchange (EDI) or extensible markup language (XML), radio frequency identification (RFID), innovative use of smartphone technology or packaging features such as special inks, holograms on cases of product or on each pallet allows the centralisation of data and more real-time access (Manning, 2016; Badia-Melis *et al.*, 2015; Bosona and Gebresenbet, 2013; Spink *et al.*, 2010). Bar codes, data loggers and RFID can be described collectively as Automatic Identification and Data Capture (AIDC) technologies. EDI is commonly used for electronic data exchange in the B2B environment enabling a sequence of messages between two parties, with either being originator or recipient and can be used efficiently by organisations with mature IT capabilities (Thakur and Hurburgh, 2009). RFID as a technology uses radio waves to automatically identify objects, including stored information such as a serial number held on a microchip that is attached to an antenna, the RFID tag (Kelepouris *et al.*, 2016). RFID is of value with identifying continuous batches, e.g. grain, milk, but the systems must be in place to remove the tracing device from the final product (Dabbene *et al.*, 2014). Using XML can facilitate the sharing of structured data across different information systems, especially using the internet, e.g. the system TraceCore for grain (Thakur and Hurburgh, 2009).

Challenges to the use of RFID in supply chain traceability are: the lack of uniformity of format standards and challenges over information sharing; the high volumes of data initiated in the traceability process; the reading range; the ability to detect faults and isolate them; cost, knowledge and skillset in their use and the level of granularity, i.e. are they operating at item, case or pallet level; the degree of integration with chemical sensors and recycling issues; physical limitations that influence the electromagnetic waves; and lastly the harsh environments in which the technology is used, such as hot, cold, wet (Ruiz-Garcia and Lunadei, 2011).

Further technologies such as electronic identification tags (EID), Geographic Information Systems (GIS), Global Positioning Systems (GPS), Remote Sensing (RS) can be applied in traceability systems too (Aung and Chang, 2015; Bosona and Gebresenbet, 2013). Indeed Musa *et al.* (2014:176) argue that:

> ongoing rapid developments in RFID, the evolution of communication and localisation technologies (such as XML, ebXML, EDI, Bluetooth, WiFi, WiMax, WiBro, Zigbee, Ultra-Wide Band, RuBee, IEEE 802 family of standards, infrared, indoor messaging), MEMS-based small sensors and actuators, web services, multi-agents, together with the digitisation of public infrastructures in the era of "internet of things" (IoT) have ushered in several methods, systems and architectures for achieving visibility of products classes and instances across supply chains.

As research in this area develops then the range of technologies and tools that can be used, as well as the associated data libraries, will expand.

The requirements for traceability data can be voluntary or mandatory (Bosona and Gebresnbet, 2013:36, citing Folinas *et al.*, 2006). Depending on legislative or market requirements, traceability data can include: lot or batch number, product ID, product description, supplier ID, quantity, unit of measure, buyer ID, supplier's name, contact information, receipt date, country of origin, date of pack, trade unit, transportation vehicle ID, logistics service provider ID, buyer's name, and dispatching date. Traceability data can be either static, i.e. features that do not change (country of origin, variety, duration date), or dynamic and change over time, e.g. lot number and dispatch date, and as such should be differentiated in this way (Folinas *et al.*, 2006).

Traceability data management frameworks provide the structure to support information flow transparency and effective decision making in four phases: identification and classification, transformation and modelling, processing and presentation of traceability data (Folinas *et al.*, 2006). In this respect transparency of a supply chain network can be described as: "the extent to which all the network's stakeholders have a shared understanding of, and access to, product and process related information that they request, without loss, noise, delay and distortion" (Buelens *et al.*, 2005:482). The management tools, systems and technologies described in this chapter enable greater data and actor transparency. Transparency in itself is embedded in the mechanisms for demonstrating the degree of food integrity in the supply chain.

Transparency: Food integrity and traceability

The issue facing society, as supply chains lengthen and multiple actors become involved, is one of food integrity. This challenge is not new, yet the problem is becoming more convoluted and nuanced, requiring greater ingenuity in the efforts employed to detect and control malpractice, malevolent behaviour and opportunism in modern more elongated supply chains. The emerging and evolving themes of traceability and transparency demonstrate the expanding scope of what the food industry and stakeholders, including regulatory bodies, need to address and verify. The technologies and tools of value in food material integrity and provenance verification have been previously drawn together (Table 3.1).

Food integrity as a subject will in the future be discussed as freely as food safety or food quality is today. Food integrity encompasses four elements: product integrity, process integrity, data integrity and people integrity (Manning, 2016).

- **Product integrity** can be said to describe the inherent quality attribute of totality or completeness (Manning and Soon, 2014), i.e. the intrinsic nature and quality of the food.

- **Process integrity** encompasses the design, assurance, monitoring and verification of processes within the product life-cycle to ensure that they remain authentic and intact (Manning, 2016), i.e. the extrinsic characteristics or quality of the food. Verification of process integrity is, and will continue to be, a challenge with regard to management traceability, regulatory traceability, consumer traceability and public traceability (Mol and Oosterveer, 2015).

- **Data integrity** concerns the consistency and accuracy of data throughout the food product life-cycle, what has been described in this chapter as information quality.

- **People integrity** considers the honesty and morals exhibited by individuals, either in their own right or on behalf of an organisation.

Traceability as a transactional activity informs stakeholders on the degree of integrity in a given supply chain. As has been previously outlined, IP and the technical and social constructs of food integrity are becoming increasingly important credence attributes that add economic value to a product.

This critique of current literature on traceability supports the postulation of the essential technical requirements of a traceability system, and the underlying elements of tracking and tracing, and how traceability can be effectively implemented in the food supply chain. The use of electronic forms of traceability data control and the integration of data management systems will underpin future developments in food traceability and the means to demonstrate technical transparency to stakeholders.

Concluding remarks

The literature that surrounds the use of the term 'traceability' is vast and multi-faceted. This chapter has sought to draw together a number of themes and used two contemporary issues in traceability: geographic origin and traceability, through intelligent packaging systems to consider how traceability systems are technically evolving with regard to managing and also verifying food supply chains. Whilst traceability as an operational activity and as a notional construct has been well explored by the industry, existing supply chain management controls still focus on process and data verification rather than product verification. New technologies and tools such as those described in Table 3.1, have the potential to make product verification more real-time, and with some techniques avoid the destruction of the product during the testing or verification process, thus reducing cost. Whilst improved traceability systems address one aspect of an organisation's social responsibility to deliver safe and consistent food, a consequence of being able to detect non-conformance more readily is the potential for food waste to rise, which will impact negatively on another aspect the organization social responsibility to minimize waste. It is important to reflect too that whilst traceability is seen on the one hand as a technical or transactional construct it also has social characteristics. Thus traceability will increasingly be used by organizations to act against opacity and ambiguity in supply chain management, and to promote transparency and the integrity of stakeholders themselves and in terms of the food product produced.

References

Arana, V.A., Medina, J., Alarcon, R., Moreno, E., Heintz, L., Schäfer, H. and Wist, J. (2015), Coffee's country of origin determined by NMR: The Colombian case, *Food Chemistry*, **175**, 500-506

Asioli, D., Boecker, A. and Canavari, M. (2014), On the linkages between traceability levels and expected and actual traceability costs and benefits in the Italian fishery supply chain, *Food Control*, **46**, 10-17

Aung, M.M. and Chang, Y.S. (2014), Traceability in a food supply chain: Safety and quality perspectives, *Food Control*, **39**, 172-184

Badia-Melis, R., Mishra, P. and Ruiz-Garcia L. (2015), Food traceability: New trends and recent advances. A review. *Food Control*, **57**, 393-401

Bechini, A., Cimino, M., Marcelloni, F. and Tomasi, A. (2008). Patterns and technologies for enabling supply chain traceability through collaborative e-business. *Information and Software Technology*, **50**(4), 342-359

Bertolini, M., Bevilacqua, M. and Massini, R. (2006), FMECA approach to product traceability in the food industry, *Food Control*, **17**, 137-145

Bosona, T. and Gebresenbet, G. (2013). Food traceability as an integral part of logistics management in food and agricultural supply chain, *Food Control*, **33**, 32-48.

BS EN ISO 22000 (2005), *Food Safety Management Systems – requirements for any organization in the food chain*, BSI London.

Beulens, A.J.M., Broens, D., Folstar, P. and Hofstede, G. J. (2005). Food safety and transparency in food chains and networks relationships and challenges. *Food Control*, **16**(6), 481-486

Charlebois, S. and Haratifar, S. (2015), The perceived value of dairy product traceability in modern society: An exploratory study, *Journal of Dairy Science*, **98**, 3514-3525

Chen, R-Y. (2015), Autonomous tracing system for backward design in food supply chain, *Food Control*, **51**, 70-84

Chiocchini, F., Portarena, S., Ciolfi, M., Brungnoli, E. and Lauteri, M. (2016), Isoscapes of carbon and oxygen stable isotope compositions in tracing authenticity and geographical origin of Italian extra-virgin olive oils, *Food Chemistry*, **1**(202), 291-301

Dabbene, F., Gay, P. and Tortia, C. (2014), Traceability issues in food supply chain management: A review, *Biosystems Engineering*, **120**, 65-80

Dabbene, F. and Gay, P. (2011), Food traceability systems: Performance evaluation and optimization, *Computers and Electronics in Agriculture*, **75**, 139-146

Dalvit, C., De Marchi, M. and Cassandro, M. (2007), Genetic traceability of livestock products: A review, *Meat Science*, **77**, 437-449

Delone, W. and McLean, E., (1992), Information system success: the quest for the dependent variable, *Information System Research*, **3**(1), 60–95

EU (2002) EC/178/2002 laying down the general principles and requirements of food safety law, establishing the European Food Standards Agency and laying down procedures in matters of food safety OJ L/31 1.2.2002 pp. 001 – 024

Fallon, M. (2001), Traceability of poultry and poultry products, *Revue Scientifique et Technique*, **20** (2), 538-546

Folinas, D., Manikas, I. and Manos, B. (2006), Traceability data management for food chains, *British Food Journal*, **108**(8), 622-633

Foras, E., Thakur, M., Solem, K. and Svara, R. (2015), State of traceability in the Norwegian food sectors, *Food Control*, **57**, 65-69

Galimbert, A., De Mattia, F., Losa, A., Bruni, I., Federici, S., Casiraghi, M., Martellos, S. and Labra, M. (2013) DNA barcoding as a new tool for food traceability, *Food Research International*, **50**, 55-63

Ghaani, M., Cozzolino, C.A., Castelli, G. and Farris, S. (2016), An overview of the intelligent packaging technologies in the food sector, *Trends in Food Science and Technology*, **51**, 1-11

Golan, E. Krissoff, B. Kuchler, F. Calvin, L. Nelson, K. and Price, G. (2004), *Traceability in the U.S. Food Supply: Economic Theory and Industry Studies*, Economic Research Service, U.S. Dept. of Agriculture, Agricultural Economic Report No. 830. (AER830)

Han, J. H., Ho, C. H. L. and Rodrigues, E. T. (2005). Intelligent packaging. In J. H. Han (Ed.), *Innovations in Food Packaging* (p. 151). Amsterdam: Elsevier Academic Press.

Kelepouris, T., Pramatari, K. and Doulidis, G., (2016), FRID-enabled traceability in the food supply chain, *Industrial Management and Data Systems*, **107**(2), 183-200

Kerry, J. P., O'Grady, M. N. and Hogan, S. A. (2006). Past, current and potential utilisation of active and intelligent packaging systems for meat and muscle-based products: a review. *Meat Science*, **74**, 113-130.

Kher, S. V., Frewer, L. J., De Jonge, J., Wertholt, M., Davies, O. H., Luijckx, N. B. L. and Cnossen, H.J. (2010). Experts' perspectives on the implementation of traceability in Europe. *British Food Journal*, **112**(2), 261-274.

Leat, P., Marr, P. and Ritchie, C. (1998) Quality assurance and traceability – the Scottish agrifood industry's quest for competitive advantage, *Supply Chain Management*, **3**, 115–117

Li, S. and Lin, B. (2006), Accessing information sharing and information quality in supply chains, *Decision Support Systems*, **42**, 1641-1656

Li, S., Rao, S.S., Ragu-Nathan, T.S. and Ragu-Nathan, B. (2005), Development and validation of a measurement instrument for studying supply chain management practices, *Journal of Operations Management*, **23** (6), 618–641.

Lin, F., Huang, S. and Lin, S. (2002), Effects of information sharing on supply chain performance in electronic commerce, *IEEE Transactions on Engineering Management*, **49** (3), 258–268.

López, M.I., Colomer, N., Ruisánchez, I. and Callao, M.P., (2014), Validation of multivariate screening methodology. Case study: Detection of food fraud, *Analytica Chimica Acta*, **827**, 28-33

Manning L. Baines R.N. and Chadd, S.A. (2006), Food safety management in broiler meat production, *British Food Journal*, **108** (8), 605-621

Manning, L. and Soon, J.M. (2013), GAP Framework for fresh produce production, *British Food Journal*, **115** (6), 796-820

Manning, L and Soon, J.M, (2014), Developing systems to control food adulteration, *Food Policy*, **49** (1), 23-32

Manning L. (2016), Food fraud, policy and food chain, *Current Opinions in Food Science*, **10**, 16-21

McCormack, K., (1998), *What Supply Chain Management Practices Relate to Superior Performance?*, DRK Research Team, Boston, MA.

Medini, S., Janin, M., Verdoux, P. and Techer, I. (2015), Methodological development for 87Sr/86Sr measurement in olive oil and preliminary discussion of its use for geographical traceability of PDO Nîmes (France), *Food Chemistry*, **171**, 78-83

Mehari, B., Redi-Abshiro, M., Chandravanshi, BS. and Combrinck, S. (2016), Profiling of phenolic compounds using UPLC-MS for determining the geographic origin of green coffee beans from Ethiopia, *Journal of Food Composition and Analysis*, **45**, 16-25

Moe, T. (1998), Perspective on traceability in food manufacture, *Trends in Food Science and Technology*, **9**, 211–214.

Mol, A.P.J, and Oosterveer, P. (2015), Certification of markets, markets of certificates: Tracing sustainability in global agro-food value chains, *Sustainability*, **7**(9), 12258-78

Musa, A., Gunasekaran, A. and Yusuf, Y, (2014), Supply chain visibility: Methods, systems and impacts, *Expert Systems with Applications*, **41**, 176-194

Olsen, P., and Borit, M. (2013), How to define traceability, *Trends in Food Science and Technology*, **29**, 142-150.

Opara, L.U. (2003). Traceability in agriculture and food supply chain: a review of basic concepts, technological implications, and future prospects. *Food, Agriculture and Environment*, **1**(1), 101-106.

Petersen, K. (1999), The effect of information quality on supply chain performance: an inter-organizational information system perspective. Unpublished dissertation. Michigan State University, MI.

Peres, B., Barlet, N., Loiseau, G. and Montet, D. (2007), Review of the current methods of analytical traceability allowing determination of the origin of foodstuffs, *Food Control*, **18**, 228-235

Petrini, R., Sansone, L., Slejko, F.F., Buccianti, A., Marcuzzo, P. and Tomasi, D. (2015) The 87Sr/86Sr strontium isotopic systematics applied to Glera vineyards: A tracer for the geographical origin of the Prosecco, *Food Chemistry*, **170**, 138-144

Pizzuti, T. and Mirabelli, G. (2015), The global track and trace system for food: General framework and functioning principles, *Journal of Food Engineering*, **159**, 16-35

Riedl, J., Esslinger, S. and Fauhl-Hassek, C. (2015), Review of validation and reporting of non-targeted fingerprinting approaches for food adulteration, *Analytica Chimica Acta*, **885**, 17-32

Ringsberg, H. (2014), Perspectives on food traceability: a systematic literature review, *Supply Chain Management: An International Journal*, **19**(5/6), 558-576

Ruiz-Garcia, L. and Lunadei, L. (2011), The role of RFID in agriculture: Applications, limitations and challenges, *Computers and Electronics in Agriculture*, **79**, 42-50

Smith, G.C., Tatum, J.D., Belk, K.E., Scanga, J.A., Grandin, T. and Sofos, J.N. (2005), Traceability from a US perspective. 51st International Congress of Meat Science and Technology Baltimore, USA, 7-12 August. *Meat Science*, **71** (1), 174-193

Spink, J. Helferich, O.K. and Griggs, J.E. (2010), Combating the impact of product counterfeiting, *Distribution Business Management Journal*, **10**(1), 6.

Thakur, M. and Hurburgh, C.R. (2009), Framework for implementing traceability system in the bulk grain supply chain, *Journal of Food Engineering*, **95**, 617-626

Vanderroost, M., Ragaert, P., Devlieghere, F. and De Meulenaer, B. (2014) Intelligent food packaging: The next generation, *Trends in Food Science & Technology* **39**(1)

Zhou, H., Shou, Y., Zhai, X., Li, L., Wood, C. and Wu, X. (2014), Supply chain practice and information quality: A supply chain strategy study, *International Journal of Production Economics*, **147**, 624-633

4 Supply Chains and Horizontal and Vertical Integration: Coordination through the Food Industries

Jane Eastham

Introduction

This chapter examines two well respected forms of collaborative activity, and leads on from Chapter 3, from the premise that information sharing is not only an important dimension to ensuring food integrity but also the generation of innovative ideas, and business practices across a spectrum of social, economic and ecological concerns. The major focus in this chapter is, however, the value of collaborative activity in economic terms.

Innovation is an important stimulant of economic growth and social change, as has been highlighted in the work of the Viennese scholar Schumpeter, and following the devastation of the 2nd World War, countries including Italy and Japan looked to regenerate their economies through different forms of collaborative activity involving horizontal and vertical orientated networks.

By the 1980s, the business solutions developed were exposed to global academic communities and became the subject of much interest, due to their apparent success as mechanisms not only for economic growth but also as sources of competitive advantage.

This chapter takes us through the nature of these initiatives and questions whether these governance structures offer a long term solution to the distribution of economic value in the food supply chain.

The emergence of supply chain management and new or Marshallian industrial districts

4

Across intellectual disciplines, there is the view that the sharing and collective action between groups, tribes or businesses offers greater opportunities than individuals or businesses operating on their own. It is seen to enable more efficient use of such resources as time and effort in the attainment of goals. Collective activity is seen to be a means by which parties can attain solutions that go beyond their own limited vision (Westley and Vrendenburg, 1991) and 'social capital', the close ties and solidarity between parties within the collective, is critical to the formation and sustainability of such communities (McMillan and Chavis, 1989; Staber, 2007) particularly in the context of localised initiatives.

Lehner (1993) in the Future of Industry in Europe programme, *Forecasting and Assessment in Science and Technology* (FAST) suggested that in the light of global competition, there was a need for new forms of organisation and governance structures to promote economic growth. The European Commission opened up the debate on industrial policy in its "communication on industry policy in an open and competitive environment" (otherwise known as the Bangemann communication) in 1990. At this stage the economic and political collaboration between western and southern European states, now known as the European Union, had been established for over three decades. Within the commission, calls were made, as a consequence of research into both the 'Third Italy', Silicon Valley in California, and initiatives within Japan, for the mastering of the supply chain and the development of collaborative behaviour. In a climate of global economies in order to compete, Europe needed to promote innovation, (Lehner, 1993) intelligent production systems, learning innovation and rapid adaptation.

To this end, policy makers promoted horizontal and vertical collaboration in supply chains. In the context of food, the European Commission, and national and regional governments were and remain committed to promote the restructuring of food supply chains, an initiative in the UK that is promoted through rural development strategies. Rural development strategies now fall under Pillar 2 of the Common Agricultural Policy. Emphasis is currently particularly upon cooperatives and producer organisations, although a range of collective governance models can be identified over the last decades, including 'New/Marshallian industrial districts' (MIDs) and 'supply chain management' as derived from the

Toyota production system and Japanese Keiretsu, each of which are now becoming increasingly criticised in terms of their efficacy as catalysts for economic growth, including rural development and regeneration.

Whilst MIDs and 'lean' supply chain governance structures emerged in the 1980s, both have their roots in earlier intellectual ventures and are a backlash against large scale units of production and vertically integrated corporations (Loveman and Sengenberger, 1991). In what has been described as the 'post productionist' era, SMEs are identified as drivers for economic growth, which is distinct from the earlier position of academics such as Chandler (1977), who firmly believed that the era of the small business was over. The underlying premise in this renewed interest lies in the idea that whilst individual small businesses alone may be under-resourced to compete in highly competitive globalised markets, the case is other when they are involved in collaborative coalitions.

Theoretical underpinning of Marshallian industrial districts and supply chain management

Implicit in work as early as the 1920s, small businesses have been recognised as seedbeds for new enterprises (Marshall, 1920), and seen to be capable of challenging established businesses (Beesley and Hamilton, 1984). Often, lead by idea generators or entrepreneurs, they have also been labelled as sources of innovation, particularly where there is access to key skills (Karlsson and Olsson,1998). Schumpeter (1947) defined innovation as new ways of organising existing resources, which could be classified into five distinctive types: new products, new methods of production, new sources of supply, exploitation of new markets and new ways of organising business. Others have held that product and production innovation were central to economic growth, however in the context of this chapter, it is held that all five are significant in our exploration of supply chains, and in particular that of new ways of organising business.

■ The nature and emergence of new/ Marshillian industrial districts

The first innovative collaborative governance structure to be discussed in this chapter is that of MIDs, particularly those developed in Italy. MIDs have been seen as an alternative to the Fordist production model of large integrated enterprises, which were emerging as the dominant governance structure in the first part of the last century (Piore and Sabel, 1984; Andersson and Ejermo, 2004). They represent a pendulum swing away from the earlier dominant discourse, that small enterprises were of the past and that "economic activity is carried on by large-scale enterprises which require extensive co-ordination of managers and the managed" (Kerr, 1960: 39). SMEs were seen to be the answer to declining economies in Europe, through the development of regional economies – the so-called 'death of distance' (Cairncross, 2001).

This was explained in economic terms (Porter and Porter, 1998). but could also be interpreted as a social backlash to globalisation (Giddens, 1991), where TNCs were seen to leach out value from the regional economy (Arezki *et al.*, 2013). Equally importantly, where specific regions are in decline, local firms are seen to be less likely to retract their businesses from the area (Acs, 1992; Grabher, 1993).

The key feature of MIDs was that they offered specialised clusters of firms bounded in specific territories. These were symbiotic in nature and focused on a range of food and associated industries. The strength of such associations is that they shared and developed local resources including, human, physical and financial, with the specific purpose of developing local capacity, local skills and competence, and a sense of community (Ray, 2000; Chiarveso *et al.*, 2010).

The theory behind industrial districts assumes that economic development is based on local participation and commitment to territorial development, engendering a feeling of ownership. It has been considered a self–centred localised and conservative form of growth (Iaciponi *et al.*, 1995), which requires local social mobilisation, locally agreed allocation of resources with the specific purpose of developing local capacity, local skills and competence, thus allowing benefits to be retained within the local area (Van der Ploeg and Long, 1994). These ideas are inherent to the theory of endogenous growth. Investment in human capital, social capital, technological and intellectual knowhow generated by one business will spill over and benefit the wider economy, generating innovation in products, production, new sources of supply and markets, which leads to the internalisation of the multiplier effect and thus greater economic growth (Porter and Porter, 1998). The size of the regional multiplier depends on the extent to which the inter-industry effects are transmitted to the region (Harris, 1997).

One such example of the conglomeration of businesses in agri-food and food sectors/supply chains is that of Emilia Romagna in Italy which brought about a significant volume of literature that showed the decline of GDP and employment had been stemmed by greater integration of agrarian with non agrarian structures (e.g. Pyke *et al.*, 1990; Baptista and Swann,1998).

Case study: The Third Italy and Emilia Romagna

The North East of Italy is comprised of six regions, Umbria, le Marche, Veneto, Friuli, and Trentino-Alto Adige/Südtirol, and is frequently referred to as the Third Italy. Whilst branded together, each of the regional goverments of these regions has, over time, adopted a distinct approach to industrial policy, from the quite laisser-faire approach of Veneto to the highly interventionist approach of Emilia-Romagna. It is with Emilia-Romagna that we start our story; a region which includes nine provinces: Bologna, Ferrara, Forlì-Cesena, Modena, Parma, Piacenza, Ravenna, Reggio Emilia and Rimini, with a current population of around 4.4 million, and the second largest of the six regions, after Veneto.

The regions have been characterised by some tens of thousands of small and medium-sized businesses and cooperatives, and are documented to have enabled economic growth through economies of scope. In Emilia-Romagna there are three key federations of cooperatives: the *Lega* group, which represents the political left; *Confcoop*, the Catholic cooperative; and the smaller centre-left cooperative *Associazione*, which were re/established after the second world war following the downfall of the fascist regime. There were also 90,000 manufacturing enterprises, which were predominantly small or medium enterprises (SMEs). One person in twelve was self-employed or owned a small business.

Since the late 1940s and reforms to the Italian constitution which allowed for cooperatives to be formed, the region has produced the highest GDP per capita in the country. Additionally, two thirds the population of Bologna belonged to a co-op and over 45% of the GDP was generated by co-ops. The Third Italy had a strong political left and Catholic tradition, a contributory factor to its history of collaboration and cooperatives.

The high density of cooperatives and SMEs in Emilia-Romagna, have been seen to epitomise the economic value of business clusters, and allow the formation of complex and dynamic partnerships between cooperatives and small manufacturing companies, from which cost advantages are thought to emerge as a consequence of the close proximity of specialised suppliers, subcontractors and specialised labour markets (Pyke *et al.*, 1990). Research had suggested that a shared culture and a network-based organisational structure enhances trust, and ultimately reduces transaction costs (Diez-Vial and Alvarez-Suescun, 2011). Furthermore, evidence suggested that external knowledge stocks cluster in the region (Belussi *et al.*, 2010) and were diffused via formal and informal knowledge transfer systems including buyer/seller relationships, know-how trading among experts, communities, the monitoring of competitors and mobility of workers.

In conjunction with cooperatives, the region put in place a whole series of initiatives designed to rebuild the much needed housing, small businesses and agriculture – programmes that nurtured both cooperatives and SMEs, rebuilding small, locally owned enterprises and creating high value jobs in a region known for its high quality artisan production. Private companies and cooperatives began to work together in flexible networks that combined a number of smaller firms into joint projects.

The fluidity of knowledge transfer has been seen to give rise to a collective learning process that, besides enhancing knowledge diffusion between firms, individuals and local institutions, turns private knowledge into a public good; that is knowledge that is open to all (non-excludable) and the use of which does not inhibit its use by others (non-rivalled). Cooperatives were also able to form larger networks/consortiums to bid for larger projects and then share the work out among their members.

The local governments also played a positive role, in creating sector-based service centres that assisted smaller companies, and a regional development agency designed to facilitate development, the ERVET, (*Ente Regionale per la Valorizzazione Economica del Territorio*), created in 1973. This initiative was supported by banks and trade associations and provided analysis and support in defining regional industrial policies. Since the 1980s ERVET has offered businesses services to enable restructuring, e.g. professional training, the use of IT, and the provision of infrastructure, as well as policy advice. In conjunction with cooperatives, in a form of private-public partnership, it has contributed to the development of financial institutions and financing pools to supply the growing firms with equity and debt capital.

■ New industrial networks as a longer term solution: Continued innovation

In essence the innovations demonstrated included the exploitation of new markets, new sources of supply, new ways of organising business, but, certainly in the early days, less evidence of new products and new methods of production. The whole essence of the 'Third Italy' and the made in Italy brand was traditionalism, authenticity, integrity and a sense of local. In this next section, questions are raised as to the extent to which this model of economic growth is sustainable.

Whilst there has been considerable interest in the value of industrial districts as mechanisms for economic growth, certain academics demonstrated a level of scepticism as to the real value of socially embedded regional networks (e.g. Harrison, 1994). In late 1980s and 1990s, MIDs were experiencing difficulties and in second half of the 1990s the Italian economy suffered a significant slowdown. In the growing globalization of the marketplace, there are new challenges to the Emilia model.

There are a number of factors suggested to be the cause of such downturns. Hadjimichalis (2006) suggests that there has been over emphasis on the agglomeration, the collectivism and the spill-over generated by MIDs without any real consideration of how small family firms operated in Italy. It is suggested that the key ingredients to the flexibility of micro artisanal businesses in MIDs were poor working conditions including low pay, long working hours, unlimited time contracts, and poor health and safety conditions. Low costs of labour were also supported through formal and informal women and child labour, which was embedded in a culture, which was patriarchal, family centric and focused upon social relations, and which enabled tax evasion, multiple job holding and moonlighting (Hadjimichalis, 2006).

These were supported by protectionist measures put in place by the Italian state, in particular in the form a low rate of exchange for the Lira until the establishment of the Euro in 2001, and statutory measures in the form of the Statuto Dei Labouratori (in 1970), which ensured that firms with under 15 workers – 'artisan firms' – were exempt from responsibilities of contribution to unemployment, tax, welfare, and health and safety regulations. Regulations such as 317/91 and 140/99 were also to the advantage of these artisan firms, in that they allowed specific subsidies to be paid to micro firms.

The inability to keep up with the growing global competition at the end of the last century was as much a consequence of the growing numbers of graduates within Italy, who were uninterested in the low paid craft-based industries inherent to the Third Italy, as it was of the reduction in demand for luxury goods as a consequence of the recession. When faced with the expansion of economies such as China, India, and Romania, they were unable to compete against their lower labour costs, particularly as artisanal skills in Italy were on the decline. In addition, the Italian government has now less control over the economy, and consequently political influence over the MIDs, since entry to the Euro.

As a consequence, the industrial base has been restructured. There have been a number of changes in specialisms of firms, international and innovation strategies and the governance structures of entrepreneurial activity (Rabellotti *et al.*, 2009). Whilst traditional manufacturing sectors included artisanal food, textile, wood and leather production, which had evolved synergistically to be the pillars of 'Made in Italy' production, there have emerged both new industries and strategies for existing industries in the Third Italy. These have varied across the six regions: the food industry has remained concentrated in Parma, Modena and Bologna, alongside the mechanical and automotive industry, whilst in others there has been the development of high tech industries.

The key strategies identified have included:

1 The emergence of new forms of enterprise organization – vertical integration and the appearance of leading medium firms.

2 Outsourcing, FDI and participation in global value chains

3 Employment of non-EU workers

4 The innovation strategies being adopted in districts (ICT diffusion, process and product innovations).

The emergence of new forms of enterprise

There have been a series of mergers and acquisitions, and the formation of large, vertically integrated firms with subcontractors or outsourcers located outside the region; examples of such enterprises include Prada, Benetton, Zara, SASIB, Diesel and Nike, who are recognised worldwide and have total control of their brand and value chain. The direct switch to subcontractors in remote locations, such as India and China, particularly in production, as well as the re-location of machines and Italian technical supervisors to closer destinations, including Slovenia, Romania, Hungary and Poland, allowed these large focal organisations to reduce costs, especially by using the cheaper labour force in these countries. Veneto, Lombardia, and Emilia-Romagna were three of the key regions which effected these strategies, and within these the highest level of de-localisation was in Vicenza (47% of industrial value).

The search for cheaper labour in the Third Italy has contributed to the immigration problem in Europe. Many of the immigrants come from Romania and Poland, employed as cheaper workforces at a period prior to their membership of the EU. Moroccans also formed a significant part of the workforce, and by 2000 represented 34.8% of recruitment of immigrants within the area of the Third Italy. Calls were made for quotas to control these levels, in order to stem the growth of indigenous unemployment. These measures have proved unsuccessful and Italy, in places such as Prato, is now a destination of choice for immigrant workers from China (Raffaetà *et al.*, 2015).

New sectors: The innovation strategies being adopted in districts

As a consequence of the downturn in economic growth in Italy, there has been a need for a re-evaluation of industrial districts. The importance of innovation continues to be highlighted, and as such is recognised in the update of legislation in Italy e.g. (Law 26/2007). Among the issues highlighted by policy makers and academics are that whilst MIDs have been considered to be hot beds for innovation, their ability to adapt is inhibited. The importance of transforming industrial districts into technological districts was seen to require considerable inputs both for the old districts and the development of new districts in high tech sectors. Within Emilia-Romagna new technological districts have emerged, particularly in the area of medical technology, mechanical engineering, agro-food, construction and energy. Traditional artisanal industries continue, but the valorisation of the region is based on the emerging sectors.

Technological districts have been promoted through multi-actor collaboration. In Emilia-Romagna, there is a consortium, ASTER, which is composed of regional policy makers, together with regional universities, other research organisations, chambers of commerce and business associations in order to increase innovation and its diffusion in the regional productive system. ASTER has favoured networking among these institutions, through various initiatives which facilitate the transfer of specialist knowhow between universities and firms, and allows access to social funds for business in the area to support innovation. From 2007, these actions have been organised into technological platforms, corresponding to the strongest industries in the region, namely mechanical engineering, agro-food, biomedical, energy and construction. The aim of these high tech networks is to strengthen interactions among regional innovative actors and raise the critical mass of research.

Further initiatives include the development of skills through the educational system. In December 2010, the regional regulation GPG/2010/2427 provided a legislative framework for the development technical high schools (*Istituti tecnici-superiori*), where in line with the industry of the province, they will educate technicians with competencies and knowledge useful for the key industries, including the agro-food industry. It is evident that the region remains innovative, but there is doubt as to the role of the SME in the delivery.

■ Supply chain management

In essence, the description given by Bellandi *et al.*, (2015) of the new networks in the Third Italy bears much in common with those of the Japanese Keiretsu and the Toyota Production System found within literature on Lean supply chain management, although the two literatures are distinct and separate. Nonetheless there is considerable scope for the cross fertilisation between the two areas of research.

In each body of research, it is interesting to note that there is a recognition that industrial success depends upon the interactions and interconnectivity between flows of information, materials, money, manpower and capital equipment (Mentzer *et al.*, 2001). Again, in each body of research there is a focus on attaining competitive advantage through innovation, with a clear understanding of the function of small and medium sized businesses within this activity.

But whilst researchers involved in the study of industrial districts originally considered the issue to be related to the embeddedness of networked social relations, the emphasis in supply chain management, and in particular lean supply chain management, is on coordination and information flow between supply chain tiers. Although certain research in lean thinking suggests that social relations are important, it is the ability to be more efficient than other agri-food chains and allow innovation in the chain, that presents businesses with competitive advantage (Christopher, 2016).

Types of supply chains

Whilst supply chains are more often considered as an alignment of firms that bring products/services to market or as a network of organisations involved through upstream or downstream linkages in the different processes that produce value in order to deliver to the ultimate customers (Christopher, 2016) this suggests that a supply chain consists of multiple firms, both upstream (i.e., supply) and downstream (i.e., distribution), and the ultimate consumer. Indeed Mentzer goes further and differentiates between direct, extended and ultimate supply chains, in which the distinction is made between the degrees of supply complexity.

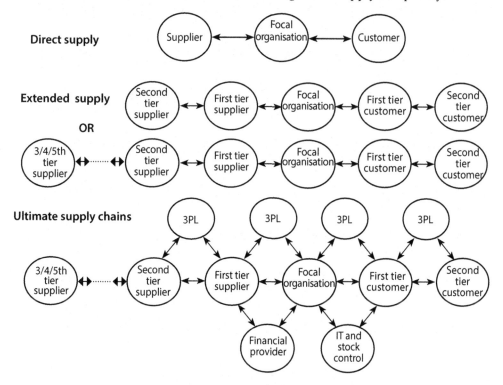

Figure 4.1: Supply chains

In a direct supply chain a focal organisation has a buyer and supplier (see Figure 4.1) who are involved in the flow of products/services, information and finance. Whereas in extended supply chains, there are a greater potential number of intermediaries, upstream and downstream through which products and information flow (Mentzer *et al.*, 2001). In what Mentzer calls 'ultimate supply chains', the complexity of information and product flow is significantly increased. As companies concentrate more on core activities, finance, logistics, warehousing even information management may be outsourced to external specialist parties. Yet, these representations are overly simplistic and fail to recognise the fact that any one organisation can be part of numerous supply chains.

Definitions of supply chain management

The term or discipline of supply chain management became recognised from the early 1990s, becoming a hot topic by 1998 (Ross, 1998). At the time of publication of this text, supply chain solutions and supply chain managers are common features of businesses. Yet there remains a lack of clarity in the meaning of the term supply chain management and consensus between the parties that use it. Furthermore definitions vary according to their academic role or relationship with the supply chain.

At one level SCM is seen to be a philosophy, taking a systems thinking approach to viewing the supply chain as a single entity and not disassociated parts, with each part serving its own function, but mutually dependent upon the other (Cooper *et al.*, 1997). In this context, SCM philosophy suggests that the effective delivery of end value is contingent upon not simply external relationships but the internal interconnectivity between other internal business functions.

The problem of defining supply chain management has exercised many academics, which, it is suggested, can lead to "confusion and misconception" (Stock and Boyer, 2009: 692). Stock and Boyer suggest that the variety of different definitions is a consequence of variations in scope and description, in that some focus upon material flows and inter-organisational collaborations, others on the final consumer.

The constructs of SCM strategies

The concept of supply chain management can be seen to have emerged from the scientific strand of management, and the concept of 'lean'. There is a distinction in terms of the thrust of the arguments for lean as against those for horizontal networks in the form of MIDs. The popularity of the concept with academics and practitioners has been attributed to trends in global sourcing and the emphasis of global companies on time and quality-based competition. The globalization of supply has forced companies look to remove inventory buffers and find more effective ways to coordinate the flow of materials into and out of the company.

It is held that in order to effect such coordination there is a need for closer relationships with suppliers. The discourse also suggests that in order to compete, companies in particular and supply chains in general need to focus more on the efficient and effective delivery of their products, so ensure that defect-free products reach the customer faster.

Thus the emergence of supply chain management (lean thinking) dispersed across global economies with the objective of achieving cost reductions, improved efficiencies and lower losses through wastage, effort, time and space.

The principles of lean supply chain management

Central to supply chain management is the concept of value. The principle idea is that all activities that do not add value are waste: wasted effort, time and money. Value should flow through the system on demand, and these considerations should be made throughout the supply chain. Organisations and supply chains should look to continually focus on improving the process of delivering value, removing what is described as *muda* (Womack *et al.*, 1990).

The first stage in lean thinking is defining business operations and the supply chain – what value is and what activities and processes are absolutely necessary. What is left is waste or muda. The concept of *value* is often interpreted loosely and at times confused with *added value*. However, the process of creatively identifying improved innovative, leaner processes, that is re-engineering the business and its processes, requires clarity as to what is of value to the customer. In the process of producing beef, it could, hypothetically, be argued that all processes from birth to butchery are muda, and that the value for the customer is only the fillet steak. This is quite extreme, but it enables the thinker to look to re-engineer the business activity in innovative, creative ways. But, with that supply chain there are a series of processes that do not in themselves add value but without which the value, in this case the fillet steak, could not be delivered. The calf needs to be born, fed for up to 30 months, slaughtered, butchered, delivered to a point of sale etc. This leads us to differentiate between two forms of waste:

- Muda 1, waste activities which are necessary and cannot (at least at present) be removed
- Muda 2, which can be removed.

At this point in time calves have to be born, and this is thus muda 1. Although over time technological innovations may change this situation, and arguably already has if one considers the advent of 3D printing.

Once value is defined, it is then possible to map the value stream, from end to end, identifying activities and processes that generate value, as well as those that are muda 1 and muda 2. The identification of value and value stream mapping, and the removal of muda are key to the improvement of supply chain performance.

A further characteristics of lean supply chain management, the absence of which leads to loss of efficiency or muda, is that it assumes just-in-time leanness. As indicated in Table 4.1, products and services are pulled through the supply chain on demand. Demand for a product has to be predictable in order that this can take place. This is distinctive from traditional supply chains, where products and services are pulled through the supply chain rather than pushed, which leads to high inventory levels, one of the key mudas (see Table 4.2). The process of pulling products in line with demand requires transparency and effective information sharing throughout the supply chain. The pursuit of a lean supply chain is, however, a continuous improvement process, i.e. there is constant revaluating of the activities and procedures within the supply chain. Even where muda is eliminated through the redesign of business processes or more effective communication, the analyst is constantly reviewing value in order to expose activities, which are now not essential to the business of creating value. Womack *et al.* (1990) identified seven sources of muda within supply chains, although an eighth has been subsequently identified (Nylund, 2013).

Table 4.1: The principles of Lean

- **Specify value:** Value is defined by customer in terms of specific products and services
- **Identify the value stream:** Map out all end-to-end linked actions, processes and functions necessary for transforming inputs to outputs to identify and eliminate waste
- **Make value flow continuously:** Having eliminated waste, make remaining value-creating steps 'flow'
- **Let customers pull value:** Customer's 'pull' cascades all the way back to the lowest level supplier, enabling just-in-time production
- **Create transparency of strategies and costs within the supply chain:** Competitive advantage must be understood from the perspective of the supply chain and not the individual firm
- **Pursue perfection:** Pursue continuous process of improvement striving for perfection

Factors that affect the presence of muda relate to product and information flow, which lead to unevenness of flow (*muri*) and over burden on resources where overburden (*mura*) can lead to either overuse of resources and potential breakdown of processes as well high inventory levels.

Table 4.2: The eight sources of muda

	Description	Significance
Over-production	Supply chain running a demand levels not at full capacity.	Most serious muda, and leads to some of the other 7 wastes e.g. inventory, non-value added processing etc.
Waiting	Time when service/production capacity is standing idle.	This is a time dimension , under-utilisation of resources. Often the easiest to remove.
Transportation	Distance products travel excessive movement can cause delays.	A particular challenge in global supply chains, one might need to transport to deliver to consumers but it isn't the transport that adds value.
Non-value added processing	The consequence of overcomplication or repeating processes. The perception is usually that all processes are required.	Value stream mapping and root cause analysis can help reduce this waste.

Defects	Defective products, or even items which are a by-product, such as bones in meat production	These can be complicated to remove, see example of the beef production on page 77.
Unnecessary inventory	The ideal is to have zero inventory and have material pop up exactly when required. Almost impossible to achieve in the real world due to variation and uncertainty. But inventory optimization is possible if the variation and uncertainties in the business are handled well.	Central to the concept of lean supply chain optimization, capability studies, variation studies, inventory modelling can help reduce this waste.
Unnecessary motion	If you can limit motion while doing a process, you can reduce the time and energy required for that process. However, it is still a waste and in obvious cases should be removed.	Usually one of the harder ones to reduce significantly and does not provide as big an impact to the total value stream as removal of other wastes. Time and motion studies can help reduce this.
Unused creativity	Under-utilisation of people's talents and skills	Recognising the knowledge and understanding of operatives is important in the continuous improvement process

4

Case study: Supply chain management at Tesco PLC

The implementation of supply chain management at Tesco PLC has received considerable interest since first explored by Womack *et al.*, in 1990, where they presented a value stream analysis of the humble tin of baked beans. As the third global food retail company, operating in 14 countries, Tesco are often heralded as the epitome of lean (e.g. Open University 2004; T882 module), and known for the extent to which they have adopted value stream mapping.

The adoption of lean practices within the UK food retailer supply chain became more prevalent, with the outbreak of foot and mouth in 2001. Following the epidemic, the UK government commissioned the so called Curry report, and exposed the both efficiencies and risks associated with the existing infrastructure within the UK food supply chain (Curry, 2002). Two key bodies, the Food Chain Centre and the English Food and Farming Partnership, were set up after the publication of the commission report which expressly identified the IGD as the body who should take the proposed food chain centre forward. The key purpose is to generate business improvement and information flow in the food supply chain to which effect value stream analysis was extensively deployed within key companies in the UK agricultural supply chains including, those located in red meat industry, fresh produce and dairy.

Tesco continued to be perceived by many to be at the front of the focus on the development of long term partnerships with its suppliers. Since 2007 for instance, Tesco have worked directly with 600-800 farmers with various herd sizes, to whom they guarantee prices and agree long term contracts through the Sustainable Dairy Group (TSDG). The dominant narrative with respect to this initiative is that given the surplus of milk on a world market post removal of the milk quotas in Europe, this enables them to protect the interests of their suppliers. In 2016, Tesco extended their commitment with a working partnership with Muller Milk ingredients allowing the continued working with farmers and dairy farmers,). This partnership has extended their involvement with the dairy sector, where there is already a long-standing relationship with Arla the other major dairy company involved in UK liquid milk, under the pre-mentioned Tesco sustainable Dairy group. The company reports that they hold around 20 strategic partnership agreements with supply partners, to create "more integrated and shortened supply chains which allow farmers, growers and processors to invest directly in standards, animal welfare and innovation". Other strategic partnerships include: Samsworths, Hilton Food Group, G's, AMT and Branston.

■ Questioning the value

It is notable that over the last two decades there has been an number of competition investigations into the supplier-buyer relationships of Tesco, and in recent activity in the media, and how Tesco has leveraged value growth through the application of lean. Whilst purporting the value of value stream mapping and lean thinking, to what extent did the company really adhere to lean principles, which surely are about equal distribution of value throughout the supply chain. To what extent has the sheer size of Tesco in the market place had a negative impact on prices received by farmers in the UK.

Farmers are often state that Tesco place considerable pressure on prices, and 'bully farmers' for price reductions, and that they are called upon to subsidise promotions, even though promotions are a key cause of increased costs in production directly and through the bullwhip effect. Claims are that their buyers do not even understand basic lean concepts. Recent responses, at Tesco have been to reduce the product offering and not the promotional strategy, unlike their competitors at Asda/Walmart who offer everyday low prices strategies and are attempting to remove promotional offers.

Alternative practices in supply chain management

The problem identified in the Tesco case study with respect to promotional activities, relates to the impact of unpredictable levels of demand or forecast errors on the smooth flow of demand information in one direction and the flow of goods in the other. Unpredictability in demand can be a consequence of either changes in volume of demand with standard products or high levels of product choice. Where promotions are offered the consumer, demand becomes unpredictable and causes a lag in response time and supply difficulties in particular the 'Forrester or bullwhip effect'. The bullwhip effect describes the amplification of demand order variability, that is to say that where there is uncertainty in customer demand, the supplier will tend to have a larger buffer stock than the buyer. This means that:

- Inventories grow in successive echelons of the supply chain as demands get amplified in the upstream direction,

- Inventory expansion leads to rising levels of lead time,

4

Accurate forecasting and intelligent use of information are key in the reduction of the bullwhip effect.

Although we note in Chapter 1, that there has been a decline in the 'buy one get one free' strategies deployed by UK retailers, they still remain, which will generate excess stock in the supply chain, which is problematic in terms of lean, furthermore there is unpredictability on daily basis, which is a function of a whole range of factors such as weather.

In essence, the ability to respond to actual demand is inhibited by the limited time available between knowledge of the demand and the demand pull. Time compression is considered as a competitive weapon in many markets, including food, and this generated a rethinking of lean, and the emergence of nimble or agile supply chains. Agile supply chains have focused more on responsiveness, rather than lean, which is doing more with less (Christopher, 2016), and as such require greater coordination and communication between partners.

While the lean and agile paradigms are different, they can also be combined into 'leagile' or a hybrid supply chain strategy (Mason-Jones et al., 2000). Agility uses market knowledge to exploit opportunities in volatile markets whilst minimising the cost, and leanness allows for the removal of muda or waste. However, as noted in Chapter 1, the production and distribution of food is not in very real terms conducive to either lean or agile supply chains. Whilst demand is growing, with considerable switches in choice behaviour as there emerges a growing number of affluent consumers in BRIC and MINT countries, total demand for food is predictable over time, but with seasonal or promotion-driven fluctuations which may or may not be predictable.

Yet, it is not simply demand that is influenced by unpredictable events; the process of producing food is also affected by weather, pests, disease, and other natural and manmade interventions that affect the volume produced. Furthermore, perhaps more importantly in the context of supply chain strategies, the determination of the volume to be produced is required some considerable time ahead of demand. Lean – true lean – is for the most part problematic, and similarly for agile. Work undertaken by the Cardiff school in the 1990s put forward the idea of leagile, a hybrid concept is appropriate for certain supply chains, so that potentially food supply chains could be lean from the farm to storage or first stage production with a nimble, agile response in line with demand (Towill, 2001).

Critiquing collaboration: Effectiveness, power, freeriding and opportunism

The post-War focus on horizontal and vertical inter-firm collaboration in the form of both MIDs and supply chain strategies has been in the pursuit of innovation, through knowledge sharing and coordination of activities, and innovation as a means of improving business and economic growth. For the academic communities and regional and industry bodies, these remain significant practice, though it could be argued that there is a tendency to accept the two paradigms as *de facto*, and where there is evidence that either supply chain strategies and MIDs have not delivered the expected results, the theory is not seen to be disproved, merely adjusted. This is possibly due to some extent, to the problematic nature of measuring impact experienced by a number of researchers in both research areas, to the extent in supply chain management they have utilised 'happiness' and 'trust' as a proxies for measures of success (Beamon, 1998).

There has been considerable debate as to the value of supply chain management strategies. Whether there is any real evidence to suggest that they are an effective way of delivering value to the businesses within the supply chain, and whether the innovations, for instance the 4000 plus new products that are launched each year, deliver value to the consumers. A further issue of concern with respect to lean, is one of food security, given the elimination of stock within supply chains. There were illustrations, during the Icelandic ash cloud in 2010, where the movement of goods by air was inhibited by the excessive ash within the atmosphere – an event which fortunately was not of extended duration and thus did not result in a food shortage. Others have raised the issue of the increasing fallibility of antibiotics and the impact of an epidemic on the availability of food, again linked to the minimisation of stock levels within the retail supply chain.

The evolution of SCM, as in the emergence of agile and leagile theoretical frameworks, is a consequence of perceptions that lean is not universally appropriate, or always effective. Explanations as to why the adoption of lean may not be effective extend beyond the unpredictability of demand and supply into relational strength and the impact of traditional practices on the extent to which information could be shared between organisations, in instances of failure of supply chain strategies (New, 1997).

In contrast, Martin and Sunley (2003) have suggested that researchers examining the concept of clusters (MIDs) have tended to accept on faith rather than rigorously test their benefits. With the shift in emphasis in the Third Italy explored above from socially embedded regional networks to globally outsourced companies, Bellandi and De Propris (2015) explain that MIDs needed to adapt in order to meet both the challenges of the increasing "science-based knowledge" of industries and the "globalisation of production" (p 82). There are potentially two issues here, that in very real terms they have redefined MIDs in order to fit in with the continued belief that they are an effective governance structure, when plainly they weren't. The MIDs are no longer socially embedded, indeed even where production has remained in Italy, there is growing strife between the immigrant Chinese and the Italian populations. Coupled with this position, it is a failure to recognise the contingency of governance with market conditions as explored in transaction cost economics (Williamson, 1975)

■ Power, opportunism and the freeriding

In transaction costs economics, it is suggested that how businesses govern operations and define their boundaries is contingent upon the relative transaction costs of one governance structure versus the alternatives. The theory is based on the behavioural assumption that transacting parties behave opportunistically, particularly where a business is reliant upon the transaction and where there is a level of uncertainty relating to the nature of the markets.

The suggestion is that partnerships are not a viable option for a business where the product/service supplied or exchange relationship is critical to the business. This is because of the risk that the partner will act opportunistically and exploit the dependency of their buyer or supplier. Whilst the implications of such have been examined within the context of supply chain management and specifically in the food supply chain (Cox and Chicksand, 2005) in which it has been identified that enterprises such as Wal-Mart, and other major retail groups utilised the dependency of their suppliers as a means of putting pressure on the value they passed on, i.e. the negotiated price.

Where there is perhaps a gap, is the consideration of the problem of opportunistic behaviour or uneven distribution of power in Marshallian industrial districts and on their ability to function effectively. Opportunism and opportunistic behaviour is seen to be at the root of many of the failures in collective action. Work on cooperatives (Cook, 1995) presents the idea that individuals within collectives will seek to gain benefit from cooperative action without paying the costs – what is known as the freerider problem – and this has been known to undermine the stability of cooperatives. This may similarly, particularly with respect to who generates social capital, technological and intellectual knowhow that spills over to the wider community, enable free riders to exploit the effort of others. This could be a root cause of the need to intervene in the form of education by policy makers in the Third Italy, in order to facilitate innovation.

Concluding remarks

Collective action, horizontal or vertical, within the supply chain, has been proposed as an important ingredient in the development of economic growth through innovative practice. Research has been extensive in the areas of industrial districts and supply chain management. The theories have evolved over time adapted to better fit the conditions observed, particularly those of the markets and supply chains.

Initial enthusiasm by the academic communities as to the efficacy of these alternative governance structures for economic development and innovation has for some dwindled. Yet, both are still highly supported by policy makers across sectors including agri-food, and perhaps there is room for more rigorous questioning and investigation. Drawing once more on the philosophical constructs of systems thinking, as well as the precepts of transaction cost economics, are collaborative structures contingent on market or other conditions. This chapter suggests that despite the continued popularity of horizontal and vertical collective activity, there is some value in being more critical of their relative value. Small may or may not be beautiful and the appropriateness of alternative collective governance structures need more in depth consideration.

References

Acs, Z. J. (1992). Small business economics: A global perspective. *Challenge*, **35**(6), 38-44.

Andersson, M. and Ejermo, O. (2004). Sectoral knowledge production in Swedish regions 1993-1999. *Knowledge Spillovers and Knowledge Management*, 143-170.

Arezki, R., Rota-Graziosi, G. and Senbet, L.W. (2013). Capital flight risk. *Finance and Development*, **40**(3), 27.

Baptista, R. and Swann, P. (1998). Do firms in clusters innovate more?. *Research Policy*, **27**(5), 525-540.

Beamon, B. M. (1998). Performance, reliability, and performability of material handling systems. *International Journal of Production Research*, **36**(2), 377-393.

Beesley, M. E. and Hamilton, R. T. (1984). Small firms' seedbed role and the concept of turbulence. *The Journal of Industrial Economics*, **33**, 217-231.

Bellandi, M. and De Propris, L. (2015). Three generations of industrial districts. *Investigaciones Regionales*, **32**, 75-87.

Belussi, F., Sammarra, A. and Sedita, S. R. (2010). Learning at the boundaries in an "Open Regional Innovation System": A focus on firms' innovation strategies in the Emilia Romagna life science industry. *Research Policy*, **39**(6), 710-721.

Cairncross, F. (2001). *The Death of Distance: How the communications revolution is changing our lives*. Harvard Business Press.

Chandler, A.D. (1977). *The Visible Hand*, Belknap Press, Cambridge, MA.

Chiarvesio, M., Di Maria, E. and Micelli, S. (2010). Global value chains and open networks: the case of Italian industrial districts. *European Planning Studies*, **18**(3), 333-350.

Christopher, M. (2016) *Logistics & Supply Chain Management.* Pearson Higher Ed.

Cook, M. L. (1995). The future of US agricultural cooperatives: A neo-institutional approach. *American Journal of Agricultural Economics*, **77**(5), 1153-1159.

Cooper, Martha C., Douglas M. Lambert, and Janus D. Pagh. Supply chain management: more than a new name for logistics. *The International Journal of Logistics Management,* 8(1), 1-14.

Cox, A. and Chicksand, D. (2005). The limits of lean management thinking: Multiple retailers and food and farming supply chains. *European Management Journal*, **23**(6), 648-662.

Curry, D. (2002). *Farming and Food a Sustainable Future: Policy commission on future of farming*, London: Cabinet Office.

Diez-Vial, I. and Alvarez-Suescun, E. (2011). The impact of geographical proximity on vertical integration through specific assets: The case of the Spanish meat industry. *Growth and Change*, **42**(1), 1-22.

Giddens, A. (1991). *Modernity and Self-Identity: Self and society in the late modern age*. Stanford University Press.

Grabher, G. (1993). *The Embedded Firm*, London: Routledge.

Harris, P. (1997). Limitations on the use of regional economic impact multipliers by practitioners: an application to the tourism industry, *Journal of Tourism Studies,* 8(2), 50 -61.

Harrison, B. (1994). The Italian industrial districts and the crisis of the cooperative form: Part I. *European Planning Studies*, **2**(1), 3-22.

Hadjimichalis, C. (2006). The end of Third Italy as we knew it?. *Antipode*, **38**(1), 82-106.

Iaciponi, L., Brunori G. and Rovai, M. (1995). Endogenous development and the industrial district, in J.D. Van der Ploeg and G. Van Dijk, *Beyond Modernisation, the impact of endogenous rural development*, Van Gorcum Assen.

Karlsson, C. and Olsson, O. (1998). Product innovation in small and large enterprises. *Small Business Economics*, **10**(1), 31-46.

Kerr, C., Harbison, F.H., Dunlop, J.T. and Myers, C.A. (1960/1996). Industrialism and industrial man. *International Labour Review*, **135**, 383-392.

Lehner, F. (1993) *The Future of Industry in Europe, Vol. 1 New Markets, New structures and new strategies*, Future of Industry paper series, FOP 365

Loveman, G. and Sengerberger, W. (1991). The re-emergence of small-scale production: an international comparison. FAST Documentation.

Marshall, A. (1920) *Principles of Economics*, London: MacMillian

Martin, R. and Sunley, P. (2003). Deconstructing clusters: chaotic concept or policy panacea?. *Journal of Economic Geography*, **3**(1), 5-35.

McMillan, D.W. and Chavis, D.M. (1986). Sense of community: A definition and theory. *Journal of Community Psychology*, **14**(1), 6-23.

Mason-Jones, R., Naylor, B. and Towill, D.R. (2000). Lean, agile or leagile? Matching your supply chain to the marketplace. *International Journal of Production Research*, **38**(17), 4061-4070

Mentzer, J.T., DeWitt, W., Keebler, J.S., Min, S., Nix, N.W., Smith, C.D. and Zacharia, Z.G. (2001). Defining supply chain management. *Journal of Business Logistics*, **22**(2), 1-25.

New, S.J. (1997). The scope of supply chain management research. *Supply Chain Management: An International Journal*, **2**(1), 15-22.

Nylund, J. (2013). Improving Processes through Lean-Management: Case study. PhD thesis.

Piore, M. and Sabel, C. (1984). *The Second Industrial Divide: Possibilities for Prosperity*, New York: Basic Books.

Porter, M. E. and Porter, M. P. (1998). Location, clusters, and the 'new' microeconomics of competition. *Business Economics*, 7-13.

Ross, D. (1998). *Competing through Supply Chain Management*, New York: Chapman & Hall.

Pyke, F., Becattini, G. and Sengenberger, W. (Eds.) (1990). *Industrial Districts and Inter-firm Co-operation in Italy*. International Institute for Labour Studies.

Rabellotti, R., Carabelli, A. and Hirsch. G. (2009). Italian industrial districts on the move: where are they going?, *European Planning Studies* **17**(1), 19-41.

Raffaetà, R., Baldassar, L. and Harris, A. (2015). Chinese immigrant youth identities and belonging in Prato, Italy: exploring the intersections between migration and youth studies. *Identities*, 1-16.

Ray, C. (2000). Endogenous socio-economic development in the European Union-issues of evaluation, *Journal of Rural Studies*, **16**, 447-458.

Schumpeter, J.A. (1947). The creative response in economic history. *Journal of Economic History*, **7**(2), 149-159.

Staber, U. (2007). Contextualizing research on social capital in regional clusters. *International Journal of Urban and Regional Research*, **31**(3), 505-521.

Stock, J. R. and Boyer, S. L. (2009). Developing a consensus definition of supply chain management: a qualitative study. *International Journal of Physical Distribution & Logistics Management*, **39**(8), 690-711.

Towill, D. (2001). Logistics and information management, in Eastham, J., Sharples, L., & Ball, S. (Eds.). (2001). *Food Supply Chain Management*. Taylor & Francis.

Van der Ploeg, J. D. and Long, A. (1994). *Born from Within: Practice and perspectives in endogenous rural development*, The Netherlands: Van Gorcum.

Westley, F. and Vredenburg, H. (1991). Strategic bridging: The collaboration between environmentalists and business in the marketing of green products. *The Journal of Applied Behavioural Science* **27**(1), 65-90.

Williamson, O.E. (1975). *Markets and Hierarchies: Analysis and Antitrust Implications*. New York: Free Press.

Womack, J.P., Jones, D.T. and Roos, D. (1990). *The Machine that Changed the World*. Simon and Schuster.

4

Part 2
Food security and sustainability

5 Food Resources and Human Evolution

Anne Eastham

Introduction

The human journey from forager to producer is a long one, encompassing nearly two million years of human prehistory. In some respects the development may be considered a retrograde one; a move away from seasonal to market forces, from seasonal abundance of a limited range of goods in the gathering of which all members of society played a part, at the expense of sporadic intensity of effort for maybe 2-4 hours a day, to an economy requiring the application of labour at any time during 24/7 by a workforce engaged in producing seasonal surpluses that supported increasingly specialist trades making goods that the primary food producers had no time to manufacture for themselves.

There were a number of factors in a fluctuating environment that exercised a powerful influence on the history of economic evolution. The most important were major oscillations in climate that periodically rendered parts of the globe inhospitable to human settlement either through flooding as sea levels rose with warmer global temperatures, or through the formation of ice caps across the continents, with a consequent drop in sea levels, exposing more of the land mass but equally making many of the northern parts of Europe, for instance, uninhabitable. The time span of these glacial and interglacial periods is indicated in the Timeline (Figure 5.1, p. 112)

The effect of these oscillations on human demography was crucial, since the availability and range of resources changed with the advance and retreat of the ice and it was the resources for subsistence that determined the size of animal or human population a given area of land within a region was able to support.

The early hominid record

"And God said, Behold, I have given you every herb bearing seed which is upon the face of all the earth, and every tree, in the which is the fruit of a tree yielding seed: to you it shall be for meat. And to every beast of the earth, and to every fowl of the air, and to every thing that creepeth upon the earth, wherein there is life, I have given every green herb for meat:

And God said, Let us make Man in our own image, after our likeness: And let them have dominion over the fish of the sea, and over the fowl of the air, and over the cattle and over all the earth, and over every creeping thing that creepeth upon the earth."

Genesis Chap. 1. 26. & 29-30

5

Hominid records take the 21st century research archaeologist back to around 2 million years before the present day and, if recent discoveries are authenticated, possibly more. All we have from the earliest phases of human development are intermittent bone deposits revealing the taphonomy of what happened to them and the relationships between predators and their prey – who hunted whom for food and who ate it. There is no question of studying their 'balanced diet' because the evidence for organic materials does not survive, but in many circumstances, especially in very dry climatic zones or in calcareous soils, bones of animals are preserved. It is clear in tracing the development of hominid species from their primate origins that dietary staples changed with climate. As the environment became more arid, there was a decrease of fruit bearing trees and permanent woodland during the mid Miocene, c. 15-8 million years ago. The early hominid species of Africa and Europe changed from a diet mainly of fruit to a greater dependence on leaves and roots. Evidence for this change may be traced in the development of dental adaptations to a change of diet (Klein, 1989). At the same time, with the reduction in the level of forest cover, they began to walk upright in the more open landscape. This in itself had its effect on foraging strategies.

Fossils discovered mainly in south and east Africa, originating around 4 million years ago but concentrated within a period 1.2 - 0.7 million years, include a number of species of Australopithecines and from 1 million years two species of hominid, *Homo erectus* and *H. habilis* evolved. These species were bipedal, walking upright and capable of running, although still agile tree climbers.

The most famous sequence of these fossil hominids was researched during the second and third quarters of the 20th century by the Leakey family and others in the ancient lake beds of the Olduvai gorge, Laetoli and Koobi Fora in northern Tanzania. Work on the teeth of *Australopithecus robustus* and *A. boisie* indicates that these hominids were largely vegetarian needing to chew their way through considerable quantities of low calorie fruits, roots and leaves. His more gracile cousin, A. africanus, a group that included the well-known 'Lucy', was more eclectic, taking eggs, lizards and small mammals for food; and tooth wear on both *Homo habilis* and *H. erectus* indicates that they were becoming increasingly carnivorous.

Since they did not have the large canines for tearing at animal carcasses and meat of other primates, these early hominids made and used stone tools of increasing sophistication for cutting, scraping, hammering and making further tools from wood or bone, in ways that facilitated the economic use of the resources available. Wear analysis on the tools can indicate quite clearly the use to which they have been put, and development of the tool types also gives a clue as to the development of resource utilisation. In the ascending lake beds, at Olduvai, was found a progression from simple unifacial tools, 'choppers' to bifacial, 'chopping tools' to complex handaxes of what is known as Acheulean type. In any form these are the best instruments for butchery and it is thought that their evolution may indicate the increasing importance of animals in the diet.

It is clear from cut marks on the bones found in the Olduvai studies, notably at muscle attachment points, and from wear analysis on the stone tools that meat was being taken for food, but there are also signs of scavenging of the carcasses killed by other predators, as happens amongst the Hadza hunters of northern Tanzania at the present day (O'Connell *et. al.*, 1988). Nevertheless, although the level of predation vs. scavenging by these hominids is still controversial, there is no doubt that a proportion of their nourishment was still gathered from roots and, seasonally, from fruits and shoots. Traditionally, gathering has been regarded as the role of the female members of many more recent hunter-gatherer groups.

There is also the evidence throughout the Palaeolithic, the period of the old stone age, for other animal predators and scavengers, like hyenas, both attacking hominids and consuming them and/or using their habitation sites, sometimes on the basis of seasonal exchange of occupation, especially where the habitat is a cave.

Evidence of controlled, as opposed to wild, natural fires was seen at the Olduvai Gorge sites and other east African sites in a context characterised by Acheulean handaxes dateable to around 500,000 years ago (Harris and Isaacs, 1976). This matches the earliest dates for man-made fires in both China at Zhoukoudian Cave and in Europe. However, the making of fires or burnt bone does not necessarily predicate cooking. Mammal bone, in particular, is an excellent fuel, with a high calorific value on account of its fat and collagen content and originally, the need for warmth may have been a primary purpose for making fire, more than for cooking.

The European scene

In Europe the Pleistocene is marked by a series of major climate oscillations between stages of warm temperate and cold periods when ice covered large areas of northern Europe, making much of the continent inhospitable to both man and animals, and much of the evolution and progress of hominid settlement is a consequence of the need to adapt to the demands of these fluctuations and the changes in the physical environment.

It is worth noting that climate change was an important long term feature of the Palaeolithic period. It manifests itself in major fluctuations in annual mean temperature lasting anything between tens of thousands of years and a few hundreds of years. During the warm phases, known as interglacial periods, the typical large herbivorous mammals grazing the land would have been the elephant, rhinoceros, and occasionally, a species of hippopotamus, red deer, various species of fallow deer, cattle and bison; but always horse, usually the heavy horse, *Equus caballus*. Predators included lion, sometimes the cave lion, bear and most important as an intruder or neighbour in cave occupation sites, hyena.

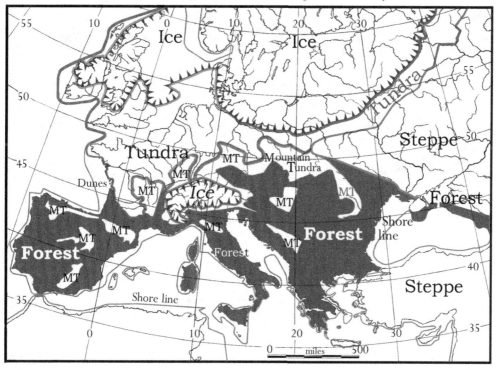

Figure 5.1: LGL extent of European ice cover and vegetation zones

The onset of colder climatic conditions not only caused a change in the animal fauna but also made considerable changes in the human demographic, especially in northern Europe, where habitable zones became restricted to the limits of the coverage of the advance of the ice. During these glacial phases levels of afforestation were considerably reduced and much of temperate Europe became covered by tundra and taiga vegetation, creating a suitable habitat for reindeer, bison, musk ox, the woolly rhinoceros and the mammoth, the hairy species of elephant, as well as a smaller species of horse *Equus caballus przewalski*, a species that may still be seen occasionally in parts of eastern Europe. Typical mammalian indicators of these colder environmental oscillations were the rodent populations and study of these and their evolution has made it possible to chart not just climatic change but also to calibrate the passage of time. Rodents, like the arctic and brown hares, voles, mice and rabbits were regularly predated by carnivorous mammals including man and by raptorial birds.

The food supply, both animal and plant, was in part seasonal, especially on the periphery of climate zones affected by glacial advance.

■ Neanderthal settlement in Europe

In terms of the evidence, there are few sites in Europe where *Homo erectus* has been firmly identified. The hominid remains in the majority of early Middle Palaeolithic occupation sites at this time have been found to belong to an early form of modern human, *Homo sapiens neanderthalensis*, who had a much larger brain capacity than his predecessors. Besides some examples in Africa and Asia, their settlements have been discovered all over Europe and Britain. Many of the Neanderthal occupation sites may be characterised by a continued use of beautifully crafted handaxes made from flint or quartzite stone cores, but also the use of retouched flint flakes to create an increasingly complex toolkit.

The older recorded specimens were mainly recovered in Spain, France and Germany: Mauer, Steinheim, Ehringsdorf, Arago, Le Lazaret, Fontechevade, Petralonia and Atapuerca are all classic locations. The fossil bones reveal not only the changes in dentition and bodily physique but, where feasible, current research into the chemistry of the bone may indicate the staple foods in their diet.

Early discoveries in Britain, include the remains from Barnfield Pit, Swanscombe in the Thames gravels (Waechter, 1973), that included both tools and animal remains. More recent work at Boxgrove in Sussex, also a quarry for gravels and marine sand, showed a discrete pattern of flint knapping areas and a very wide range of animal fauna from a warm temperate climatic phase known as the Cromerian (Roberts and Parfitt, 1999). Animal species included nineteen species of birds, the majority of them wildfowl or waders, and large mammals: a species of elephant, a large horse, rhinoceros and red, roe and fallow deer as well as the rarer giant deer, Megaloceros sp.

It was concluded that, although it was possible that these hominids were scavenging on the carcases of the abandoned prey of the many carnivorous mammals that were also present at Boxgrove, the balance was in favour of assuming that man was himself the hunter in this situation. One horse scapula was pierced by a semicircular wound apparently from a projectile point. Together with the frequent cut and scrape marks on bones from other species besides horses, this indicates considerable human modification of animal carcases. Since many of the marks are cuts designed to fillet the meat from the bone or crack the marrow bones it is clear that consumption for food was the primary motive; flint chips were found, embedded in bone during marrow extraction. This highlights the huge requirement for lipids, fats, in hunter–gatherer subsistence and besides the large mammals; wildfowl are another excellent source of dietary fats. It is a requirement that persists in the relict hunter-gatherer societies of the present day. No evidence of butchery was discovered on avian bones, which are usually divided by dislocation and dismemberment of the joints.

Other British sites of Neanderthal peoples include La Cotte de St Brelade, Jersey, dated to around 238,000 years BP (Callow and Cornford, 1986) and Pontnewydd, close to the river Elwy near St Asaph, North Wales, and dated to between 200,000 and 230,000 years BP, where there were bones of Bewick's swan, and four species of wild geese, all of which would have been taken in a winter season on their feeding grounds along the marshes of Liverpool bay, some seven kilometres from the cave. This would seem to indicate some signs of a move from an opportunistic to a planned hunting strategy (Aldhouse Green, 2012).

■ Homo sapiens as hunter-gatherers

With the arrival of anatomically modern humans, *Homo sapiens sapiens*, around 40,000 years BP, the population dynamics of Europe began to change. There is ongoing discussion about the origin in Africa of modern humans and indeed the route of their expansion into Europe, but increased numbers of individuals and settlements gradually transformed the way in which resources were accessed and distributed. Subsistence hunter–gathering remained the way of life and groups became infinitely adaptable in the use of available resources. As already noted, the settlement of Europe was considerably influenced by sequential fluctuations in the advance and retreat of the glaciers and human adaptations to them, a progression marked archaeologically by developments in their toolkits of stone and bone, outlined in the timeline, Table 5.1 (page 112).

■ Upper Palaeolithic subsistence

Recent research has concerned itself with investigating some of the details of Stone Age life and economy, especially during the time between the last Glacial

Maximum around 18,000 years BP and the beginning of the Post Glacial or Holocene period around 10,000 years BP. At the maximum extent of the ice, Northern Europe was almost uninhabitable and we find human occupation in Britain were restricted to regions south of the Thames, and south of a line across Denmark and the North German plain to Russia. Zones of permafrost tundra, blending into taiga, polar forest, which extended across central France to the Balkans. On both the Alps and parts of the Cantabrian mountain cordillera permanent snow continued into our own era, the Holocene.

Much of our understanding of hunter-gatherer life in the cold of winter during the last glaciation is derived from deposits in the numerous caves, especially those of continental Europe. Summertime habitations were probably mainly camps in the open air and with a strong subsistence base in a variety of plant shoots, roots and kernels and fruits. Unfortunately, as noted, plant remains seldom survive at this period in the soil.

Caves offered shelter in winter and protection from many of the carnivorous predators, despite the existence of cave lion and cave bear who could make shared occupation hazardous. In many regions reindeer and horse, along with less frequent woolly rhinoceros and mammoth ,were the staples of subsistence at times of maximum glacial expansion and as it receded and forest cover increased, cattle, bison, red deer and musk ox reappeared, along with other forest species of roe deer, pig, hare and rabbit. In highland zones, chamois and ibex were common.

Tracing the relationship between human demography and the biomass, obtained from ungulates between the Last Glacial Maximum at 18,000 years BP and its final end around 11,000 years BP, Francoise Delpech (1999) demonstrated from findings based on the faunal lists of over 30 occupation sites in the Aquitaine region of France from within these dates, that there was a steady increase in the use of these animals that only declined after 11,000. She found that there were two major periods of animal migration, into and away from the sampling area, as the availability of suitable open habitats for these species expanded or reduced with the changes in the environment. Just before the Glacial Maximum at around 19,500 years BP, large animals were moving into the region, away from less favourable habitats to the north and east, and between 12,500 and 11,500 the reverse migration was in progress and biomass availability from these sources gradually reduced.

Calculations to estimate the effect of the changes in the availability of animal biomass on human demography across the inhabited parts of Europe have indicated that the estimated population of the region at:

18,000 years BP: < 0.75 persons per 100 square kilometres

16,000 – 14,000 BP:< 8.25 persons per 100 square kilometres

14,000 – 13, 000 BP:< 17.2 persons per 100 square kilometres

12,000 BP: a sharp drop in population density

11,000 BP onwards:< 0 .80 persons per 100 square kilometres in forest areas.

Some sites exemplify the changes in the pattern of animal distribution towards the latter stages of this time span extremely well. Two neighbouring settlements in the Landes and the Atlantic Pyrenees span this transition. At the Abri Dufaure, set in a group of rock shelters beside the Gave d'Oleron, the hunters took up residence from the early months of the winter into the spring. In the levels dated to 15,000 years BP, half of the carcases on the site were reindeer and from other evidence it appeared that the occupants were moving seasonally with the dwindling herds of reindeer between the Pyreneen foothills and the Atlantic coast to benefit from coastal vegetation at certain times of year and to avoid the flies during the summer. By 12,500 year BP, red deer, roe deer and wild boar had replaced the reindeer. The other site, some 14 kilometre away, the Grotte de Bourrouilla at Arancou, a site situated above the Bidouze river, red deer were the main ungulate present throughout the Late Glacial sequence and by 8,000 years BP, the Mesolithic phase on the site, the forest species of deer and wild boar were the only source of protein from the medium sized ungulates. By the beginning of the Holocene occupation in Europe, as large herbivores declined as a food source, exploitation of fish resources increased (Le Gall, 1992) and a similar increase occurred in the hunting of birds.

Fishing

Fish was an important element of the diet throughout the Palaeolithic period and was readily available both from the sea and freshwaters. Fish remains have been recorded from the sites of early hominids, and Neanderthal exploitation is well attested from sites in France, Italy and Spain. Evidence of fishing is recorded from many of the Upper Palaeolithic, *Homo sapiens* sites, especially in the region of Aquitaine that is blessed with an extensive river system through a largely calcareous geological substrate. Each of the Upper Palaeolithic cultures that have been named in sequence: Aurignacian, Gravettian and Solutrean took fish and the late glacial inhabitants of Europe, the Magdalenians, were clearly master fishermen, taking a wide range of freshwater species at various times of year (Cleyet Merle, 1990). The most commonly recorded species in western Europe were the salmonids, salmon and trout, the pike, the cyprinidae, carp, roach, dace and perch. Eels were taken and on some sites there are signs indicating sea fishing; images of flat fish appear among the drawings of cave walls and in the portable art, along with images of seals, possibly whales, and in one instance a possible dolphin.

The equipment became increasingly specialised and elaborate, frequently carved with personalised motifs. Fish spears and tridents, harpoons and hooks have been recovered on many sites. The main season for freshwater fishing in late glacial times appears to have been at the beginning and towards the end of the 'good season' (the time when most food was readily available). Some site studies on salmonid bone have shown that the spring run produced the largest catch.

Post glacially too fishing remained important. Mesolithic sites reveal an increased dependence on aquatic resources, including shellfish, and extensive recoveries have been made and images recorded of nets and fish traps at settlements like that of Starr Carr in Yorkshire, and later on Neolithic farming sites and in metal-using societies into our own era.

Fowling

Goose good eating. You got to eat goose
because goose e breed up again
soon as wet e got to make egg… good eating….
Geese e can eat two hundred but e'll come.
E breed up here, egg…
Another plain, another plain, another plain.
You might get one thousand and thousand goose.

   Bill Neidje (East Alligator River)

Avian resources were not neglected. Some of the bones recovered in association with human occupation appear to represent seasonal additions to the hunter-gatherer diet in the form of meat, fats or eggs.

The most useful sources of nourishment in the spectrum of bird fauna, and some of the most easily captured, were the wildfowl and the grouse. In winter members of the grouse family tend to form groups that make them vulnerable to netting, and wintering geese and swans, when they migrate south from their separate summer breeding grounds in the Arctic, form large mixed flocks on suitable feeding grounds that makes them vulnerable to predators. At times when the European ice sheets extended further south than at the present day, the wintering grounds of these species shifted southwards to marshlands and waters within the range of local human settlements (Eastham, 1999).

By contrast to the culling in winter of wildfowl, seabirds, gulls, auks and gannets, their eggs and chicks may be culled from their nests on the cliffs during the summer. Both wildfowl and seabirds are excellent sources of animal fats, so important for a multiple of uses to hunter-gatherers and to pre-industrial societies.

Eggshell occurs on a number of sites, but species identification has proved technically difficult. A study of the eggshell from the Neolithic early farming village at Skara Brae, Orkney, scanning SEM images through a computer programme resulted in the probable collection of eggs from 18 different species.

Traditional egg collectors on the cliffs in the Scottish Islands stored those of seabirds in specially built houses called 'clets' for future use.

■ Hunting and procurement strategies

Then the little Hiawatha----
Of all beasts he learned the language
Learned their names and all their secrets,
How the beavers built their lodges,
Where the squirrels hid their acorns,
How the reindeer ran so swiftly,
Why the rabbit was so timid.

　　Longfellow

The collection of both plant and animal foods is seasonal, and an intimate understanding of seasonality and animal ethology is part of hunter-gatherer lore. Each season marks the availability of certain resources and timing is important. Among the traditional owners of the Kakadu region of northern Australia the year is divided into six seasons between the 'wet' and the 'dry', each one marking the availability of staple foods like meat, fruit, eggs and yams. Among Palaeolithic engraved bone plaques, occasional discoveries have been made that have been interpreted as calibrating the passage of time through the phases of the moon. One such from Aurignacian levels of the Abri Lartet in the Gorge d'Enfer, close to Les Eyzies in the Dordogne, was discovered in 1863 and was not fully studied until the 1970s (Marshack, 1972). A second similar plaque, recovered from a similar context in the Abri Blanchard, is now in the National Museum of Antiquities at St Germaine en Laye, and in 1991 a further, much later, example was discovered at the Grotte du Tai in the same region, interpreted as a calendar to cover three years, mapping the phases of the moon and, perhaps, the pattern of the solstices. The precise interpretation of these objects may be open to question, but the engraved marks on them may represent a notation of seasonal change and its implications for the acquisition of staple foods. The total dependence on seasonal resources is difficult to appreciate in an age when alternative supplies of most commodities are available, if not through local manipulation of the annual cycle, then imported from elsewhere at minimal cost to the consumer, but possibly considerable damage to the producing economy in terms of its own social development. And, the concept of immediate availability of out of season ingredients is a very recent phenomenon, based on technology. Even during the first half of the last century, seasonal surpluses of foodstuffs were dried, smoked, salted, cured, bottled, pickled or tinned for winter use in the western world, and other societies had their own methods of conserving ingredients for future use.

The hunting of herd animals or, in particular of large mammals, necessitated group co-operation. Although at this period no scenes of hunts were depicted, evidence for group participation, especially in the butchery and sharing of kills comes from images in cave art and on portable objects.

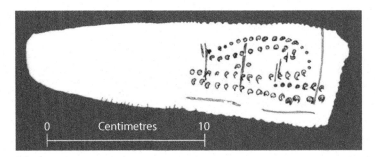

Figure 5.2: The Abri Blanchard calendar

More significantly, from the location of settlements in relation to landfall and to others, give the lead to reconstructing some of the strategies used in organising the game. Sites of occupation are frequently grouped together, usually in association with a water source close by. A primary example of an aggregation of occupations may be seen at Les Eyzies on the Dordogne. Here, hunter-gatherer communities came together, possibly at certain times of year, over a very long period of time, so that the material evidence of their stay dates from the early Mousterian during the Middle Palaeolithic to the very end of the final Magdalenian during the dying phases of the last glaciation. Other group contact sites may be found along the course of the river Lot and further south, within the catchment of the Aveyron gorge and the series of Magdalenian rock shelters along the Gave d'Oleron at Sordes l'Abbaye. A similar aggregation of sites occurred in Britain in Derbyshire in caves around the magnesian limestone outcrop of Creswell crags. One of the purposes of such aggregation sites was likely to have been to facilitate animal drives into a corral or trap, usually at the end of the good season. Another might have been purely one of social exchange.

The basic equipment of the hunter changed very little over time until the invention of the handgun in the 14th century AD (Eastham, 2006; Kear, 1990; Lewis, 2009). Pits, traps, corrals, drives and nets combine with spears and arrows were used throughout. Clap nets and similar are shown on paintings in Palaeolithic and Egyptian art, as are decoys as a means of leading animals and , especially, birds into captivity. Imitative calls are still in use, as are hides or camouflage of the person either to hide the hunter or make him invisible. Illustrating the latter stratagem, a drawing on the walls of the cave of Les Trois Frères in Ariége depicts a hunter dressed in a skin with a bow in hand, following the herd.

Locations of mass animal culls have been examined in detail in North America. The Gull Lake kill site in south western Saskatchewan in the country of the Plains Indians, revealed a sequence of bison drives into a prepared pound from AD 50 until the 13th century AD (Kehoe, 1973). European examples of mass culling on such a large scale as that which was organised in Saskatchewan province are rare. In Europe, largely mobile prehistoric hunter-gatherer communities had no use for materials that could not be rapidly consumed or occasionally, perhaps cached. A relatively nomadic way of life did not require the accumulation of possessions or the warehousing of commodities, in order to cope with the demands of subsistence. These could be dealt with from day to day and it is generally believed that they did not require a huge investment in time or expenditure of effort (Sahlins, 1972). From the relatively frequency of bones of mammalian and avian scavengers profiting from leftovers around the living floors of human occupation areas, it would appear that a surplus of supplies was more common than scarcity and distribution an activity to be considered.

Because of the difference in social organisation, the utility of planned mass animal kills in Europe at this time was minimal. The instance of the herd of horses crashing down the cliff at Solutré, Saone et Loire, in France is sometimes quoted as an example of a mass kill and there was evidence of human exploitation of the carcasses for meat but, even though the horse carcases were extensively butchered by successive groups, the Solutré site may not represent deliberate hunting strategy on the scale of that which took place at the Gull Lake site. It is more than probable that the horses were sufficiently terrified by the thunder and lightening of a storm such as the Rhone valley is prone to, that a stampede took them involuntarily over the cliff to their deaths.

More frequently, small groups of beasts may have been corralled and single individuals taken in traps, nets, pits or speared for immediate use. We may compare the way Cree Indian people of James Bay and the Innuit of North America are strongly influenced by their belief that animals are persons in their own right, who give themselves to the hunter so that humans may survive and their sacrifice entitles them to respect, putting the hunter under the obligation to act for their benefit (Feit, 1999; Ingold, 2000). The deliberate acquisition of surplus does not appear to be a driving force among prehistoric hunter-gatherer communities but when it occurred the proceeds seem to have been shared.

■ Resource distribution

Evidence for procurement is well attested by the large numbers of living floors and population growth during the Upper Palaeolithic; it is more difficult to trace the way supplies were distributed. Something may be learned about exchange systems and the way resources were distributed between a discrete group of people or external groups with which contact was made. It is also possible to gather some information from the art, both the images on cave walls, parietal art and on portable objects for personal decoration, weapons or bone tools. In considering this aspect, guidance from ethnographic studies of recent hunter-gatherer peoples may prove useful, although accounts are coloured by post-contact influences and the growth of mixed economies.

If there can be a general picture, it would appear that in the harsher environments, like the Arctic or desert zones like the Kalahari, cooperative hunting amongst bands or kinship groups has been regularly undertaken and represented a sharing of effort in procurement and distribution of limited resources. In the richer, often forest zones, family groups tend to gather food more independently and make more use of smaller game, and of gathering fruits, plants and honey.

Among the peoples of North America, Europe and the north of Russia, hunting has continued to be a collective occupation even post colonisation by commercial interests. Communal sharing, usually within the group, was also the norm. Very often it was the women who were responsible for organising the distribution of the game and seasonal foodstuffs. The collective process of acquiring physical as well as cultural resources was accompanied by sharing in all its aspects, not as unsolicited gifts but as an accepted response to demand, therefore eliminating any concept of obligation on either side (Ingold, 1999). Equal division of the produce resulting from the hunt within the group continues to operate among different hunter-gatherer groups at the present day and at a variety of levels. Among the Qikirtamiut Inuits of the Belcher islands in Hudson Bay, Canada, the eiderduck are culled for their skins that the women use to make clothing. Following each kill the birds are divided according to age and sex so that each household has an equal share of the most hardwearing or softest part of the skin for different parts or type of clothing (Nakashima, 2002). The reciprocal sharing of food resources is common amongst groups from the Amazon and Argentine to South Asia, Australia and the Arctic.

Where gift exchange takes place, it is on the basis of reciprocity as in the Kula ceremonies among the Trobriand islanders of the Pacific (Malinowski, 1922) or the ceremonial exchange gatherings of the villagers of Mount Hagen in New Guinea (Strathern and Strathern, 1971). We have no physical evidence of such gatherings in Palaeolithic hunter-gatherer life but there is evidence that points towards contact or exchange between groups. Some themes in the depictions in cave art have been traced across considerable distances within the regions of Aquitaine and Cantabria in northwest Spain; for example, specific types of conventional symbolism in, for instance the representation of the female form (Lorblanchet, 2010). At different periods the uniform dispersion of manufacturing styles and methods in the shaping of flint and stone tools and other culturally significant materials, indicate a highly mobile society establishing regular contacts between other dispersed groups, intermittently sharing aggregation sites and festivals.

Skins, bone, fats, guts, feather and fibre

Food was only one aspect of the use of animals and plant materials as a major resource in everyday life. There were signs even as early as at Boxgrove, that carcases had been skinned, notably there is evidence of skinning of a bear skull.

As the average temperatures periodically declined during the onset of glacial phases, besides a need for lipids in the diet and for other applications, there was an increasing requirement for skins, fats and bones in the household management of hominid settlements.

Hides of all kinds were almost as valuable as meat. But all parts of an animal were put to use. It may be heard in traditional sayings like "you can't make a silk purse out of a sow's ear", or, "I'll have your guts for garters".

Clothing was one priority, but there was a considerable range of other every-day equipment and goods that leather was there to supply. Large mammal skins like those of bison and bovids were ideal as coverings for tents and other shelters. Open air shelters were covered with hides. Reconstructions of these habitations such as Kostienki I in Eastern Europe, Pushkari in Russia or Konnersdors in Germany, show a basic round or oval cabin with a frame usually constructed of mammoth tusks and covered with skins held down with stones. Pincevant, a Late Glacial site beside the river Seine, revealed a series of circular living floors, with post holes forming a a dwelling similar to a tepee, that on the interior ground surface was insulated against the damp with a layer of iron ochre mixed with animal fat. This combination of red ochre and animal fat forms an excellent pre-servative and was used to coat the body and clothing of the youth named 'the Red Lady', buried ceremoniously in Paviland Cave on the coast of Gower, South Wales around 27,000 years BP (Aldhouse Green, 2000).

Pushkari, Ukraine, 23,000 BP

Mammoth bones and tusks

Hearth

Figure 5.3: Hut reconstructions at Pushkari, Ukraine, showing the use of skins as durable coverings. By the author.

Animal fats were extremely important in the diet of hunter-gatherer groups, especially those occupying peri-arctic and tundra zones at the onset and early retreat of the Last Glacial Maximum, when the daily calorific requirement in the diet was high. However, in addition to the nutritional value and the water repellent qualities of lipids, animal fats were used for illumination. It is only necessary to consider the quantity of whale and other oils burnt in domestic lamps, prior to the use of coal tar products or electricity, to realise this. Oil lamps fashioned from stone, but otherwise very similar in shape to those used in Roman times have been recovered from a number of Palaeolithic sites and particularly in association with cave wall painting.

Just as mammal skins were a primary need for all types of clothing and covering, so it was inevitable that avian plumage should be important for insulation either as down or as skins. Both are in use for clothing among the relict populations of peri-arctic peoples, besides the fashion trades of industrialised societies. In 1942, research by the American Army concluded that the tog value of goose down was higher than any other insulation material except reindeer skin, but the latter was disadvantaged by its total lack of compressibility. Sadly, although there are many ethnographic examples of Eskimo and other feather parkas in museums, there are no archaeological survivals. Similarly, we have no direct evidence of feathers used for decoration or ceremonial purposes, although there are wonderful instances recorded in tribal societies. There is one curious phenomenon cropping up at the end of the Last Glaciation amongst certain groups of people in parts of Aquitaine in France. Large numbers of snowy owls, these days associated with the high tundra zone, were culled and processed apparently to remove the skin and feathers. The hollow bone was extensively used in the manufacture of tubes. Both the primary motivation for these kills and the use to which they were put is still under consideration and interpretation depends upon the length of time over which such pursuit operated, but it is worth bearing in mind that both males and females of the species have spectacular white or speckled plumage, that would have had its attraction.

Animal bone

Bone and ivory was sometimes an important material in construction. As late as the 3rd and 4th Millenium BC, early Neolithic farmers at Skara Brae on Mainland Orkney were constructing the roofs of their stone built houses using whale ribs for the roof trusses. Even during a climatic optimum, there was little timber available on the island but the alternative was at hand. Besides some Eastern European examples, like Kostienki on the river Don, mammoth tusk structures have been found, even within caves in the Palaeolithic habitations in the west, and a good example appeared at Arcy sur Cure on the river Yonne, a tributary of the Seine, dated to the early years of the Upper Palaeolithic, where a shelter supported on mammoth tusks was constructed for increased protection inside the cave. Another concentrated study by Gaussin (1980) sponsored by CNRS of late, upper Palaeolithic open air sites in France in the valley of the river Isle, south west of the town of Perigueux has revealed a high level of uniformity among these summer residences. They were built with internal stone paved floors, as protection from the damp of low-lying ground; sides and walls were supported by timber or bone posts and covered with hides, held down by river pebbles: all materials present in the immediate locality.

Bone also furnished a large part of the toolkit required for daily living and for personal decoration or ceremonial. Whilst stone in the form of flint or quartzite could be made into every sort of cutting, scraping or digging implement and arrow tips; bone supplied much of the hunting equipment in the form of spear throwers, harpoons and spatulas for hides and fulfilled a great many cultural needs besides. Even skulls make effective receptacles for liquids.

It was not only mammalian bone that was used in the manufacture of everyday objects. Bird long bones, of the wing and hind limb in particular, because of being hollow were extensively used from the earliest settlement times of modern humans. Storage and transfer of liquids and powdered pigments was an obvious use. Blow pipes to apply pigment in body painting or for images on cave walls was another and as containers for small objects that might be carried around on the person. Excavation has recovered such tubes with traces of red ochre at, for example, the late Magdalenian site of Bourrouilla, Arancou and tubes were useful for the safekeeping of the very fine sewing needles used in the production of garments at this period.

The relatively leisured existence led by a large proportion of many of these Stone Age hunter-gatherers is evidenced not only in the painting and engraving of caves but also in the decoration of items of equipment, spear throwers, harpoons and the like, with the purpose perhaps to personalise the instrument to its owner. Yet besides decoration on essential tools even more elaborate carving may be seen on items of personal adornment, pendants and beads for necklaces or arm bands using decorative or symbolic items like carved animal teeth, bone, fish vertebrae, or shells. Much of this art expresses a theme of plenty, of ample beasts at the best time of the year, with little bone figurines displaying human pulchritude. A primary motive for the taking of animals may have been for nourishment but their inherent significance may have been expressed in the accompanying works of art and be related to a philosophic approach not too far distant from that amongst the Innuit of the North American plains (ibid). And, like the North American Indian peoples. their lives allowed for sufficient leisure to record their ideas in bone and pigment. Like art, music would not appear to be relevant cultural factor in the context of animal exploitation, yet instruments in the form of

5

pipes, whistles and flutes, manufactured from avian bone are known from some of the earliest settlements of modern man. Some of these may have been used in hunting as imitating animal or bird calls but a number have recently come to light in the Swabian Jura, that have a sufficient number of notes to be played as flutes. At Hohlefels in the Ach valley 20 kilometre from Ulm a five hole flute, fabricated from a radius of vulture, was recovered in 2008 (Connard *et al.*, 2009). Nearby in the Lone valley at Geissenklosterle, another three hole flute was found with the remains of several others. These finds have been dated to between 35,000 and 40,000 years BP (Conard and Bolus, 2003). Elsewhere in France a number of bird whistles have been identified from the early Upper Palaeolithic, at caves in the Dordogne, La Roche and La Roque, in deposits dated to 30,000 years BP, while further south in Aquitaine in the cave of Isturitz with a similar date a cache was discovered of some twenty two pieces of vulture bone flutes hidden as though for use at future ceremonies in or near the cave. Less well dated is the Veyreau flute from the Aveyron region. Also made from a vulture ulna it is a complex instrument of uncertain age despite its similarity with the Palaeolithic examples, since it was found amongst funerary debris of the Copper age (Fage and Mourer Chauviré, 1983). The use of bird bone for musical instruments is not restricted to Europe; a cache of over 30 flutes made of crane ulnae was found among the ruins of the 8,000 year old city of Jiahu in Wuyang county of Henan province of China.

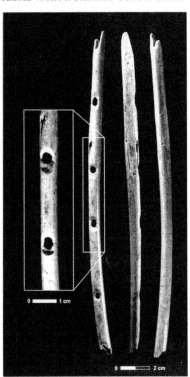

Figure 5.4: Hohlefels flute

■ Economic change in the early Holocene

The end of the Pleistocene was marked in Western Europe by a series of minor climatic oscillations between 15,000 and 10,000 years BP, when there were alternate phases of warming and deterioration of the climate. These phases may be traced in the history of the pollens and in the gradual disappearance of animal species like the reindeer from the encroaching forest zones. The Middle Stone Age was characterised by the reduction in large animal prey, the beginning of a rise in sea level due to the warming of the climate and retreat of the ice and a reduction in the human population in line with the reduction in the larger game species. Regional variations apart, forest species like red deer and roe deer took the place of reindeer, bison and musk ox and horse. As a result there was an increase in dependence on rabbits and hares, fish, shellfish and wildfowl, with a commensurate diminution in the size of the flint element in the equipment required for the pursuit of smaller game. By 8,000 years, BP the density of the population per kilometre square is calculated to have fallen by half, as resource availability reduced. Nevertheless, evidence of Mesolithic presence is very widespread across the continent of Europe, Britain, and the Middle East.

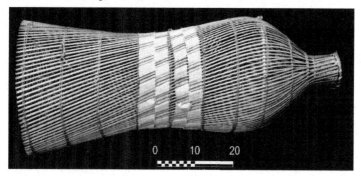

Figure 5.5: Middle Stone Age fish trap type as used in 21st century Vietnam.

■ Neolithic farmers

The amelioration of the climate in western and northern Europe following the end of the Ice Age had its corollary in the drying up of the fertile areas of the Middle East and a marked reduction in the availability of the herds of gazelle and other ungulates that had been a major staple of hunter-gatherer life in that region. Fortunately, the Fertile Crescent was the home of many wild cereals that were gathered and then systematically cultivated by around 9,000 years BP. Cultivation in the fertile floodplains of Egypt and Mesopotamia demanded a more settled life style and agriculture required a more constant labour force across the seasons, with the result that as the practice of raising crops spread across the Aegean and the Balkans, along the Danube corridor, or through the Mediterranean, gradually communities comprising family groups expanded into village settlements. In the more fertile areas, because these early agriculturalists were able in good years to produce a surplus and store harvests, settlements began to develop into urban communities, with the growth of specialist trades.

However, cultivation using stone or wooden hoes or digging sticks was only suitable on relatively light, sandy or alluvial soils and the early agriculturalists found a considerable problem in maintaining soil fertility. In order make use of land in temperate zones, they had first to fell and burn the trees, thus increasing the available phosphates in the soil. To begin with, since their tools were unsuitable for heavy clay soils, they could only cultivate successfully light or thin soils, like those of the Kentish Weald or upland areas. After a few years these became impoverished and they had to move on to a new site and carry out the process of slash and burn once more. Any form of settled agriculture in northern Europe only became possible once a form of the plough came into use in the Bronze Age, around 1,600 years BC.

Hunting, and to some extent the gathering of wild produce, continued, as it does to the present day, but with a shrinking population of wild animals in relation to the demographic rise in the human population it became necessary to manage the herds. Pastoralism of wild herds, of native cattle and of sheep, whose ancestors were native to Cyprus and the Middle East, and of reindeer in the north became important ways of ensuring subsistence levels. Over time, management advanced to controlled breeding and domestication, so that instead of moving with the herds in search of pasture, animals could be raised adjacent to the cultivated land and used to maintain its fertility. Nevertheless pastoral mobility continued at least into the 20th century. In the South of France, for instance, shepherds continued to lead their flocks between the Camargue and the lower slopes of the Alps - often by train in recent times - and in Spain the village herds of sheep and goats were led out each day to feed on the open meseta, guarded by the shepherd boy and his dogs.

Figure 5.6: Afgan shepherds with sheep and goats, the Pastoral way of life. Photo by the author

The mechanisms of human demographic distribution created problems for producers even before the Middle Ages. Cattle, sheep and even geese reared in surplus in rural communities had to reach the consumer. When the Romans traded for hides, for which Britain was famous, for their armies, they were transported by sea, but in order to reach markets outside the immediate distribution catchment area of local fairs, the animals were walked along drovers' roads, across country from the West Country, Wales or Scotland to markets in the major centres of population, even as far as London and, in the 14th century, to supply the armies of the British king in France (Toulson, 1977; 1992). There is archaeological evidence for such long distance imports at Stonehenge and Durrington Walls in Wiltshire during the Neolithic of the mid third millennium BC. It was discovered by isotope analysis that large numbers of cattle and pig bones from the middens had belonged to beasts reared in Cornwall, Devon or West Wales and more rarely from further north in Scotland (Parker Pearson, 2012; Albarella and Serjeantson, 2002). It was a slow moving supply chain, travelling at an average of two miles an hour, escorted by professional drovers and local young people from the age of ten or twelve, giving them employment of a kind away from their home villages. The animals, even geese, required protection for their feet over long distances and were shod for the journey and along the way. However for these beasts, unlike the reindeer herds of the Palaeolithic hunter-gatherers, this was a one-way trip.

Concluding remarks

In terms of resource management, it may be considered that a hunter-gatherer lifestyle can be both economic of labour and sustainable. It was a way of living that persisted for over two million years of primate evolution. It was not exploitative of certain individuals in respect of others and the cultural remains left behind indicated a relatively leisured society that was self regulating in balance with the resources obtainable. However, a change in that environmental balance, the drying out and gradual desertification of parts of the settled world in the south combined with the loss of many large game species and an increase in the human population upset that balance. It became no longer possible to sustain the demographic increase through a hunter-gatherer way of life with its implications of low carbon output. It effectively turned man out of the 'Garden of Eden' and changed the pattern of society, dividing the population into producers and consumers, each group servicing the other to an extent. Out of it grew concepts of feudal service and slavery, specialist trades, and hunter-gathering persists today only as a form of sport.

References

Albarella, U. and Serjeantson D. (2002). A passion for pork: meat consumption at the British Late Neolithic site of Durrington Walls, in Miracle P. and Milner N. (eds). *Consuming Passions and Patterns of Consumption*. Cambridge: Cambridge University Press.

Aldhouse Green, S. (2000). *Paviland Cave and the Red Lady, a definitive report*. Western Academic and Specialist press Ltd, Bristol.

Aldhouse Green, S. (2012). *Neanderthals in Wales*. Oxbow books and the National Museum of Wales.

Callow, P. and Cornford J.M. (eds.) (1986). *La Cotte de St Brelade, Excavations by C.B.M. McBurney 1961-1978*. Norwich: Geo

Cleyet Merle, J-J. (1990). *La Préhistoire de la Peche*. Editions Errance, Paris

Conard, N. J. and Bolus, M. (2003). Radiocarbon dating the appearance of modern humans and timing of cultural innovations in Europe: new results and new challenges. *Journal of human Evolution*, **44**(3), 331-371.

Connard, N.J., Malina, M. and Munsel S.C. (2009) New flutes document the earliest musical tradition in south west Germany. *Nature* **460**, 737-740.

Delpech, F. (1999) Biomasse d'ongulés au Paléolithique et l'inférence sur la démographique. *Paléo* **11**: 19-42.

Eastham, A. (1999). Les oiseaux et la microfaune. In Chauchat, C., *L'Habitat Magdalénien de la Grotte de Bourrouilla à Arancou (Pyrénées Atlantiques) Gallia Préhistoire* **41**, 113-127

Eastham, A. (2006). Papageno down the Ages: a study in fowling methods, with particular reference to the Palaeolithic of Western Europe. *Munibe* **57**: 369- 397.

Fages, S.I. and Mourer Chauviré, C. (1983). La Flute de la Grotte de Verreau. *Bulletin de la Société Préhistorique Française* **16**, 95-103.

Feit H.A. (1999). James Bay Cree. In Lee R.B. and Daley R. eds. *The Cambridge Encyclopaedia of Hunter Gatherers*. Cambridge Univeristy Press, pp 41-45.

Gaussin J. (1980). Le paleolithique superiure de plein air en Perigord. Secteur Mussidan Saint-Astier, moyenne vallee de l'Isle. *Supplement a Gallia Préhistoire Paris*, **14**, 1-300

Harris, J.W.K. and Isaacs, G.U. (1976). The Karan industry: early Pleistocene archaeological evidence from the terrain east of Lake Turkana, Kenya. *Nature* **262**, 102-107.

Ingold, T. (1999). Paths of fire: An anthropologist's inquiry into western technology. *Technology and Culture*, **40**(1), 130-132.

Ingold, T. (2000). *The Perception of the Environment*. Routledge, London.

Kear, J. (1990). *Man and Wildfowl*. London: T. and A.D. Poyser.

Kehoe, T. F. (1973). *The Gull Lake site: a prehistoric bison drive site in south western Saskatchowan*. Milwaukie Public Museum.

Klein, R.G. (1989). *The Human Career: human, biological and cultural origins.* Chicago University Press.

Leakey, R.E. (1981). *The Making of Mankind.* Michael Joseph, London.

Le Gall, O. (1992) Les Magdaléniens et l'Ichthyofaune dulçaquicole. In *Le peuplement Magdalénien.* Comité des travaux historique et scientifique. pp. 277-288.

Lorblanchet, M. (2010). *Art pariétal: grottes ornées du Quercy.* Rodez, Edition. du Rouergue.

Lewis, B. (2009). *Hunting in Britain from the Ice Age to the Present.* Stroud: History Press.

Malinowski, B. (1922). *Argonauts of the Western Pacific; an account of native enterprise and adventure in the archipelago of Melanesian New Guinea.* London: Routledge and Kegan Paul.

Marshack, A. (1972). *The Roots of Civilisation.* London: Weidenfeld and Nicholson.

Nakashima D. (2002). Inuit women's knowledge of bird skins and its application in clothing construction, Sanikiluak, Nunavit. *Material Cultural Revue. Vol. 56* UNESCO.

O'Connell, J.F., Hawkes K. and Burton Jones K. (1988). Hadza scavenging implications for Plio/Pleistocene hominid subsistence. *Current Anthropology* **29**, 256-263.

Parker Pearson, M. (2012). *Stonehenge, Exploring the greatest Stone Age mystery.* London: Simon and Schuster.

Roberts, M.B. and Parfitt, S.A. (1999) *Boxgrove: a middle Pleistocene Hominid site at Eartham Quarry, Boxgrove, West Sussex.* London: English Heritage.

Sahlins, M. (1972). *Stone Age Economics.* London: Tavistock.

Strathern, A. and Strathern , M. (1971). *Self Decoration in Mount Hagen.* London: Duckworth.

Toulson S. (1977). *The Drovers Roads of Wales, Vol I,* London: Whittet Books Ltd.

Toulson, S. (1992). *The Drovers Roads of Wales, Vol II.* London: Whittet Books Ltd.

Waechter, J. d'A (1973). The Late Acheulean industries of the Swanscombe area. In D.E.Strong (ed.) *Archaeological Theory and Practice.* pp. 67-86 New York: Seminar.

5

Table 5.1: Time line

Date	Climate	OIS	Culture / Hominid	Site	Region	Observations
12–1900 AD	Temperate		Early Modern, Medieval to modern	Drove roads	Mainly Western Europe	Herdsmen leading stock to markets and centres of population from rearing grounds.
50 – 1500 AD	Cold/temperate		Plains Indians	Gull lake site	North America	Bison herding into kill site enclosures
55 BC– 400 AD	Temperate	1	Roman Traders	Coin hoards and evidence of pottery around western coasts.	Britain and Gaul [France]	Trading for hides, tin, lead, copper and silver
c. 3,600 BP	Warm temperate	1	Neolithic to Bronze Age onwards	a) Stonehenge and other Neolithic sites, evidence of long range sourcing fat cattle for consumption. b) Mechanical plough marks visible in soil, eg. Stackpole Warren.	Britain and northern Europe	a) Isotope analysis of teeth show that beasts were sourced at long distance from the west and north to Stonehenge. b) The use of ploughshares began to replace hoeing as a means of cultivation.
c. 8,000 BP	Climatic amelioration with rise in sea levels & tree cover	1	Neolithic revolution in food production. a)Agriculture b)Pastoralism and animal domestication		Europe, Middle and far East	a)Crop growing spreading across Europe, developing from wild cereals etc., resulting in short term settlements, employing slash and burn cultivation. b) Herding leading to mobile pastoral, groups and controlled breeding of stock
Holocene 12,000 BP	Last Glaciation, ends with onset of PreBoreal	2	Mesolithic industries in Europe	Widespread and characterised by flint scatter	Europe	Reduction in availability of large game, increase in use of small animals, fish and shellfish. Flint toolkits becoming smaller and composite.

Date (BP)	Climate	Stage	Culture / Period	Sites	Region	Notes
13,000 – 22,000 BP	Last Glaciation in Europe. [Devensian in Britain]. 4 stages of glacial advance with warmer interstadials between.	2	Upper Palaeolithic Magdalenian [Creswellian] 13-18,000 BP	Church hole, Robin Hood Cave, Creswell Derby. Dufaure, Arancou, and sites throughout Aquitaine and northern Spain	France Spain, Central Europe Britain.	Cave paintings of animals, personal ornaments and elaborate flint and bone equipment for hunting and cultural activities.
21/20,000 BP			Solutrean and Gravettian		Paviland Cave, Gower	Well retouched flint blades especially burins used as chisels on wood and bone
23 – 35,000 Years BP	Last Glaciation Temperate phase	15 3	Aurignacian, preceded by the Chatelperronian	Hohlefels, Geissenklosterle, La Roche & La Roque	Swabia, South Germany, South west France	A fine blade culture that in the early stages formed the transition from Neanderthal to Homo sapiens cultures, of which music seems part of the development.
32-38,000 years BP		4 5	Transition in Europe between Aurignacian and Neanderthal occupation	Arcy sur Cure	France, Yonne	Transition from an industry based on retouched flint flakes to one based on long cutting blades.
40 - 500,000 years BP	Fluctuations between cold and warm as ice advanced and retreated	5 6	Neanderthals in Europe	Fontechevade, Ehringsdorf, Pontnewydd La Cotte de St Brelade, Swanscombe Atapuerca Arago& Lazaret, Mauer & Steinheim,	France Germany N. Wales Jersey Thames valley Spain France Germany	Hunting and scavenging on large animal kills. The increasing use of well retouched flint flake tools with specific function within the toolkit, alongside sophisticated handaxe forms. Industrial facies referred to as 'Mousterian'. The use of caves as habitation during cold phases.
500,000 – 1,000,000 years BP	Mainly warm	13- 21	Homo erectus Homo habilis Australopithecine species	Zhouchoutien Olduvai Gorge Lake Turkana	China E. Africa	Acheulean , handaxe industry Pebble tools 'Chopper and Chopping tools'. Hominids becoming increasingly omnivorous

5

6 Land Grabbing and Land Imperialism: Historic and contemporary perspectives

Louise Manning

Introduction

The subject of land grabbing and land imperialism has a duality that is both contemporary and historic. Societal mechanisms for delivering food security in an agrarian or nomadic community have always rested on effective resource control and management. Land and water have been, and still are, the critical resources that communities depend upon to survive, although in the twenty-first century there is a physical and mental dislocation between the urban majority and the land from which their food is derived.

With secondary economic growth, and a move from a society primarily working on or living off the land to urban dwelling, this leads to a realignment of how food is produced and distributed. Industrialisation and urbanisation are the major global drivers of agricultural land conversion and peri-urban sprawl (Dadi *et al.* 2016). In developed countries such as the United Kingdom (UK), the reasons for the urbanisation of the population, whether in part voluntarily or policy driven, are lost in the mists of time. The connection of an evolved, largely urban and metropolitan population with how their food is produced is broken and fragmented. This allows a new discourse and other actors to enter the void that is created, often deriving new economic and social models for how food is produced, processed, sold, purchased and consumed, even a new dialogue as to what food actually is.

The modern rural landscape of the UK is embedded within historic activities of land enclosure and changes in land tenure, loss of access and common rights for rural dwellers and a subsequent population migration to towns and cities. Between 1604 and 1914 over 5,200 Enclosure Bills were enacted by the UK Parliament relating to just over a fifth of the total area of England, some 6.8 million acres (Parliament, n.d.). Enclosure under these Parliamentary Acts brought an end to common rights and communal management of the open fields, instead providing portions of land to individual landowners as private, personal property (McDonagh and Daniels, 2012). McDonagh and Daniels outline that there was not just enclosure of land area, but also a realignment of wider infrastructure in terms of existing roads, churches, farmhouses, drainage systems and the removal of villages and resettlement of individuals either in new model villages (villagisation) or in towns and cities (urbanisation). Land enclosure in this context can be said to be an integral component of the historical development of capitalism (Makki and Geisler, 2013).

The narrative still continues in developed rural economies, with migration of the young from rural areas and agricultural corporatisation, whether it manifests in increased farm size (Foster *et al.* 2013), mindset (Wheeler *et al.* 2012; Magnan, 2012), or reliance on technology and the loss of jobs (Phillips and McLeroy, 2004). The collective discussion also reflects concerns over biodiversity conservation, natural heritage in the evolved landscape and societal interest in how food is produced. The brokering of much of this latter conversation is by civil society through non-governmental organisations (NGOs). It is nuanced and obviously political in its most rooted sense.

Civil society and social capital

Social capital is a resource, based on trust, that multiplies in developed social networks leading to co-operation among actors, and collaboration between institutions and community organisations to facilitate the achievement of common goals (Manning, 2013; Muthuri *et al.*, 2006; Leicht, 1998). Civil society is construed as being professional associations, clubs and societies (Norton, 2001). Foley and Edwards (1996) considered the paradox of civil society and whether firstly the generation of 'social capital' and secondly delivering what is seen to be a 'public good' are essentially the same thing. Foley and Edwards (1996, citing Putnam, 1993) suggest that the public good is only of value when it is available equitably to all society and provides the effects notionally ascribed to it. Their line of argument proposes that social networks in themselves may not necessarily drive effective governance. It is only when such networks bridge and do not become politicised, that they rise above representing specific social interests and actually deliver a public good. Whilst this critique is nuanced, the contention that a politicised civil society co-exists with, but does not necessarily represent, citizens' interests is important. This is especially so when the decision makers in such private organisations become more remote from the individuals they state they are seeking to represent. In the void created by passive democratic political governance, an active politicised civil society could be considered as complementary or even a suitable substitute for governmental action. This form of civil society can then be charged with being the focal point and the advocate for society's interests and points of view (Foley and Edwards, 1998). Within the process of governance, mutually exclusive social constructs such as the political society, and differentiated public, private and non-profit economic sectors are then created (Foley and Edwards, 1996) often in themselves becoming more and more distant from the very society they were developed to represent. All these interfacing social constructs have a role to play in concert, or in conflict, with the development of food policy governance, especially around food security and more particularly nutrition security, and this context is crucial when considering the subject of land grabbing.

Social responsibility

Purchasing food and eating it as a consumer is an act that has political, economic, environmental, aesthetic, and ethical aspects (Lavin, 2013; Devinney *et al.*, 2006). In saying this, the term 'political' is being used in its core sense. In the ancient Greek, *'politikos'* means 'of, for, or relating to the citizens'. Citizenship, or the decision-making that is for, or on behalf of, all sections of society is today more usually termed as governance. Governance can be described as:

> the structures and processes that enable governmental and non-governmental actors to co-ordinate their interdependent needs and interests through the making and implementing of policies in the absence of a unifying political authority, (Krahmann, 2003: 331).

Social responsibility can be prescribed or voluntary. Spence and Bourlakis (2009) define corporate responsibility (CR) as the voluntary actions that an organisation can take, over and above compliance with minimum legal requirements, to address both its own competitive interests and the interests of the wider society. Global governance and the interrelationship between foreign direct investment (FDI), trade, shareholder return, insurance, credit rating and sustainable development are key dynamics driving corporate social responsibility (CSR) and there are increasing demands from multiple stakeholders for more sustainable investments, and compliance with internationally accepted standards and agreed instruments (Manning and Baines, 2004). The formation of multinational corporations (MNC) means that their identity will naturally transcend national culture and national identity to form a differentiated, and sometimes dissociated, corporate identity. This corporate identity, in terms of social responsibility, and the organisation's interaction with a given or indeed plural 'society' can mean that there is a homogeneous interaction, and the notion of nation states and national identity is simply subsumed.

Szántó (2001) states that it is "a peculiarity of globalisation" that a hierarchically well-placed individual within a MNC can technologically govern at a global range. Indeed, MNCs apply their own strategic techniques and tactical measures in pursuing their business interests and affiliations (Teklemariam *et al.* 2015) that operate across nation states. Stigliz (2006) argued that whilst exploitation of natural resources is a key part of the corporate globalisation model, this approach has lead to failures in resource-rich developing nations. Therefore in order for their activities to be sustainable, Stiglz suggests that MNCs need smart incentives and/or be forced to pay the true cost of their environmental and social impact. These assertions bring forth considerations of whether a corporation or a nation-state can act from an imperialistic stance in how it operates and its associated reach.

Imperialism as a mechanism to drive commerce and profit is as contemporary as it is historic. Imperialism at its simplest is the extension or imposition of power; more fully imperialism is the policy, practice, or advocacy of extending the power and dominion of a nation, (NGO or MNC) especially by direct territorial acquisitions or by gaining indirect control over the political or economic life of other areas. Thus imperialism is the exercise of power and control over political or economic activity in a given area, without any regard to the boundaries of nation states or nationhood. Nationhood in this sense is the grouping of individuals with a common language, culture economic life and an innate sense of identity. Hofstede (2011: 3) defines national culture as the "collective programming of the mind which distinguishes the members of one group or category of people from those of another." Mann (1997) argues that the rise of transnational power relations has weakened the role of the nation state. Thus it could be argued that globalisation is the set of changing conditions that transcends the nation state as a fundamental unit in terms of organisation, democratic processes or political units (Thompson, 2012), ultimately leading to high level policy processes that lack accountability (Lang and Heasman, 2015), the formation of a mobile global elites, less liberal models of identity and a deepening gap between rich and poor (Arditi, 2004).

Aspects of governance associated with food are rooted in the political. Social responsibility connected with food, at individual, corporate, institutional or national levels, is in its purest sense political. Land rights, tenure, ownership and access as a subject affords the opportunity to consider many aspects of the governance and responsibility that underpin how food is grown, processed, sold, purchased, consumed and wasted. With regard to personal social responsibility, individuals can consider their interaction with food at different times from the viewpoint of "the citizen or the consumer" (Grunert, 2006). Largely, economic drivers influence consumer behaviour with the consumerism component rather than the caring component of social responsibility often playing more of a lead role (Manning, 2013). The interplay is neither consistent across all consumers nor with a given issue or food product. Indeed, social responsibility can be a solo, product-centric purchasing decision within the shopping basket (Manning, 2013). Whilst the issue of land-grabbing is not a central focus for consumers as this book chapter is being written, that does not mean that in the future a specific incident that gains societal attention does not then focus consumers onto the topic and the wider behaviour of corporate bodies or governments who condone such activity.

In summary, the interaction between civil society and other aspects of governance is fluid and contextualised. The corporatisation of agriculture and the wider food supply chain is simultaneously blatant and subtle, and at its core demonstrates a paradox giving rise to the dilemma that as local, regional and global societies, when we purchase, consume and waste food we either accept or reject the ethical dimensions associated with how our food is produced. This is as true with regard to extrinsic characteristics of animal welfare, and bonded workers and modern slavery, as it is of land grabbing. The aim of this book chapter is to critique the contemporary literature on land grabbing and land imperialism in order to give an overview of the drivers of the activity and the strength of the governance framework that surrounds it. This approach allows for reflection on notions of corporate and consumer social responsibility and social power within food security and sovereignty.

Land grabbing

Land grabbing is the purchase or long-term lease of vast tracts of lands by foreign and/or national state-owned or private investors primarily to produce crops for regional and international markets (Hules and Singh, 2017) earning foreign exchange (Nalepa *et al.* 2016). Alternatively, land grabbing can be described as the profit-focused exploitation of the environment, and restricting of access to resources and displacement of local livelihoods causes food insecurity (Messerli *et al.*, 2013). Land grabs involve the transfer of the rights to own, use or control land through its sale, lease or concession to another entity (Nally, 2015). However, Teklemariam *et al.* (2015) propose that the definition of land grabbing is contested and whilst as a result of the 2008 global financial crisis, food price hikes, and concerns over access to energy resources and fuel, there is a food crisis-centred and farmland-centred characterisation in the literature, the reality is much different, with associations with energy security, climate change mitigation and mobilising global capital too. This has led to a competition for natural resources to underpin food, feed, fuel and textiles production at the primary level. The mining of fuel and mineral resources, provision of rubber and other land based commodities to underpin the burgeoning consumer society as global population continues, and a rise in biodiversity conservation, carbon sequestration, and offsetting projects has led to an increased pressure on natural resources too. Teklemariam *et al.* (2015) citing Mehta *et al.* (2012) suggest that water is actually the target and driver of large-scale land acquisition and term this 'water-grabbing' rather than land grabbing and that governance of land rights needs to be extended to water rights too. Mehta *et al.* (2012: 197) describe water grabbing as:

> a situation where powerful actors are able to take control of, or reallocate to their own benefits, water resources already used by local communities or feeding aquatic ecosystems on which their livelihoods are based.

The drive to secure current and future access to land, and equally the associated water resources, is complex and differentiated according to the actors involved in the discourse on land acquisition (Table 6.1). The positive vocabulary is that land acquisition drives opportunity, improvement and 'win-win' situations, whilst the negative language tends towards exploitation, opacity, displacement and loss.

Land grabbing is purchase or long-term lease of vast tracts of lands by foreign and/or national state-owned or private investors primarily to produce crops for regional and international markets	Hules and Singh, 2017
Land grabbing can be described as the profit-focused exploitation of the environment and restricting of access to resources and displacement of local livelihoods causes food insecurity	Messerli *et al.*, 2013
Land grabs involve the transfer of the rights to own, use or control land through its sale, lease or concession to another entity	Nally, 2014
Land acquisition can contribute to poverty reduction and the improvement of local livelihoods by generating local employment opportunities	Otsuka and Yamano, 2006
International Food Policy Research Institution (IFPRI) has claimed that large-scale land deals are inevitable and mechanisms should be sought to maximise opportunities while mitigating negative impacts	Von Braun and Meinzen-Dick, 2009
Inward investment may be well managed but it has 'high opportunity cost and less poverty-reducing impact' compared other options for alternative land use by the local farming community.	De Schutter, 2011
Large-scale investment in agriculture will result in a win-win solution for both investing and hosting countries, provided that inward investment is well managed.	World Bank, 2010

Table 6.1: The discourse of land acquisition. Adapted from Shete and Rutten, 2015; Baumgartner *et al.*, 2015

Land demand is being served by land areas in Africa, Latin America, and Eastern Europe. The capital being used to fund the leasing or purchase of land is being driven from three main sources:

- Private funding – equity, pensions, hedge funds, charities;
- Public funding – state owned enterprises, sovereign wealth funds, government ministries;
- Government to government deals.

Sovereign wealth funds are state owned investment funds that are invested in order to give a dividend or return. Sovereign wealth funds are created from national central bank reserves that as a result of a positive balance of payments accrue equity. The total value of global sovereign wealth funds has increased markedly since 2008 from US$3.4 trillion in that year to US$7.1 trillion in 2015 (Source: Sovereign Wealth Fund Institute). This money needs to be invested to drive a return. Suhardiman *et al.* (2015) argue that during the land reallocation process, the state has used territorialisation (a state's claims and power to control land access) and legalisation (the wealthy and connected use their power to control land through legal contracts) tactics as its means to secure control over land and thus the revenue from its sale. There is a capital powerbase as a result on the one hand of investor and sovereign wealth funds and on the other of nation states seeking to increase FDI, i.e. to convert natural capital assets into financial capital. Teklemariam *et al.* (2015) assert that in this powerbase environment the protection of vulnerable groups and wider social capital, i.e. local economies, social fabric, and cultures, should be a basic requirement of any inclusive land leasing or acquisition deal. Factors of concern with the leasing or purchase of land by investors include: resultant changes in land use, displacement of indigenous people and opacity of deals (Hules, 2013). Opacity can be described as the lack of credible information or information asymmetry, and the greater the degree of opacity the greater the level of systemic risk (Kozubovska, in press).

The motives of those leasing land has also been questioned in terms of: first, the enhancement of food security for one nation on land that is within the nation state of another; second, the level of employment generation which can be a significant positive; and third, the beneficial associated development of infrastructure (Hules, 2013). However, often employment generation is one of the 'employed' labourer rather than the 'independent' farmer, with the resultant loss of personal sovereignty that brings. Patel (2009:667) stresses that there is a "glossing-over of one of the key distinctions in agrarian capitalism – that between farm owner and farm worker." Gender often also plays a role, in that the work of the smallholder in Africa is female whereas the work of the labourer is not, meaning that corporatisation of agriculture can remove women from the workforce and reduce their personal sovereignty. Food sovereignty underpins respect for women's rights within a context of patriarchal traditions so this requires every culture to undergo transformation (Patel, 2009). Therefore land grabbing has environmental, economic and social impact in the country where it takes place. The situation in Ethiopia is used as a contemporary example to provide an exploratory case study for this chapter.

Ethiopia: Case study

Land ownership is invested solely in the state in Ethiopia, where the population is predominantly rural and smallholder agriculture plays a large role in Ethiopia's national economy (Nalepa *et al.*, 2016). This reliance on agriculture is recognised as being an economic weakness by the Ethiopian government. Despite government initiatives since 2002 to expand industrial sectors in Ethiopia, there has been little progress in terms of contribution to GDP in the national economy (Dadi *et al.* 2016). Pedersen and Buur (2016) argue that the highly centralised Ethiopian state seeks to increase federal control over land in remote regions through investment and land leasing. The nature of this discourse is important. Nation states allocating or leasing rural land to investors often characterise the areas being leased as of little innate value, e.g. barren, marginal, unused, or wasteland (Nalepa *et al.* 2016). Ethiopian officials are said to use terms such as 'empty' and 'unused' with the word 'uncultivated', with little or no reference at all to the people who currently live on and use those lands (Cochrane, 2011). The livelihoods of those making a living from this land is through 'slash and burn' agriculture, pastoralism, and agropastoralism (Nalep *et al.* 2016), what would often be seen as 'unprofessional' or 'inefficient' methods of agriculture. Smallholder households are prevalent and nearly 55% of smallholders operate on one hectare or less (Louhichi *et al.* 2016). Ethiopia has developed a universal subsidy programme, where the government imports fertilizer and distributes it through the network of cooperative unions to farmers at below-market price (Louhichi *et al.* 2016) in an effort to increase productivity.

Population reallocation has occurred with the Ethiopia's Villagisation Programme (EVP), an initiative by the Ethiopian government that was started in 1974. The aim of the EVP was and is to relocate and cluster people in villages with better access to services and infrastructure and clear the land of indigenous people to make it more freely available for external investment (Hules and Singh, 2017). Despite approaches like EVP, Ethiopia is still one of the least urbanised countries in Africa with only 17.4% of the population living in towns and cities, but with an average 4% annual urbanisation rate this population dynamic is changing fast (Dadi *et al.* 2016).

Shete and Rutten (2015) state that just because the local population does not have land tenure rights, it does not mean they are not using the land to sustain themselves, and as a result transfer or lease of farmland to commercial farming has worsened the local food insecurity situation and resulted in a loss of income within local communities.

6

Furthermore, the authors argue that the approach of leasing out farmland for large-scale agricultural investment is risky, does not influence and benefit local food markets if all the output derived is exported out of the locality or the country, and that diligent verification of current land-use patterns by local communities should be undertaken before land transfer takes place. A further challenge is that the land may be leased, but then is not actively farmed, so the local people do not have access to grow their own food, there is no resultant increase in employment and the productive capacity is lost in the short term. Baumgartner *et al.* (2015:188) assert that whilst in Africa, off-farm employment is an important opportunity for poverty reduction, conversely there may be a price to pay:

> "the uncompensated loss of direct access to natural resources and in the context of insecure labour benefits, there is a legitimate risk of negative local livelihood impacts and the exclusion of significant proportions of rural populations from the potential economic benefits of large scale land acquisition."

60-80% of food production in Ethiopia is completed by women, thus they are more directly affected by land grabbing and reassignment (Cochrane, 2011). Indeed Patel (2009) asserts that to drive food sovereignty in a given community, there must be a commitment to women's rights, not merely over property but over a full spectrum of social, physical and economic goods. Thus food sovereignty as a construct seeks to address the base equality in power in addressing food supply, which can be influenced not only by tenure, gender, culture, but also other factors too.

Nolte *et al.* highlight the target countries for land deals; the top eight being Indonesia, Ukraine, Russia, Papau New Guinea, Brazil, Argentina and Ethiopia. In Africa, 94% of the deals are by lease and concession, and the majority of deals run for at least 20 years (Nolte *et al.* 2016). The Ethiopian People's Revolutionary Democratic Front (EPRDF), has ringfenced in a federally delineated land bank millions of hectares of land described as marginal (Nalepa *et al.* 2016). Nalepa *et al.* argue that the lands designated for investment that are described as marginal are located in areas with associated surface water, but have yet to be permanently used for intensive agriculture, and in doing so this promotes land valuation based solely on the land's perceived macro-economic development potential. Franco *et al.* (2013) assert that formal water and land management have become disconnected, creating ambiguity, increasing local level uncertainties and complexity that powerful actors can navigate, but alternatively leading to the exclusion of the poor and marginalisation.

The paradox that Hules and Singh (2017) and Nalepa (2016) describe is that whilst the Ethiopian Investment Agency (EIA) is actively promoting the production of cash crops for exports, and organisations such as Saudi Star Agricultural Development plc., an Ethiopian company, plans to invest US$100 million in Ethiopia, between 2007 & 2011, the World Food Programme (WFP) provided US$116 million in food aid (230,000 tonnes of food) for Ethiopia's 4.6 million people. Nalepa *et al.* (2016) suggest that 40% of Ethiopians are undernourished. Indeed in 2016 (USAID, 2016), 9.7 million Ethiopians were in need of relief food assistance, whilst a further 8 million Ethiopians were described as chronically food insecure in a total population of 100 million (8%).

The current Ethiopian population compares to a population in 1966 of only 25.6 million people, showing the dramatic challenge of feeding a growing population in a country of finite natural resource that may, or may not, serve to feed the indigenous population. However the nutrition insecurity paradox is not unique to Ethiopia. Relief food assistance is global. The original Food Stamp Program that ran in the US from 1939-1943 supported 4 million people from a population of 130 million (3.1%),. In 1969, around 2.8 million people (1.4% of the population) received Supplemental Nutrition Assistance Program (SNAP) support, but over the last decade participation in the US programme has increased dramatically from less than 20 million people (6%) to 46 million in 2012 (14.6%) in the wake of the post-2008 recession (Caswell and Yaktine, 2013). More than 40% of SNAP recipients live in working households and nearly half of the recipients are children. The US SNAP federal food assistance programme spent US$80 billion on nutrition assistance in 2012 (Gregory and Deb, 2012). Thus nutrition insecurity is not just the province of the developing world.

Cochrane (2011) seeks to differentiate between food security, availability and access to sufficient safe food, and food sovereignty, i.e. the ownership and the rights of local people to define local food systems, without first being subject to international market concerns. Land grabbing can hinder access to the land and water required to produce such food, affecting food security and food sovereignty, especially if the food produced is destined for an export market (Tscharntke *et al.* 2012). Borras *et al.* (2012:850) framing on land grabbing as actually being 'control grabbing', i.e. "grabbing the power to control land and other associated resources such as water in order to derive benefit from such control of resources".

Control grabbing involves political power relations (Borras *et al.* 2012) in ring-fencing resources and where possible making them a private rather than a public or common good. The Ethiopian example highlights the challenge of land grabbing from the viewpoint of political and social power relations.

6

Concluding remarks

This chapter has considered the subjects of land grabbing and land imperialism in light of the global realignment of how food is produced and distributed to an increasingly urbanised population. The opacity between nation state and globalisation has been discussed. Evans (1997) argues in this context that access to capital and technology depends far more on strategic alliances with those who control global production networks that it does on controlling any particular piece of territory. Further Evans poses that the state can be reconceptualised as a "vehicle for rent". The processes of power are complex and opaque (French and Raven, 1959) especially in a nuanced area such as land grabbing. There is a dilemma at play between ensuring, at the national scale, both food security and food sovereignty. Power can express itself in many forms including political and social power.

Food security exists when "all people, at all times, have physical, social and economic access to sufficient, safe and nutritious food which meets their dietary needs and food preferences for an active and healthy life" (FAO, 2003:29). This means that to demonstrate food security there must be a series of valued outcomes that are met. Fiske and Berdahl (2007) define valued outcomes as physical (access to food, shelter), economic (in terms of material or financial wellbeing to meet personal needs) and social (in terms of social belonging, social shared understanding, social control, self-enhancement and social trust). Food has a role in delivering such affective, social outcomes. However the social sense of belonging to land itself is broken in the event of land leasing or sale. Lyons and Westoby (2014) speak to the privatisation of development causing the indigenous population to now being seen as illegal encroachers and trespassers on land to which once they had free access, and highlight the challenge of local people ensuring food security and maintaining connections to sites of cultural significance. Whilst the seven Principles of Responsible Agricultural Investments (PRAI) code of conduct has been developed (UN, 2010) and been built upon by the Committee on World Food Security Principles for Responsible Investment in Agriculture and Food Systems (FAO, n.d.), they are voluntary and non-binding. This means that their adoption in a given situation relies on the social responsibility of the actors involved. In conclusion, land grabbing is a power process and, despite there being moves to develop principles of best practice, is still very much a form of privatised development in which food, and the resources used to produce it, becomes a private rather than a public good. The broken governance system employed in Europe and elsewhere in the developed world of a dissociation of food production, and water supply, as a private market-orientated private good and alongside the land based activity being required to deliver public good is not worthy of replication.

The challenge is the total lack of governance for all rural policy within an increasingly urbanised population; political society, private and non-profit economic actors, especially as highlighted by Foley and Edwards (1996), become more and more distant from the society they were developed to represent. The current shape and definition of land imperialism and the development of power-bases is nuanced and specific to the time, but as has been demonstrated in this chapter with the drive for globalization and international governance this has reduced the focus on national self-sufficiency and the requirement for national governments to address food security on behalf of their citizens, instead leaving that responsibility to civil society, as has been seen in the reliance on food aid in Africa and the growth of food banks in the US and UK. Latouche (2004) argues that proponents of contraction, as opposed to growth, want to create integrated, self-sufficient materially responsible societies with greater equity across their citizenry. In this chapter, land grabbing has been used as a lens to consider contemporary issues in the food supply chain and also to introduce some of the contextual topics that will evolve in coming years, such as growth vs. de-growth, food security and food sovereignty.

References

Arditi, B. (2004). From globalism to globalization: the politics of resistance. *New Political Science*, **26**(1), 5-22.

Baumgartner, P., von Braun, J. Abebaw, D. and Müller, M. (2015), Impacts of large-scale land investments on income, prices, and employment: Empirical analyses in Ethiopia, *World Development*, **72**(1), 175–190,

Borras, S.M., Franco, J.C., Gomez, S., Kay, C. and Spoor, M. (2012) Land grabbing in Latin America and the Caribbean, *Journal of Peasant Studies*, **39**(3-4), 845-872.

Caswell, J.A and Yaktine, A.L. (eds.) (2013), Committee on Examination of the Adequacy of Food Resources and SNAP Allotments, Food and Nutrition Board; Committee on National Statistics; Institute of Medicine; National Research Council ISBN 9780309262941. http://www.ncbi.nlm.nih.gov/books/NBK206911/pdf/Bookshelf_NBK206911.pdf. Accessed 15 May 2016.

Cochrane, L. (2011). Food security or food sovereignty: The case of land grabs. *The Journal of Humanitarian Assistance*, **5**. https://www.researchgate.net/profile/Logan_Cochrane/publication/291166891_Food_Security_or_Food_Sovereignty_The_Case_of_Land_Grabs/links/569ed16608ae21a56424ef61.pdf. Accessed 29/01/2017.

Dadi, D., Azadi, H., Senbeta, F., Abebe, K., Taheri, F. and Stellmacher, T. (2016), Urban sprawl and its impact in land use in Central Ethiopia, *Urban Forestry and Urban Greening*, **16** (1), 132-141

De Schutter, O. (2011). How not to think of land-grabbing: three critiques of large-scale investments in farmland. *Journal of Peasant Studies* **38** (2), 249–279.

Devinney, T.M., Auger, P., Eckhardt, G. and Birtchnell, T. (2006), The other CSR: consumer social responsibility, *Stanford Social Innovation Review*, Fall, Leeds University Business School Working Paper No. 15-04. https://ssrn.com/abstract=901863

Evans, P. (1997). The eclipse of the state? Reflections on stateness in an era of globalization. *World Politics*, **50**(01), 62-87.

FAO (2003). *Trade Reforms and Food Security – Conceptualizing the linkages*, Rome: FAO, (Food and Agriculture Organisation)

6

FAO (n.d.) Committee on World Food Security Principles for Responsible Investment in Agriculture and Food Systems. http://www.fao.org/fileadmin/templates/cfs/Docs1314/rai/CFS_Principles_Oct_2014_EN.pdf. Accessed on 28/12/2016.

Fiske, S. T. and Berdahl, J. L. (2007). Social power. In A. Kruglanski and E.T. Higgins (Eds.), *Social psychology: A handbook of basic principles* (2nd ed.). New York: Guilford, 678-692.

Foley, M. W. and Edwards, B. (1996). The paradox of civil society. *Journal of Democracy*, **7**(3), 38-52.

Foley, M. W. and Edwards, B. (1998). Beyond Tocqueville: Civil society and social capital in comparative perspective. *The American Behavioral Scientist*, **42**(1), 5.

Foster, H., Whittaker, J., Handmer, J., Lowe, T. and Keating, A. (2013). Regional Victoria in 2021: changes and implications for the emergency management sector. *Australian Journal of Emergency Management*, **28**(2), 51.

Franco, J., Mehta, L. and Veldwisch, G.J. (2013). The global politics of water grabbing. *Third World Quarterly*, **34**(9), 1651-1675.

French, J. R. and Raven, B. (1959). The bases of social power. In D. Cartwright (Ed.) *Studies in Social Power*, Ann Arbor, Mich.: Institute for Social Research, pp 150-167.

Gregory, C.A and Deb, P. (2015), Does SNAP improve health? *Food Policy*, **50**, 11-19

Grunert, K. G. (2006). Future trends and consumer lifestyles with regard to meat consumption. *Meat Science*, **74**(1), 149-160.

Hofstede, G. (2011). Dimensionalizing cultures: The Hofstede model in context. *Online Readings in Psychology and Culture*, **2**(1). http://dx.doi.org/10.9707/2307-0919.1014. Accessed 28/12/2016).

Hules, M. (2013). India's quest for resources in Africa: Land grabbing and its implications for India and Ethiopia. University of Vienna. Department of International Development (Master thesis.).

Hules, M. and Singh, S.J. (2017), India's land grab deals in Ethiopia: Food Security or global politics? *Land Use Policy*, **60**, 343-351

Kozubovska, M. (in press) The effect of US bank holding companies' exposure to asset-backed commercial paper conduits on the information opacity and systemic risk. Research in International Business and Finance. http://dx.doi.org/10.1016/j.ribaf.2016.09.013

Krahmann, E. (2003). Conceptualizing security governance. *Cooperation and Conflict*, **38**(1), 5-26.

Lang, T. and Heasman, M. (2015). *Food Wars: The global battle for mouths, minds and markets*. Routledge.

Latouche, S. (2004). Degrowth economics. *Le Monde Diplomatique*, **11**.

Lavin, C. (2013). *Eating Anxiety: The Perils of Food Politics*. University of Minnesota Press. http://www.jstor.org/stable/10.5749/j.ctt32bcnz

Leicht, M. (1998) Facing globalization: More social capital and the ability to act as a global player as a response from the EU, *Swiss Political Science Review*, **4**(4), 197-214. http://onlinelibrary.wiley.com/doi/10.1002/j.1662-6370.1998.tb00257.x/pdf. Accessed 6/12/2016.

Louhichi, K., Riesgo, L. and Paloma, S.G. (2016). Modelling farm-household level impacts of fertilizer subsidy programs on food security: The case of Ethiopia. http://ageconsearch.umn.edu/bitstream/235927/2/Louhichi%23%208847.pdf. Accessed on 21/12/16.

Lyons, K. and Westoby, P. (2014). Carbon colonialism and the new land grab: Plantation forestry in Uganda and its livelihood impacts. *Journal of Rural Studies*, **36**, 13-21.

Magnan, A. (2012). New avenues of farm corporatization in the prairie grains sector: farm family entrepreneurs and the case of One Earth Farms. *Agriculture and Human Values*, **29**(2), 161-175.

Makki, F. and Geisler, C. (2011), Development by dispossession: Land grabbing as new enclosures in contemporary Ethopia, Paper presented at the International Conference on Global Land Grabbing 6-8 April. University of Sussex.

Mann, M. (1997). Has globalization ended the rise and rise of the nation-state?. *Review of International Political Economy*, **4**(3), 472-496.

Manning, L. (2013) Corporate and consumer social responsibility in the food supply chain, *British Food Journal*, **115**(1), 2-29

Manning, L. and Baines, R.N. (2004), Effective management of food safety and quality, *British Food Journal*, **106**(8), 598-606.

McDonagh, B. and Daniels, S. (2012), Enclosure stories: narratives from Northamptonshire, *Cultural Geographies*, **19** (1), 107-121. ISSN 1474-4740

Mehta, L., Veldwisch, G.J. and Franco, J. (2012). Introduction to the special issue: Water grabbing? Focus on the (re) appropriation of finite water resources. *Water Alternatives* **5** (2), 193–207.

Messerli,P., Andreas Heinimann, A., Giger, M., Breu, T. and Schönweger, O. (2013). From 'land grabbing' to sustainable investments in land: potential contributions by land change science. *Current Opinion in Environmental Sustainability* **5** (5), 528–534

Muthuri, J., Moon, J. and Matten, D. (2006), Employee volunteering and the creation of social capital, Research Paper Series No. 34, International Centre for Corporate Social Responsibility, Nottingham University. www.nottingham.ac.uk/business/ICCSR/research.php?action=download&id=46. Accessed 6/12/2016.

Nalepa, R.A., Short Gianotti, A.G., and Bauer, D.M. (2016), Marginal land and the global land rush: A spatial exploration of contested lands and state-directed development in contemporary Ethiopia. *Geoforum*, http://dx.doi.org/10.1016/j.geoforum.2016.10.008

Nally, D. (2015). Governing precarious lives: land grabs, geopolitics, and 'food security'. *Geographical Journal*, **181**(4), 340-349.

Nolte, K., Chamberlain, W. and Giger, M. (2016). International land deals for agriculture. Fresh insights from the land matrix: Analytical Report II. Pretoria: Centre for Development and Environment, University of Bern: Centre de coopération internationale en recherche agronomique pour le développement; German Institute of Global and Area Studies; University of Pretoria; Bern Open Publishing.

Norton, A. R. (Ed.) (2001). *Civil Society in the Middle East.* (Vol. 2). Brill.

Otsuka, K. and Yamano, T. (2006). The role of rural labor markets in poverty reduction: Evidence from Asia and East Africa. FASID Discussion Paper Series on International Development Strategies, No. 12-007.

Parliament (n.d.), Managing and owning land. http://www.parliament.uk/about/living-heritage/transformingsociety/towncountry/landscape/overview/enclosingland/ Accessed 6/12/2016.

Patel, R. (2009). Food sovereignty. *Journal of Peasant Studies*, **36**(3), 663-706.

Pedersen, R.H. and Buur, L. (2016) Beyond land grabbing. Old morals and new perspectives on contemporary investments, Editorial, *Geoforum*, **72**(1), 77-81

Phillips, C. D. and McLeroy, K. R. (2004). Health in rural America: remembering the importance of place. *American Journal of Public Health*, **94**(10), 1661-1663.

Putnam, R.D. (1993), *Making Democracy Work: Civic Traditions in Modern Italy,* Princeton: Princeton University Press.

Shete, M. and Rutten M. (2015) Impacts of large-scale farming on local communities' food security and income levels – Empirical evidence from Oromia region, Ethiopia, *Land Use Policy* **47**(1), 282–292

Spence, L. and Bourlakis, M. (2009), The evolution from corporate social responsibility to supply chain responsibility: the case of Waitrose, *Supply Chain Management*, **14**(4), 291-302.

Stigliz, J.E. (2006), *Making Globalization Work*, Allen Lane, London.

Suhardiman, D., Giordano, M., Keovilignavong, O. and Sotoukee, T., (2015), Revealing the hidden effects of land grabbing through better understanding of farmers' strategies in dealing with land loss, *Land Use Policy*, **49**, 195-202

Szántó, B. (2001) The paradigm of globalism, *Technovation* **21**, 673–687

Teklemariam, D., Azadi, H., Nyssen, J., Haile, M. and Witlox, F. (2015) Transnational land deals: Towards and inclusive land governance framework, *Land Use Policy*, **42**, 781-789

Thompson, J.R. (2012). Food talk, in Frye J.J and Bruner, M.S. *The Rhetoric of Food – Discourse, Materiality and Power.* Routledge, New York

Tscharntke, T., Clough, Y., Wanger, T.C., Jackson, L., Motzke, I., Perfecto, I., Vandermeer, J. and Whitbread, A. (2012). Global food security, biodiversity conservation and the future of agricultural intensification. *Biological Conservation*, **151**(1), 53-59.

UN (United Nations Conference on Trade and Development) (2010) The Principles for Responsible Agricultural Investment (PRAI). http://unctad.org/en/Pages/DIAE/G-20/PRAI.aspx. Accessed 28/12/2016.

USAID (2016) Food Assistance Fact Sheet – Ethiopia, Available at: https://www.usaid.gov/ethiopia/food-assistance. Accessed on 6/12/2016.

von Braun, J., Meinzen-Dick, R. (2009). 'Land grabbing' by foreign investors in developing countries: Risks and opportunities, http://www.ifpri.org/sites/default/files/ publications/bp013all.pdf. Accessed 10/03/10.

Wheeler, S., Bjornlund, H., Zuo, A. and Edwards, J. (2012). Handing down the farm? The increasing uncertainty of irrigated farm succession in Australia. *Journal of Rural Studies*, **28**(3), 266-275.

World Bank (2010). *Rising Global Interest in Farmland: Can it Yield Sustainable and Equitable Benefit?* International Bank for Reconstruction and Development/World Bank, Washington, DC.

6

7 The Global Economy: Food Security

Luis Kluwe Aguiar

Introduction

The issue of food security has been one which has taken a prominent position on the world stage. Food security has been defined variously, but is seen by the United Nations committee to be concerned with the condition of people and their need to have physical, social and economic access to sufficient safe and nutritious food that meets their dietary needs and food preferences for an active and healthy life. This chapter puts forward the question as to what is the right action to take in order to deliver food security, given the predicted growth in global populations, changing consumption patterns and increased food wastage. Solutions up until recently have been predominantly driven by the economic constructs, but could the solution be more utilitarian to deliver the greatest good to the greatest number of people?

The chapter explores the current paradoxes and problems faced both in developed and developing countries in the delivery of sufficient safe and nutritious food. One key paradox is that whilst there is sufficient food globally to feed current populations, in both developing and developed countries there are haves and have-nots, there are the over-nourished and the under-nourished, and this is potentially a function of the present political economy of food. Current political economies, although built upon welfare economics, are failing or avoiding effective compensation of the losers, whilst the winners are more than adequately rewarded. Growing affluence amongst certain fractions results in higher consumption of meats, dairy products and added value highly processed meals, whilst poverty has led to food insecurity and social dislocation with the poor pushed out of the mainstream of society. Land availability offers further challenges for food security. With the increased demand for meat, more land is required both for the production of sufficient meat to feed the total population, and the production of sufficient animal feed; a factor which will heighted the gap between the haves and have-nots. The position is exacerbated where there are conflicting demands on land for alternative renewable fuels.

The management of food security needs to be carefully considered along with our systems of food delivery, the dominant political economic frameworks, consumer consumption trends and demands, and the shift towards a drive for the re-localisation of electorate experience and identity. The determination of these to effectively deliver global food security will require considerable deliberation and innovative thought.

Global shifts in the consumption of food

The food and drink culture we experience today is totally different from that prior to World War II. Millstone and Lang (2003) highlighted in the *Atlas of Food* the interconnectivity of internationalised supply chains, which enabled most con-sumers to have continual access to food. The majority of the world's consumers do not need to think where the daily bread, rice, noodles or porridge might be coming from.

The way some foods reach the plates of an entire globalised population depends on very complex links and exchanges, which also reflect a cultural shift in the role that food has taken, especially in more economically developed coun-tries. Yet, the transformative nature of the changes of the links and exchanges has been relatively fast and encompassed the whole world. Seldom are there places where this cannot be felt, thus, the transformation of the food supply chains has affected not only societies in more developed economies but also in less economi-cally developed societies. In the process, their food cultures have indeed been transformed. In the African, Asian and South American continents, instead of the traditional food staples, wheat has become the predominant carbohydrate consumed at breakfast, lunch and dinner. Out went the tortilla, congee, yam with honey, baked sweet potatoes and couscous, and in came the bread roll, the pasta and the sandwich. What, where and how people eat, according to Millstone and Lang (2003), is dependent upon a growing interconnectivity of international trade. International supply chains are increasingly elongated and dependent on many stages of production, where value is added. No longer is the local food system sufficient to provide consumers' needs, and increasing amounts of the food eaten today have to be imported.

In less than a century, changes in consumption have taken place, which ini-tially were slower and more localised, but in more recent decades have intensified

7

and become the norm. Changes to food and drink culture have been complex (Millstone and Lang, 2003) changing the whole nature of how consumers relate to food. In Table 7.1, some of the main drivers behind cultural shifts and their consequences are summarised. As can be seen, these shifts are predominantly linked in the movement of populations from the rural towards an urban domain (UNICEF, 2015) leading to the need to transport food from the rural areas of production to urban areas.

Table 7.1: The shifts of food and drink culture. Source: adapted from Millstone and Lang (2003)

From an agrarian economy...	...to industrial capitalism	...to post capitalism
From rural dwellings ...	... to a life in villages...	...to mass urban existence
From living within the constraints of food subsistence...	... to accessing food from an expanded network	... to beyond
From eating restricted diets...	... to eating mainly seasonal diets...	...to eating unrestricted diets
From local ...	...to regional...	...to global structures

The shift from rural to urban, some argue, has had mixed results. On the one hand, more food has been produced, feeding more mouths than ever before. The foods eaten are arguably of a better quality and a more varied range, thus allowing consumers more choice. On the other hand, there is a need to intensify the use of technology throughout the food supply chain. At farm level, capital intensive machinery is used by farmers to produce food. At food processing and manufacturing level, technology is also key in the transformation of raw materials into added value branded foods. In the distribution sector, technology has facilitated the organisation of a global logistics system, not to mention the exchange of capital through payment and credit. The end result is that consumers have the chance to access a wider range of processed foods, which in comparison to consumer purchasing power are priced at an all time low. Advances in technology have enabled large scale transformations regarding the sizes of tractors and combine harvesters, the speed at which machines can churn out tonnes of potato crisps or bread rolls. Technology has also transformed the way food reaches consumers, with food retailing being accessible 24 hours a day, seven days a week.

Furthermore, advances of technology have also been transformative in households. In the kitchen, intensively processed foods are convenient for the consumers, but at the same time, more gadgets are needed to cope with ever quicker meal preparations. This is a far cry from preparing a meal over four to five hours before World War II. Now food preparation takes a matter of minutes.

Implications of technology

For consumers who can afford ready, pre-prepared and easy to cook meals this can be considered a 'consumer nirvana' or heaven, where technology has triumphed. Nonetheless, for others the gains have not been so evident. The access of highly processed foods, which are manufactured outside the home, can have a detrimental effect on the 'naturalness' of food and the dissociation of consumers from seasonality. Some argue that the dissociation of the consumer from natural cycles has had a detrimental effect on the environment by depleting from most of its non-renewable resources (soil, water, minerals and petroleum); an effect which is irreversible (Rockstrom *et al.*, 2009). The changes in consumption are seen to be very real contributors to the acceleration of the effects of climate change. Not least, as to deliver the predominant food production system there has been a need to utilise marginal land to produce food on fragile ecosystems, causing a loss of biodiversity and irreversible environmental damage.

Furthermore, despite 'superior' organoleptic qualities, excess consumption is detrimental to human health. Foods science has enabled the enhancement of products through the use of additives in the manufacturing process. Many food products depend on the use of artificial ingredients such as colourants, stabilisers, flavours and aromas, which added to the basic food ingredients, i.e. sugar, carbohydrates, fat, dairy, meat and salt, are key constituents of much of the food being purchased from supermarket shelves and fast food, popular and quick service restaurants.

However, continued consumption of these foods, which are fast to prepare and quick to eat, has resulted in the rise of healthcare costs in many economically developed economies, as a consequence of diet related diseases. Non-communicable diseases such as type 2 diabetes, cardiovascular diseases, tooth decay in pre-school children and obesity, to mention but some, are prevalent in developed countries, and are now becoming more prominent in emerging economies. The longitudinal study on lifestyle and behavioural risk factors in the USA and the works of Barry Popkin and Samara Nielsen on the ubiquitous presence of sugar on western diets, to mention some, provide small snapshots of the growing size of the problem (Popkin and Nielsen, 2003). But more alarmingly is the news from China, where part of its population, usually urban and young, are facing issues of over-nutrition.

7

Food insecurity

As an example, it is remarkable that in China, a country where many provinces had experienced food insecurity until the late 1970s, and had to endure many episodes of hunger and starvation, over-nutrition has become a problem. China is presently a country in food transition, where the haves and have-nots are usually represented by urban and rural populations; the efficiencies of the modern food supply chain have brought food which is cheap to many, but the issues of hunger and malnutrition in the rural areas have not been addressed.

On the other hand, poverty is usually considered to be the number one root cause of food insecurity (FAO, 1992). Many in more economically developed countries still have the false impression that poverty is a condition affecting more remote countries. However, poverty is also concealed in more economically developed societies. In recent years, the growing number of consumers accessing food banks in the UK, France, Germany, Italy, Spain, the USA, Mexico, and Brazil is an indication that either the world food system is unequal or the present political economy of food model is unstable. The present day food system allows for the coexistence of subsystems, which promote malnutrition either through over or under nourishment. Access to insufficient food of nutritional value, can cause obesity or undernourishment. The clear effect is that this creates an intrinsic problem of social dislocation, where different groups of people end up being pushed to the margin of the mainstream society because they are outside the norm. This is where the problem of hidden hunger or malnutrition comes to light impacting society as a whole, since the consumption of essential mineral, vitamins and amino-acids do not meet daily requirements.

Moving forward, how then can the present day food supply chain meet the needs of an expected population of 9.6 billion by 2050? The issues to be faced relate to:

- Whether further globalisation processes are the solution to access and circulate more food.

- Can we enable access to the wealth of food, currently enjoyed by western societies, to the increasingly affluent in emerging economies in Asia, Latin America and Africa?

- To what extent can we expand production and access to food using traditional farming methods?

The problem is complex, and as in many economic and social problems one man's gain is another's loss, and therefore policy makers, industry and indeed you, the reader, need to reflect on the ways in which solutions may be found. The problem is one of utility maximisation, and choosing an action that promotes the greatest good for the greatest number of people (Mills, 1861). This is potentially the time to shift away from welfare economics, in which policy makers and economists are concerned with who gains and who loses, and place a predominant focus on the compensation of the loser. This is particularly so in an economic context, where the cost and feasibility of compensation becomes more problematic.

■ Emerging from the neo-liberal economy?

Until very recently, it has been thought that further intensification of food production was the solution, through the creation and implementation of more and more technological knowhow. This is the main argument made by the supporters of the neo-Malthusian philosophy to address the issues of the lack of food when faced with a growing population. The acceleration of the intensification of food production is presumed to lead to the narrowing of the gap between the population needs and the actual food produced.

■ Sustainable intensification: a technical or political solution?

In recent years the term 'sustainable intensification' has gained prominence in many circles. It has been coined around a report from the Royal Society entitled *Reaping the Benefits: Science and the sustainable intensification of global agriculture*, published in 2009. Since the resources available in the planet cannot be considered as an endless font of factors of production, the notion of producing more food sustainably is in principle a good solution. It also reconciled polarised viewpoints regarding conventional high input-high output food production and those advocating a more sustainable agenda. It thus accommodated the notion that in the future there will be a need for a food system that not only produced more food more intensively but also delivered it in a way that embodies sustainable precepts.

In practice, according to Garnett and Godfray (2012), sustainable intensification is more of an aspiration than practical solution. The term implies the need for alternative practices; tailored and adapted to each and every condition. Yet caution is required; sustainable intensification may not be 'the solution', and in fact, may be perceived as 'greenwash'.

It is apparent that we need to be wary of solutions purporting to deliver food security if they are solely technological, as political considerations are equally if not more important. As this book goes to press, we note a sea-change in the discourse of political leaders on both sides of the Atlantic. We are faced with growing evidence that suggests that in the future there would be a greater polarisation in the political arena. Where hitherto, the WTO, national and regional governments have promoted globalisation, there is a regression by certain leaders and the electorate towards protectionism measures and the localisation in trade. Certain consumers/electorates, from more economically developed countries have from their position of plenty chosen political systems that promote the interests of their farmers, processors and other parties within the local supply chain over the interests of those in developing countries, with the design to inhibit the further internationalisation of the food supply chain. It is intriguing to note that in rejecting internationalisation, the same consumers who have taken advantage of the globalised food supply chain, which allowed them access to cheaper food, now hold a more favourable view of local and domestic food supply chains.

The shift towards local and domestic would most certainly have a huge impact on the food systems that have emerged as a consequence of international economics. Furthermore, a local and domestic food network wouldn't necessarily provide affordable food for the majority of the population. Thus, the problem of those who would have access to food and those who have not, continues to be unresolved.

Much of the reduction of the world's food insecurity was expected to be resolved on the back of the neo-liberalising waves of the 1980s. At that time, the understanding was that trade liberalisation and the reduction of import duties, especially on food, coupled with freer market access would improve food security. In the early 2000s the signatories of the World Trade Organisation expected that a new trade order would help rebalance the inequalities especially regarding access to food. Nevertheless, nearly forty years later, evidence shows that perhaps the more economically developed countries have benefitted the most. Many of the neo-liberal predictions, which favoured the elimination of trade barriers and the decline in terms of terms of trade between more industrialised and less industrialised countries, presumed that greater equalities would prevail.

The inability of developing countries to gain from the deterioration of the terms of trade is, as suggested in the Singer-Prebisch hypothesis, a consequence of the increase in price of manufactured, or high value added products, in relation to agricultural commodities, and this can be related to the distribution of gain within the supply chain. Farmers have had to ever increase their production to compensate for the loss of relative revenue in order to acquire manufactured goods. From a country's perspective, agricultural commodity exporting dependent countries would have to produce more coffee, soya, cocoa, sugar, rice, chicken, etc. and export more to compensate for the international decline of food prices.

Yet, by the mid-2000s, there were already signs that the economic status quo was changing and that an over reliance on cheap food would not last forever. In addition, the final awakening of those giant emerging economies of, for instance, Brazil, China and India, would play havoc with world's commodity system in both hard and soft commodities, (where hard commodities are natural resources mined or extracted and soft resources are agricultural products).

Coupled with this, the food price inflation of the mid 2000s, which could be attributed to the drought in both Russia and Australia and other unusual climatic patterns, helped to change the dominant notion of agricultural sector as being a purveyor of cheap raw material basic food staples (wheat, maize, sugar, vegetable oil and rice) to one of primary concern.

The sharp rise of international commodity prices, especially affected by the supply of wheat in the world, sent ripple effects around the markets. These had also to face additional problems such as panic buying, especially as part of some key countries' food policy instruments, which practiced the subsidising of food for their population. This was the case of India and China whose buying of food staples in the world market further contributed to the price spike, fuelling the rise to almost all major food and feed commodities (vegetable oil, meat, rice, sugar) at the time. Food price inflation was particularly an issue for the more vulnerable people who live on the poverty line. Any shift in food price pushes a lot of people into dire food insecurity. It is thus of the interest of countries to subsidise the food for its population.

Choices of food products to subsidise may vary from country to country. In China, pork is not only a staple food but also the most preferred type of meat for its population. In the context of India, access to affordable rice by its population, similarly to China, is key to social cohesion. Furthermore, food stock speculation and price inflation has had a profound impact in other countries in Africa, Latin America and Asia as has been discussed earlier in Chapter 1.

Since the end of the Cold War, the emergence of the neo-liberal economic order forced governments, who previously were heavily involved in balancing supply and demand through the management of a food policy based on minimum agricultural prices and intervention buying, to relinquish their control to the private sector. Free trade policies supported by the last GATT Uruguay Round initiated a drive by major players such as food retailers and manufacturers to become the controllers of the stocks within the supply chain. In the process, the supply chains have become leaner by minimising stock levels, thereby driving costs down and retaining market share. The implications of this for developing countries are that they have been unable to attain buyers for their stock during periods of bumper harvest/excess supply. Conversely, in periods of scarcity, food inflation causes food insecurity.

How do we achieve food supply security?

Given the impact of the current political and economic frameworks one has to ask: which type of food system would be better in delivering a more secure food supply chain at a global economic level? This is particularly so where there are increasingly rival demands on the use of foodstuffs, with worthy opponents to the production of food for direct human consumption such biofuels, and food for animal consumption. Although it is evident recently that many, including environmentalists, have questioned the value of the practice of producing biofuels, there is a rising demand for the production of foodstuffs such as feed wheat, maize and sugar for use in the delivery of renewal fuel. Biofuels were promoted as clean solutions to reduce pollution and be less harmful for the environment. Thus the issue of food security is complex with conflicting demands on resources. The FAO (2009), proposed that the dilemma faced by policy makers and society is the management of the rival demands from:

■ Food for human consumption

■ Food for animal consumption

■ Food for fuel consumption

■ Food that is wasted

However, before examining the problem in more depth, some clarification on the definition of food security is needed. According to Naylor (2014:7) the term 'food security' can have many dimensions and thus "can be an elusive good" as it is a complex and multifaceted problem (McDonald, 2010: 2). McDonald also remarked that food security could be defined "at its most general level as the availability of adequate food at all times and the people's ability to access it". Martindale (2015:1) proposed the term 'food security' embodied many attributes which were difficult to describe as "it was a sum of many aspects not only concerned with the immediate supply of protein or energy, but also the sustainable supply of a healthy diet that promoted wellbeing". Similarly, Lang and Heasman (2015) posited that food security is more about the appropriateness of food supply rather than its simple sufficiency. A more widely accepted definition of 'food security' was established during the World Summit of Food Security, with the concept that "all people all the time should have access to sufficient, safe and nutritious food necessary to lead an active and healthy life" (FAO, 2009).

The debate on food security has been evolving to include, more recently, the human security dimension, which includes the "vulnerability from threats that are sudden, unexpected and persuasive" (McDonald, 2010). McDonald understood that the food security that enabled human security had to account for the different economic aspects of food availability, access, utilisation and stability, as well as health, environmental, personal, community and political security (Naylor, 2014). These dimensions are all interdependent, thus food security that enabled human security should shelter people, particularly the most vulnerable, from the many worries of daily life and enable resilience. For the purpose of this chapter, the term 'food security' will have to be used in its broader sense. Narrowing its focus and concentrating on a couple of its dimensions would fail to depict the more pressing likely issues.

It is when attempting to unpack the issues that more arise. For example, the per capita consumption of meat (particularly poultry and livestock) has been growing for the past six decades at a steady 4% rate per decade. Should the global population reach the predicted plateau at 9.6 billion people by the year 2050, if the current trends in demand for meat are kept at the current level, it is expected that between 50 to 73% more meat would need to be available in the future (Bonny *et al.*, 2015). Furthermore, Bonny *et al.* also posited that since the current capacity of conventional meat production is reaching its limit, it is likely that by 2050 there will not be enough animal protein for everyone. They estimated that only 8 billion people would have access to meat, whilst 1.6 billion would be deprived of eating it. In the light of this, Goodwin and Shoulders (2013) have indicated that conventional meat production would no longer have the ability to satisfy its future population demand.

Following the premise that humans should have the inalienable right to food (Lang *et al.*, 2009), in the future all consumers should also have the right to eat meat since food entitlement is also a facet of food security. If the premise of Bonny *et al.* (2015) if fulfilled, negating the access to eating meat to 1.6 billion people, who are likely to be the poorest, would be unethical to say the least.

Nonetheless, much of the worries around the expected future demand of meat and dairy products are that modern resource maximising initiatives ensuring efficient meat producing systems depend on giving nutritionally balanced feeds to animals. These are formulated with all the essential vitamins and minerals for best animal performance using bulk material such as wheat, maize and soya. It is obvious that animals that would naturally be grazing and are now reliant on formulated feed. This means that land is required to produce animal feed instead of producing food for direct human consumption. One cannot negate that the ingestion of animal and dairy protein plays an essential role in the nutrition of the majority of the population. However, Hopkins (2015) mentioned that animals are not *per se* good food energy efficiency converters, and beef and dairy are some of the lowest efficient food energy conversion systems. Thus the reliance on low animal feed energy conversion systems (Galusky, 2014) is arguably not wise.

From the above notion of the food security problem, one can add to that the classic food security model proposed by the Food and Agriculture Organisation

(FAO) and the World Health Organisation (WHO). In the FAO and WHO model, proposed as a result of the World Food Congress of 1974, food security would be achieved provided that system delivered food availability, food stability, food access and food utilisation (nutrition). Figure 7.1 is an attempt to illustrate the complexities of addressing these issues. When the classic food security model is put in the light of the four major food security problems, it is necessary to assess the relationships and the likely impact they might have at local, regional, domestic and international levels.

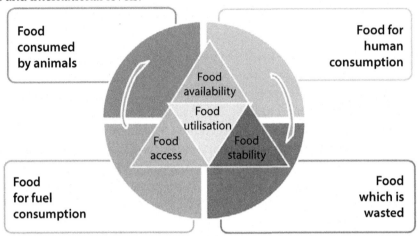

Figure 7.1: The food problem and classic food security model. Adapted from FAO (2009)

Food wastage

We are not suggesting that there is any simple answer to the issue of food security, and it is perhaps too obvious to suggest that there should be an effort to level out consumption between the affluent and the poor. Whilst there are other more radical proposals with respect to the reorganization of business relationships and marketing channels, one major hindrance to food security rests in the level of food wasted. The extent of waste has become so significant in recent years as a consequence of the elongation of supply chains, the growth of regulatory frameworks to preserve food integrity and the measures adopted by retailers and processors to demonstrate due diligence and maintain market share.

As seen in Chapter 5, the phenomenon of waste, as food or by products of food has emerged with the development of more complex human societies. The management of waste in pre-agricultural societies was achieved through the utilisation of all parts of the animal, and using only seasonally available food products. In pastoral and agricultural societies, the potential for waste grew, as society became more complex with a greater division of labour, and waste became a natural by-product of economic and social activity (Schneider, 2008). Food and drink waste can be classified into kitchen, edible and avoidable wastes, which, according to the EU Directive 2008/98/EC, derives from "any substance discarded as a result of human consumption" (EU, 2008). Despite food waste being a world-wide issue, the case of the UK will be used to better contextualise the problem.

Case study: The UK experience

Measures to tackle the issue of food waste in UK began to be adopted in the last decade and became more intensive following the publication of the *Household Food and Drink Waste in the UK* report (WRAP, 2009).

The report is of interest to consumers, food manufacturers and authorities, regarding the need to reduce the amount of waste generated, in order to reduce the use of scarce and non-renewable resources deployed in the production of food and drink, and thereby increase food security.

The *Household Food and Drink Waste in the UK* report was based upon previous studies which built on earlier data published by the Waste and Resources Action Program (WRAP) such as the *Food We Waste* report published in 2008, which provided evidence of the scale of the waste at household level; the Kitchen Diary Research of 2007, the Food Composition Analysis of 2008, both by WRAP; the Waste Data Flow collected by Local Authorities; and the Review of Municipal Waste Composition. Data was collected, analysed and classed according to the Food Waste Hierarchy typology (Table 7.2 below). Such a typology has since become part of the Waste (England and Wales) Regulations (GOVUK, 2009).

Table 7.2: Food waste hierarchy typology. Source: WRAP (2009)

Avoidable	Edible food and drink disposed of which has been cooked, prepared and/or served in over-large quantities.
Possibly avoidable	Food and drink wasted as part of food preparation which could still be used, such as bread trimmings and crumbs, edible fruit and vegetable skins, leaves and stems, bruised fruit and vegetables, as well as foods that are close to or past their sell-by dates, have gone mouldy or rotten, looked, smelt or tasted bad.
Unavoidable	Food and drink discarded which could not be used for consumption, such as egg shells, bones, tea bags etc.

The findings from the report show that about 22% of all food and drink purchases by weight is actually wasted. As for the composition of the waste, the largest amount derived from fresh vegetables and salads (25%), drinks (16%), fresh fruit (13%) and bakery (10%) respectively. The report also provided indications of liquid food waste such as gravy, milk (some 7% of all milk purchases is wasted) or other liquids and fats which are discarded in sewers (WRAP, 2009). As a result, it was estimated that some 8.3 million tonnes of food and drink is wasted per year, approximately 330Kg for each household in the UK. This is from a population of 62 million people from a small island. Should these figures be extrapolated to the whole world population, the volume of food wasted can be very alarming.

When considering the avoidable fraction of the food and drink wasted only, it was estimated that the total waste would cost about £12 billion or some £480 per household in the UK every year. In addition, the equivalent greenhouse gas (GhG) emissions would be approximately 20 million tonnes of carbon dioxide per year, roughly 2.4% of the GhG emissions regarding all consumption in the UK. It also highlighted the need for the local authorities to consider the overall impact food and drink waste has relating to the volumes needed to go to landfills and down sewers. The cost incurred in the collection and treatment of waste, as well as the environmental and social impacts it might have is sometimes difficult to quantify. However, by estimating the total amount of food and drink waste generated by UK households, a better understanding of the potential scope for collection and treatment of such a waste was made possible (WRAP, 2009).

Waste needs to be managed, so that the costs to society of dealing with waste, including the environmental costs, are minimised. More importantly, the quantification of how much waste is being produced could be of benefit for authorities which could re-use or recycle some these resources. Food waste is a cost to all parties within a supply chain. Food wasted at household level, involves wasted resources on the farm, in the distribution to manufacturers, at the manufacturing stage, in the storage and distribution to retails and food service operations as well as within the retail or food service outlets. Yet there is more – household food waste does not account for food which is lost along the supply chain. In some countries the combined food loss and waste can sometimes represent over 50% of all food which is produced (WRAP, 2009); in theory, 50% more people could be fed!

Concluding remarks

Our journey through food security has raised many issues, and perhaps very few solutions. Food security is a central part of our society's discourse. At the crux of the matter is that there are simply far too many of us, and these figures are predicted to grow. We have restricted land resources and increasing pressure on these land resources to produce a sustainable, safe, nutritious diet for the many rather than the few, when there are competing demands by animal feed, and alternative fuels on this scarce resource.

On our televisions, tablets and other forms of mass communication we are given images of starving children, of children who through poverty are unable to afford necessary operations to regain sight in order that they may take an active part within their community. In the west there is increasing concern over obesity, poor diets and diet related illnesses. Yet the dominant solutions delivered by industry, academia, and policy makers is to deliver more with less, as discussed in the next chapter, using more technology to manage land use, soil structure, targeted use of petrochemicals through robotic intervention, strategies that heavily links a core issue of how the management or removal of waste within supply chains. One core waste – which with careful holistic thought might be reduced, is that of food which is produced throughout the supply chain which remains unconsumed, at least by humans. Yet, the question remains. What our options, and how do we develop a more utilitarian approach to the delivery of food?

References

Bonny, S.P.F., Gardner, E.G., Pethick, D. W. and Hocquette, J-F. (2015). What is artificial meat and what does it mean for the future of the meat industry? *Journal of Integrative Agriculture.* **14** (2), 255-263.

EU (2008). EU Waste Framework Directive 2008/98/EC. http://ec.europa.eu/environment/waste/framework/

FAO (1992). Human nutrition in the developing world. http://www.fao.org/docrep/w0073e/w0073e03.htm.

FAO (2009) The state of food in-security in the world: economic crisis, impacts and lessons learned. FAO. http://www.fao.org/3/a-i0876e.pdf

Galusky, W. (2014). Technology as responsibility: failure, food animals and cultured meat. *Journal of Environmental Ethics.* **27**, 931- 948.

Garnett, T. and Godfray, C. (2012). Sustainable intensification in agriculture. Navigating a course through competing food system priorities. Food Climate Research Network and the Oxford Martin. Programme on the Future of Food, University of Oxford.

Goodwin, J.N. and Shoulders, C.W. (2013). The future of meat: a qualitative analysis of cultured meat media coverage. *Meat Science.* **95**, 445- 450.

GOVUK. (2009). Waste hierarchy. Available from: https://www.gov.uk/waste-legislation-and-regulations. Date accessed: 29/12/2013.

Hopkins, P. D. (2015). Cultured meat in western media: the disproportionate coverage of vegetarian reactions, demographic realities, and implications for cultured meat marketing. *Journal of Integrative Agriculture.* **14** (2), 264-272.

Lang,T., Barling, D. and Caraher, M. (2009). *Food Policy: Integrating health, environment and society.* Oxford University Press.

Lang, T. and Heasman, M. (2015). *Food Wars, 2nd ed.* Earthscan.

McDonald, B. L. (2010). *Food Security.* Polity.

7

Mills, S. (1861, 1998). *Utilitarianism*, Roger Crisp (ed.), Oxford: Oxford University Press

Millstone, E. and Lang, T. (2003). *Penguin Atlas of Food: Who eats what, where, and why.* Penguin.

Naylor, R.L. (ed.) (2014). *The Evolving Sphere of Food Security.* Oxford University Press.

Popkin, B. and Neilsen, S. J. 2003. The sweetening of the world's diet. *Obesity Research.* **11**(11), 1325–1332.

Rockstrom, J., Steffen, W., Noone, K., Persson, A., Chapin, F.C., Lambin, E. F., Lenton, T.M., Scheffer, M., Folke, C., Schellnhuber, H.J., Nykvist, B., de Wit, C. A., Hughes, T., van der Leeuw, S., Rodhe, H., Sörlin, S., Snyder, P.K., Costanza, R., Svedin, U., Falkenmark, M., Karlberg, L., Corell, R. W., Fabry, V. J., Hansen, J., Walker, B., Liverman, D., Richardson, K., Crutzen, P. and Foley, J.A. (2009). A safe operating space for humanity. *Nature* **461**.

Schneider, F. (2008). Wasting food-an insistent behaviour. Proceedings Waste – The Social Context, 8. http://www.ifr.ac.uk/waste/Reports/Wasting%20Food%20-%20 An%20Insistent.pdf. Accessed 03/01/2014.

UNICEF (2015). The state of the world's children 2015: reimagine the future innovation for every child. https://www.unicef.org/publications/files/SOWC_2015_Summary_ and_Tables.pdf. Accessed: 19/09/2016.

WRAP (2009). Household Food and Drink Waste in the UK. http://www.wrap.org. uk/sites/files/wrap/Household_food_and_drink_waste_in_the_UK_-_report.pdf. Accessed: 13/11/2013.

8 Alternative Production Systems: Moving away from Farming the Land

Andrew M. Beacham, Jim M. Monaghan, Luis Kluwe Aguiar and Jane Eastham

Introduction

Following on from Chapter 7, where we raise the issue of the complexity of delivering food security, when faced with both constraints in availability and conflicting demands on resources, specifically in the context of expected increases in global population levels, the jury is out as to how food security may be achieved.

The dominant discourse is that an increase in the number of mouths to feed requires an increase in productivity, but there are well reported pressures on land available for food production that might inhibit 'sustainable intensification' of food production (Garnett *et al.*, 2013). This chapter examines some of the recent technological developments for the production of food that are reputed to redress this issue.

Technological developments have been varied, and included the use of digital technology for, for instance, the production for in vitro meat and meat substitute, 3D food printing, precision farming, as well as innovative use of space as in Urban and vertical farming. This chapter follows on from Chapter 7, which suggests that some radical thinking must be undertaken with respect to the food supply chain, and in particular the rethinking of the political economic framework, and the issues of managing supply and food waste. This chapter provides a brief introduction to current initiatives, which based on the productionist neoliberal framework, are being put forward to redress the issue of the delivery of sufficient food for growing populations. It examines the ways in which land resources and technologies are deployed in order to produce more for less. It states that the issue of feeding populations is about the volume and costs of production. The chapter then moves on to consider how the production of sufficient food is not a function of primary production but of food manufacturing, and manufacturing through the vehicle of nanotechnology. We start with the use of land resources and consider the developments of urban and vertical farming.

Urban and vertical farming

As the global population increases, many additional demands are being placed upon food production. An increase in the number of mouths to feed requires an increase in productivity but pressures on land available for food production requires 'sustainable intensification' of food production (Garnett *et al.*, 2013), not only in terms of the quantity of crop that can be produced per hectare but in the location of farmed land as well. In addition to population pressures, climate change is affecting the area of cultivable land available by altering not only the growing temperature and seasonal variability, but water availability, soil nutrient and salinity levels and the frequency of damaging weather events, such as flooding, storms and drought (Beddington, 2012).

In addition, urban expansion may also reduce the availability of farmland as more and more is turned over to housing an increasingly urban population. Globally, more people now live in urban areas than in rural areas, with 54% of the world's population residing in urban areas in 2014. In 1950, 30% of the world's population was urban, and by 2050, 66% of the world's population is projected to be urban (UN, 2015). However, urban areas also provide an opportunity to reclaim some of this lost land for food generation, and in doing so help increase global food production, via the adoption of so-called 'urban farming' schemes, whereby food is produced from setups located in urban areas.

Urban farming is not a new means of feeding urban communities. The use of allotments and gardens in urban areas for growing produce is common around the world both in developed (Mok *et al.*, 2014) and developing economies (Orsini *et al.*, 2013). However, the scope of urban farming projects is changing and it is the adoption of large-scale commercial systems that is currently expanding in popularity and, if suitably popular, could provide a useful means to augment food production by making use of urban spaces to grow crops. An increasing number of companies that produce crops in such environments are emerging and are developing innovative approaches to meet the challenges of urban agriculture in a sustainable manner. These new approaches can provide opportunities for increased efficiency, new technologies, patterns of food supply and beneficial urban spaces (Thomaier *et al.*, 2015).

Urban farming systems can range from conventional ground-level plant growth, for example in city parks and other open spaces, to sophisticated growing environments with highly regulated conditions, which can be found in unusual locations wherever space permits. Rooftops are a common site for urban crop production as they provide large flat spaces, which are raised above the shady street level and provide good illumination for growing plants (Figure 8.1) (Orsini *et al.*, 2014). Such locations have been described as 'zero-acreage farming', as no additional land is used in their operation (Thomaier *et al.*, 2015). Rooftop production can be performed uncovered, particular in warmer countries, although this may lead to concerns about crop contamination from pollution sources such as vehicle exhaust fumes (Tong *et al.*, 2016).

Figure 8.1: The Long Island City rooftop farm, part of Brooklyn Grange Rooftop Farms, New York, USA (Image from www.brooklyngrangefarm.com).

Urban farming is often performed in greenhouses, as these provide a series of benefits. Greenhouses allow the growing environment to be heated and allow natural light to the plants. Supplementary artificial lighting can also be used in low light level periods, such as during the winter months to maintain crop production (Bergstrand and Schüssler 2013). Greenhouses also protect plants from external pollution and pests, and allow a degree of control over humidity. Lufa Farms Inc., in Montreal, Canada, claim to have built the world's first commercial rooftop greenhouse in 2011 (Figure 8.2) and currently produce a range of different vegetable crops including herbs, peppers and aubergines (Lufa Farms, 2014). Over 200 metric tons of vegetables are produced from their two greenhouses each year. The produce is distributed to customers along with other locally-grown food items. Similar schemes are also underway providing vegetables in other cities such as New York (Gotham Greens Local Produce, 2016).

Figure 8.2: The world's first commercial rooftop glasshouse, the Ahuntsic glasshouse, located in Montreal, Canada, operated by Lufa Farms Inc. (Image from lufa.com).

Covered, self-contained controlled environment (CE) facilities can also be used to grow plants and allow complete control over growth conditions, independent of prevailing weather conditions. Being completely enclosed, CE facilities do not require natural illumination from sunlight and so can be located anywhere in the urban environment and are not restricted to use on rooftops. Both glasshouse and controlled environment facilities require precise control of internal conditions to optimise production and plant health, and may also benefit from the provision of additional carbon dioxide which may be sourced from waste CO_2 to improve sustainability and recycling (Dannehl *et al.*, 2014).

These facilities often use light-emitting diode (LED) lighting systems which provide a high-efficiency light source comprising predominantly red and blue wavelengths that can be tailored to the needs of particular crops, but with minimal heat production, allowing the lights to be located near the plants, maximising efficiency of light use (Yeh and Chung, 2009). As LED lighting technology improves, the light spectra can be optimised for maximum benefits, for example a 10-30% proportion of blue LED lights amongst red LED lights is optimum for lamb's lettuce growth (Wojciechowska *et al.*, 2015). The largest LED farm in the world, measuring around 2500 m^2, is based in Japan, and can produce up to 10,000 lettuce heads every day (Dickie, 2014). Even more precise control and higher efficiency could be achieved with the use of quantum dot lighting technologies (Yang *et al.*, 2015) where the entire light spectrum emitted by the light source can be specified to provide maximal absorption by the crop.

Vertical farming uses stacked layers of plant beds to maximise the amount of crop that can be produced in a given area (Al-Chalabi, 2015). While vertical farming is not limited to urban areas, the high demand for space and limited dimensions of many urban farming setups have led to vertical farming being used as the method of choice for some companies. Vertical farming setups can be used outdoor, in glasshouse, or in CE facilities, but are most often employed in glasshouses. In addition, crops can sometimes be grown on inclined or vertical surfaces such as walls and so maximise the amount of urban space that can be used for cultivation (Touliatos *et al.*, 2016). For example, some companies are even using office spaces to grow indoor tomatoes and herbs, which are used in their cafeterias and aim to improve the working environment for employees (Feng, 2013).

Many glasshouse and CE urban farming systems, particularly those with a vertical farming setup, utilise a hydroponic approach, whereby plants are grown in a soilless system with a nutrient solution that circulates around their roots. Commonly, the crops grown are leafy vegetables and herbs as they grow rapidly, are relatively small and of high value. Plants are often inserted into foam or polystyrene trays, which float upon the surface of the solution and help keep the leaves and other above-ground material dry. This helps minimise crop damage and improves appearance and shelf life. The nutrient solution provided to the plants must be carefully monitored to ensure that it allows for the best possible plant health, with the composition, temperature, pH and osmolarity of the solution being of high importance for optimal growth (Touliatos *et al.*, 2016). Concentrated pre-mixed hydroponic nutrient solutions can be used; alternatively companies can concoct their own bespoke chemical mixtures that provide an ideal growing environment for each different crop type. Some hydroponic systems allow for adjustment of the nutrient solution during operation by feeding in separate elements, such as compounds of nitrogen, potassium and phosphorus, to compensate for use by the crop (Touliatos *et al.*, 2016).

An alternative to an enclosed building is to use underground facilities. A business in London uses a hydroponic production system on shelves to produce herbs and salads in abandoned London Underground train tunnels (Zero Carbon Food, 2016). Light is provided by banks of LEDs suspended above the plants. By growing in this unusual location, the presence of pests and disease is minimised, while the subterranean nature of the site helps provide a consistent growing temperature. In Australia, the 650 metre long Mittagong railway tunnel has been used as a mushroom farm since the 1950s (Li Sun Exotic Mushrooms, 2014). Mushrooms are grown on a sterilised mixture of sawdust, bran or wheat grain packed into small plastic bags (Figure 8.3). One benefit of growing mushrooms in a tunnel is the cool and humid air, with an average temperature of around 16°C and 80% humidity, which reproduce the conditions found on forest floors where the mushrooms would be found naturally.

8

Figure 8.3: Li Sun Exotic Mushrooms grow a wide variety of mushrooms in a railway tunnel in Mittagong, Australia (Image from www.li-sunexoticmushrooms.com.au).

Production of crops in glasshouses or CE facilities also allows for increased automation. Sophisticated robotics systems are being employed in indoor growing environments. For example, a business in Singapore is using a rotating vertical farming system of plant trays containing lettuce, spinach and leafy greens (Figure 8.4) to achieve sufficient light exposure for the production of the maximum possible amount of crop in a small space (Sky Greens, 2014). In addition, production is soon expected to begin from the world's first fully robotically-operated farm, using CE facilities, which aims to produce up to half a million lettuce heads per day within five years of its launch (Garfield, 2016). This technology would be well suited to smaller urban units, reducing the need for sourcing and managing labour. In contrast, an alternative approach to staffing production areas is to allow customers to harvest their own crops. As well as reducing labour costs, this also provides customer appeal by allowing them to select exactly the product that meets their requirements and specifications (Snook, 2014).

Figure 8.4: The vertical farming system of Sky Greens, located in Singapore, uses rotating stacked trays of plants to maximise light exposure (Image from skygreens.com).

An area of growing interest is aquaponics, where waste material generated from a tank containing fish is used to provide nutrients for a crop; the crop, in turn, purifies the water, which is then returned to the fish (Surnar *et al.*, 2015). The only inputs required are food for the fish and energy to heat the water and operate pumps to circulate the system. GrowUp Urban Farms, based in London, use a combination of vertical farming and aquaponics systems housed in recycled shipping containers to produce not only salad crops, but also fresh fish (Figure 8.5) (GrowUp Urban Farms, 2014). Urban Organics run a similar operation providing salads and fish for sale from a facility housed in an old brewery building in St Paul, Minnesota, USA (Urban Organics, n.d.).

Figure 8.5: The GrowUp Urban Farms system combines an aquaponics system housed in a reused shipping container with a vertical farming setup above (Image from growup.org.uk).

Sustainability and environmental awareness are key components of many urban farming operations, with the adoption of recycled materials and reduction of energy consumption, agrochemicals and water usage being important factors in the design and operation of the farming system (Orsini *et al.*, 2013). Aquaponic and hydroponic setups use a closed loop system to reduce the amount of water used for crop production (Touliatos *et al.*, 2016). For soil-based systems, soaking up water reduces run-off into drains and sewers and so helps to manage storm water (Choo, 2011). Growth in closed environments also helps reduce disease and pest occurrence, and can eliminate the need for pesticide use and improve further the sustainability and environmental benefits of such approaches. Production in urban areas minimises transport costs and environmental impact by virtue of produce being generated in close proximity to where it will be used (Orsini *et al.*, 2014). Despite striving for sustainability, there are, however, concerns over the environmental impact of urban farming, such as through soil and groundwater contamination from agrochemicals. In Lisbon, for example, it was found that fertiliser application rates on allotments exceeded uptake by crops, leading to a surplus of nitrogen that was lost to the environment (Cameira *et al.*, 2014). Fertiliser application rates should therefore be chosen to match crop uptake to reduce environmental impact.

Urban renewal is another possible benefit to in-city farming operations. Places such as the US cities of Detroit and Cleveland, where a declining population is leading to an increasing number of vacant lots, could benefit from the conversion of vacant land to farming projects (Choo, 2011). Vacant lots cost city authorities millions of dollars every year in providing basic services and from uncollected tax revenue. By using the land for farming, some of these costs can be recuperated. In such locations, land is being used not just for crops but also for holding pigs, goats and chickens. Some projects also include beehives to help with pollination of crops and improve yield. It is thought that the vacant land in Detroit has the potential to supply more than 75% of vegetables and 40% of fruit required by local residents. In other cities, such as New York, which are not experiencing economic decline, urban agriculture is seen more as a quality of life benefit that necessary for urban renewal but urban farming here may still prove popular (e.g. Brooklyn Grange, n.d.).

The level of adoption of urban farming will depend on a number of factors and will likely require longevity in order to prosper (Choo, 2011). The future of this form of agriculture will depend on perception and location. A recent study in Barcelona, where urban gardens are traditionally used for leisure, indicated that some urban agriculture was viewed as a social activity rather than a potential food production source (Sanye-Mengual *et al.*, 2016). However, urban rooftop farms, which championed innovative methods, were considered to provide potential benefits to urban fertility, highlighting that the perception of urban agriculture is dependent upon the concept involved. Demands for agricultural land, urban sprawl, the level of public and commercial interest, economics of setup, operation and distribution will all likely feature in the uptake and ultimate success of urban farming.

As urban farming becomes more popular, so management of project numbers, scale and development is another area that will need to be addressed. Competition between building and farming enterprises, or building in a manner to allow urban farming, such as providing a flat rooftop, should be considered. Urban infilling of gaps in African cities such as Kampala in Uganda is considered to decrease the opportunities for small to medium scale commercial and garden enterprises by around 60% by 2030 (Vermeiren *et al.*, 2013). In some countries, land-use regulations often lag behind the rapid increase in urban agriculture, leading many projects to operate in a grey area of legality until laws are drawn up to manage them (Choo, 2011).

Urban farming represents a potential new means of food production that may become more familiar in the future as populations, urbanisation and demand for food and agricultural land increase. This style of farming promotes the development and use of new technologies while championing environmental awareness and sustainability. In addition to providing food, urban farming can enrich city environments and promote urban renewal. Whether urban farming becomes a mainstay of global agriculture remains to be seen and will depend on productivity, profit and public support but such an approach could provide a useful resource of innovation and future-proof food provision.

Precision agriculture

An alternative way of maximising benefit from land and other resources is that of precision agriculture (PA). The drive for what is also known as precision farming is that it offers a means of increasing cost efficiency of production through the maximisation of value gained from inputs including seed, fertilisers and pesticides, and allows for greater levels of production for a lesser impact on the environment, especially in terms of the pollution of underground water and soil structure and fertility. Research in 2005 suggested that from 234 studies published between 1998 and 2005, precision agriculture was found to increase profitability by 68% (Zarco-Tejada, 2014; Griffin and Lowenberg-DeBoer, 2005). However, other sources have suggested a much more conservative estimate of circa 20% (Nesta, 2015).

Furthermore, in light of the growing concerns over population growth and food security, findings suggest that precision agricultural technologies offer the opportunity to increase crop quality and yield (Aubert *et al.*, 2012; Tey and Brinal, 2012).

This new approach has emerged from the convergence of several technologies including global position systems, (GPS) geographic information systems, miniature computer programs, automatic control, infield and remote sensing, mobile computing, advance information processing and telecommunications (Gibbons, 2000; Zhang *et al.*, 2002), computer-linked yield and nutrient monitors, and variable rate chemical applicators (Aubert, *et al.*, 2012).

PA recognizes a long known issue, which has been ignored following the 'green revolution', in that there are spatial and temporal variations in soil and crop factors within a field. Prior to the intensification of farming and the development of larger field systems, it was possible to vary inputs according to manual monitoring of the specific requirements of areas of land, but following the green revolution and the opening up of field structures, the specific needs of particular soils, and thus crops within a field were ignored.

8

Table 8.1: Types of PA technologies

PA technologies	Description
GPS (global positioning system)	Use for topographic surveying, to produce geo referenced coordinate maps of yield, salinity, and other chemical properties of soil
Yield Monitors	Collect data across the field to measure variability
GIS (geographic information system)	Stores data such as soil type and location specific information
Variable rate application	These apply seeds and fertiliser based on the information gathered from the GPS and other sensors, and are able to vary the amount applied
Crop scouting and remote sensing	Imaging devised to identify problems in crops
Controlled traffic farming	System used control the field vehicles to a minimal area of permanent traffic lanes – reduces soil compaction, and crop damage.

Agriculture has always appeared to benefit from the incorporation of technological advances as a means of increasing volume of production. The first introduction of precision agriculture emerged in the 1980s. Precision farming is a site-specific farming system, which in many quarters is beginning to be seen as vital for farmers' success, although it offers both opportunity and challenge.

Despite emerging in the 1980s its adoption has been much slower than expected, even in the last 10 years. The barriers for adoption have been predominantly identified as financial, and it has been regularly suggested that the adoption of new technology requires sufficient financial well-being (Morris and Potter, 1995; Prager and Posthumus, 2010). Yet as prices of the technological system decline, surely these barriers will be lifted.

While precision farming will no doubt benefit farmers in many aspects, they are also challenged to have site-specific information about the land, have advanced knowledge and skills for managing large bodies of information and complex equipment. Suggestions have been made that a lack of skills of farmers and farm workers, coupled with a limited focus on the user-friendliness of the digital applications has hindered the uptake of these technologies.

■ Managing variability

In effect, precision farming is the management of variability of which six types of variability that affect agricultural production, these are identified in Table 8.2.

The collection of such data has been facilitated by the continued emergence of digital and sensor technolog,y and this can be undertaken in agriculture through either a map-based or a sensor-based approach. The map-based approach utilises GPS, remote sensing, yield monitoring and soil sampling and is thought to be the easiest to implement, but there is less real time information. Decisions tend to be based on historical data. This can be used to control what is known as a variable rate applicator for the purpose of seed drilling, weed management, and the application of fertiliser including lime. The GPS operates as the positioning system.

Table 8.2: Variability in agricultural production (Adapted from Zhang *et al.*, 2002)

Variability	As measured by
Yield variability	present and historical yields
Field variability	Topography: Elevation , slope, aspect , proximity to boundaries
Soil variability	Soil fertility eg. Chemical properties (N, P, K, Ca, Mg, C, Mn, Zn & Cu) density mechanical strength , moisture, texture
Crop variability	Crop densities, crop height, nutrient stress, leaf area index nutrient stress, e.g. for nitrogen, calcium iron etc,
Management variability	Tillage practices, crop hybrid, etc
Variability of analilie factors	Infestations of weeds , nemotodes

The sensor-based, in contrast, measures those properties of the soil and plants using real time sensors. These tend to be more expensive than the map-based approaches. The implementation of PA, has moved forward and there have been some real movement to link sensor technologies with the mapped variables to facilitate the management of tillage, seeding, fertiliser and herbicide and pesticide application. Precision agriculture is most advanced amongst arable farmers and has shown real benefits with large farm and field sizes, across the EU, Australia and the USA.

Success and lack of success across Europe

It is apparent however, that whilst there are some real financial benefits delivered to farmers utilising PA systems, in parallel to the slow uptake of this technology, there has also been variable success in the application. In fruit, vegetables and viticulture, where benefits have been achieved, this has been very much linked to the management of water stress and water use efficiency. Furthermore in grape production, yield maps are seen to be particularly important in order to avoid mixing grapes of different wine qualities (Tropea and Morvan, 2014). In arable, both variable rate application (VRA) and controlled traffic methods (CTM), resulted in large savings. VRA have controlled the rate of inputs based on yield maps. CTM have reduced nutrient leaching in surface and ground water, and a system coupled with a no-till approach is seen to be particularly successful in avoiding soil compaction. Success has been also delivered in the livestock sector where there has been the development of technology (in the form of a radio activated bolus) to routinely monitor ph levels in cows as a measure of the presence of SARA (sub acute ruminal acidosis), a disease that has been connected to

Laminitis, milk fat depression, as well as parakeratosis, and the translocation of pathogens into the bloodstream causing abscessation throughout the cow's body (Tropea and Morvan, 2014).

However, it has not been all plain sailing, other studies, such as those in Denmark, have shown no economic advantage of senor-based fertiliser application, which has been linked to the need for greater understanding of the contingency of crop type, areas, region amongst other factors, in order to fully realise the value of this system in the context of food sustainability.

Cultured meat and 3D food production

In this last section, we will look at a third genre of technology, and this is of the technological production of the primary product from their chemical properties. This may some of us may seem like an extract from some horror film, none the less the use of artificially created meat through in vitro or nanotechnology has emerged as a possible solution to food insecurity.

■ Technology and meat food

Technology has been the main engine in food supply chains and food production with wide application, which has not only shaped its production but has enabled a vast number of the world population to regularly access food of consistent quality and standard. Particularly in meat production, the application of manufacturing-like production, management and control systems has been implemented at all levels of the meat chain, from animal husbandry to processing, transformation and retailing. Nonetheless, food technology innovation and diffusion tend not to be supported by food-related policies.

Meat, especially red meat, is packed with energy deriving from high-quality proteins, which are formed by the essential amino-acids, lipids, minerals and vitamins vital for human nutrition. Stanford (1999) postulated that the appetite for meat was essential to human evolution. The moment early primates introduced meat to a basically vegetarian diet, a change took place. The cognitive capacity required to organise groups to hunt and the sharing of the product of the hunt, the meat, established fundamental social skills and behaviours which formed the origins of human intelligence.

For centuries, meat, was consumed more sporadically, and often as a complement to a meal basically consisting grains, pulses and tubers. Whilst agrarian societies throughout the centuries could often guarantee adequate source of carbohydrate from the crops harvested, meat and lipids have always been relatively scarce until the late 1500s (Smil, 2013). Yet, in recent decades, and especially since the end of rationing after World War II, the intensification of meat production based on the modern livestock husbandry methods has made meat more readily available and accessible. Meat has always been important in diets because it is known that "the consumption of meat and other animal products can alleviate nutritional deficiency, particularly regarding the minerals, iron and zinc, important for physical and mental development especially in children (Delgado *et al.*, 1999; Bhat and Fayaz, 2011).

As seen in Chapter 7, the changing nutritional needs, particularly in transition economies, has increased the demand for food in general and livestock products in particular (Delgado *et al.*, 1999). The further increased appetite for more animal protein is due to projected population growth, especially in emerging economies. The growing demand is also being driven by a rising purchasing power (Hocquette *et al.*, 2015; Delgado *et al.*, 1999) particularly in emerging market economies in Asia, Africa and Latin America. Consumers in transition economies are looking for more than a simple diet of grains and tubers, they are looking for variety of foods and better food quality, which emulates the trends in consumption of more economically developed societies elsewhere.

Conversely, Gallusky (2014) noted that "meat has problems which are intimately tied to the technology of industrialisation of the meat product" *per se*. In the process of producing meat and bringing it to market, humans have increased the stress on animals and the environment. Both Harrison *et al.* (2013) and Polland (2006) have criticised the way meat production is being treated. In their view, animals have simply become protein machines. Yet, Gallusky (2014) has argued that within the means through which technology has been used in present day meat production systems, meat should be understood "as a technology, and not as the product of a technology". By accepting meat as technology it would tie us intimately with the idea of responsibility, thereby creating the need for a more meaningful mapping of the stakes involved in the contestations over animal bodies within the human food systems. The adoption of meat produced in this manner would, according to Gallusky (2014), enable the meat industry to produce better quality meat.

Thus, the notion of meat produced artificially as a means of perhaps resolving some of the traditional meat technology problems has finally come to light. As an alternative for producing meat, the launch of the first cultured meat beef burger in London attracted the attention of the general public, scholars and meat producers in August 2013. Research driven by Dr. Post and his team at Maastricht University (Langelaan *et al.*, 2010) revealed that it was finally possible to artificially create a meat protein, which could be eaten, from a laboratory.

Since the 1930s, perhaps from a more sci-fi premise, the idea of creating animal protein artificially has always been aired. However, past attempts have resulted

8

in some problems, inherent of the technology available at the time. Mattick *et al.* (2015) mentioned fish and pork tissue being produced using in vitro technique. After Dr Post's achievement, the Israeli institute of technology, Technion, made a statement on the possibility of also developing cultured chicken meat. Following the cultured meat production principle, it could indeed be a good solution for the problem of food security, world hunger and malnutrition (Bonny *et al.*, 2015). Moreover, as a very lean meat it could aid in the control of food caloric intake as well as reducing the risk to food safety (Laestadius and Caldwell, 2015).

Currently, the advocates of cultured meat technology are basing the justification for such a technology on its potential to actually address food security issues at many levels. The work of Laestadius and Caldwell (2015), when analysing the content of materials published by the American media revealed that, despite perhaps not being well articulated by the general public, there was indeed a much wider and pervasive dimension of the role of cultured meat regarding the ethical, social acceptability, health improvement capability, innovation risk and distrust, and cultural acceptance.

Before advancing further, there is a pressing need to clarify, which terminology would be most appropriately used when referring to meat that is grown outside an animal body. From the literature it becomes evident that it would not only improve the clarity of this discussion, but possibly help stakeholders, and in particular aid in enabling future consumers' acceptance too. This is because consumers tend to be sensitive to terminologies which might influence the adoption of products. Consequently, reducing the negative perception this new meat might have would be vital for managing future aversion and rejection by the general public (Goodwin and Shoulders, 2014).

In the literature many terms have been freely used. Some referred to it as 'printed meat', alluding to the fact that it could be produced from a 3-D type of machine. Others use the term 'synthetic' which gives the impression of something rather artificial. 'Lab-grown' meat was, until recently, a strong contender term, but has more recently lost impetus. Anecdotal evidence shows that referring to the new meat as lab-grown would also pass the impression to the final product of something less natural. Nonetheless, the use of 'artificial meat' can also constitute a problem for manufacturers and consumers. Usually artificial meat refers denotes food products already in the market made from vegetable protein sources. Thus, this term can be a misrepresentation of what the new meat might be as understood by (Bhat *et al.*, 2015). Moreover, other meat substitutes which are based on fungus protein replacements, such as Quorn, have also started their life in a laboratory. Therefore, artificial meat should be avoided.

There are many references in the literature on 'in vitro meat' and 'in vitro meat technology' (Chiles, 2013). The term 'in vitro meat', despite its widespread use in the literature, can provide some negative connotations as it could be misunderstood by something which is not only artificially created by the means of, for example, cloning, process, but also because human babies can be conceived by IVF (Brooks and Lusk 2011; Schaefer and Savulescu, 2014, Laestadius and Caldwell, 2015). Other terms such as 'artificial', 'tissue culture', 'cell culture', 'tissue engineered', 'cultured meat', 'myocyte culturing' (Datar and Betti, 2010), 'biotechnologically produced meat', and 'futurism food' have also been widely used.

Table 8.3: Summary of terminologies

Printed meat	Tissue culture
Synthetic meat	Cell culture
In vitro	Tissue engineered
In vitro meat technology	Biotechnologically produced meat
Artificial	Futurism food
Myocyte culturing	Cultured
Clean meat cell culture	Lab-grown

Despite its many denominations, the terminology used so far for the new meat has referred to meat deriving from an animal tissue grown in a serum-like medium (blood plasma) in test tube conditions in a laboratory. As for the process used in obtaining it, many authors (Datar and Betti, 2010; Jones, 2010; Bhat and Fayaz, 2011) have gone into great detail describing the standard methodology behind it. Moritz *et al.* (2015: 208) described the method for producing meat by using bovine muscle stem cells which are cultured in vitro. This is a "fairly standard 2-D tissue engineering technology" which according to Moritz *et al.* (2015) uses flasks containing a nourishing fluid, blood plasma, and other essential nutrients also known as medium. For the muscle tissue to grow and self-organize, it requires some scaffolding support, which can be made from various materials, and some electrical stimulation, or polarisation. The basic principles that may enable it to replace livestock produced beef in the future would be better efficiency, sustainability and mimicry (Moritz *et al.*, 2015: 208).

It is evident that the technology has been developing fast and in recent years the 'test tube' or flask conditions no longer apply. The literature now refers to a packed bed bio-reactor (Moritz *et al.*, 2015:211), which is a large receptacle where the meat tissue is grown bathed by serum medium. It has proved to increase the viability of producing meat tissue. However, more recently, discussions have erupted challenging the validity of the technology using a serum medium which is actually derived from animal sources, calf foetuses more precisely.

During the 2nd International Conference on Cultured Beef in the Netherlands in 2016, scholars highlighted the shortage of bovine serum in the market, which would be detrimental to further research, not to mention escalating the costs associated with accessing it. Alternatives to the (bovine) serum are already being tested since there would be a great need to raise livestock simply to feed the bioreactors in the future. This would potentially deflate the argument for reducing animal suffering, which will be tackled later on.

Despite the literature providing a pool of terms from which scholars have freely drawn, it is felt relevant to unify the terminology used. First, for the sake of the readers of this chapter, second so that stakeholders could unify around a terminology which would improve the general public's acceptance, and third to reduce its possible rejection due to likely negative connotations that could be attached to it. During the recent 2nd International Conference on Cultured Beef in the Netherlands in 2016, scholars, scientists and industry representatives coalesced around 'clean meat' as a unifying terminology, since the many other denominations used to-date can be scary, thus frightening more consumers instead of educating them.

Another justification behind the term 'clean meat' is the realisation that meat grown from cultured tissues would potentially be cleaner than that deriving from animals. Animals tend to be dirty and act as vectors of microbiological diseases. Some argue that when culturing meat in laboratory, it has the potential to produce a product which would be safer to humans, as it is free from animal-borne diseases. In general, Bhat *et al.* considered cultured meat as being a more reliable source of protein since it does not depend on nature and natural animal behaviour which can, sometimes, be unpredictable (Bhat *et al.*, 2015). This might not actually be the case since safety protocols in abattoirs and meat processing plants are in place to guarantee consumers' food safety protection.

■ Other 3-D foods

As with any new technology, the potential of 3D food printing has been under scrutiny for some time. However, it has the capacity to deliver novel and exciting food alternatives beyond its current industrial application (Southerland *et al.*, 2011). Sher and Tuto (2015) propose that the advent of 3D food takes us closer to a Star Trek sci-fi vision of the food replicator which could be used at home.

Yet, closer to earth, Sun *et al.* (2015) have proposed that 3D food printing has had a great impact on food processing by providing an engineering solution for customized food design and personalized nutrition control. These 3D food printing machines have come to revolutionize food manufacturing and enhance digital gastronomy by the means of allowing customisation of food shape, colour, flavour, texture and even nutrition. As a result, according to Sher and Tuto (2015) 3D food printing is the technology that might disrupt the food industry as it has the capacity to change how new products are designed, developed, produced, marketed and consumed and cooked. In Japan, with a growing aging population, Serizawa *et al.* (2014) mentioned that 3D edible gel printer extruders have been developed to make soft foods more palatable for the elderly. This has enabled soft foods to be better swallowed. Agar-agar is used for moulding the shapes.

The question remains as to whether such a means of artificially producing meat offers an effective solution to the lack of sufficient meat grown in the natural way, and whether it would be acceptable to the consumer.

In an article in the Guardian Environmental network, Jeffrey Lipton has developed a 3D food printer. Liquid versions of food are laid down dot by dot and layer by layer, and result in apparently edible meals. The technology uses liquid or melted ingredients – but the longer term aim is to create food inks made from hydrocolloids, that form gels with water. Printers have been used to make a range of products from chocolate, cheese and hummus to scallops, turkey and celery. Homaru Cantu is a chef has also made sushi on a printer, and he is enthusiastic about the implications for sustainability, particularly in terms of carbon footprint and food waste. He is pleased that that there would be less emphasis placed on the supply chain. Suggestions are that the food printer could become as commonplace in the average household kitchen as the food mixer or bread maker

Concluding remarks

This chapter has examined three novel ways in which food security may be addressed, following on from Chapter 7. In each of the three ways, innovation has taken place to ensure the maximisation of the use of one or more of the resource inputs. In the first instance, vertical and urban agriculture focuses upon the maximisation of the use of land and the use of land which is not traditionally utilised for food production, thereby increasing yields through extending the land available for food production. Alternatively, precision farming presents a way of improving yields, reducing costs and reducing environmental impact through monitoring and managing inputs according to site-specific variability in soil types. Again a means of generating more with less. In the third instance, we abandon the land as a resource and go directly to the processing stage. The latter, both in vitro and 3D production has received some interest by the food industry, although their adoption so far has been limited. Heston Blumenthal's test tube burger, created by Dr Mark Post from Maastricht University, hit the headlines in February 2012, at an experimental cost of £207,000, so there is still perhaps a little way to go.

References

Al-Chalabi, M. (2015). Vertical farming: Skyscraper sustainability?. *Sustainable Cities and Society*, **18**, 74-77.

Aubert, B. A., Schroeder, A. and Grimaudo, J. (2012). IT as enabler of sustainable farming: An empirical analysis of farmers' adoption decision of precision agriculture technology. *Decision Support Systems*, **54**(1), 510-520.

Beddington, J. (2012). *Food, energy, water and the climate: A perfect storm of global events?* UK Government Office for Science.

Bergstrand, K. J. and Schüssler, H. K. (2013). Growth, development and photosynthesis of some horticultural plants as affected by different supplementary lighting technologies. *European Journal of Horticultural Science*, **78**(3), 119-125.

Bhat, Z. F. and Fayaz, H. (2011). Prospects of cultured meat: advancing meat alternatives. *Journal of Food Science Technology*. **48** (2), 125 – 140.

Bhat, Z. F., Kumar, S. and Bhat, H.F. (2015). In vitro meat: a future animal free harvest. *Critical Reviews in Food Science and Nutrition*. **5**.

Bonny, S.P.F., Gardner, E.G., Pethick, D. W. and Hocquette, J-F. (2015). What is artificial meat and what does it mean for the future of the meat industry? *Journal of Integrative Agriculture*. **14** (2), 255-263.

Brooks, K.R. and Lusk, J.L. (2011). U.S. consumers' attitudes toward farm animal cloning. *Appetite*. **57** (2), 483-92.

Brooklyn Grange. (n.d.) Education and projects. http://www.brooklyngrangefarm.com/about/education/. Accessed 20/07/2016.

Cameira, M.R., Tedesco, S. and Leitao, T.E. (2014). Water and nitrogen budgets under different production systems in Lisbon urban farming. *Biosystems Engineering* **124**, 64-79.

Chiles, R. M. (2013). If they come, we will build it: in vitro meat and the discursive struggle over future agrofood expectations. *Agriculture and Human Values*, **30**(4), 511-523.

Choo, K. (2011). Plowing Over: Can urban farming save Detroit and other declining cities? Will the law allow it? *ABA Journal*, Aug. http://www.abajournal.com/magazine/article/plowing_over_can_urban_farming_save_detroit_and_other_declining_cities_will/. Accessed 20/07/2016.

Dannehl, D., Josuttis, M., Ulrichs, C. and Schmidt, U. (2014). The potential of a confined closed greenhouse in terms of sustainable production, crop growth, yield and valuable plant compounds of tomatoes. *Journal of Applied Botany and Food Quality*, **87**, 210-219.

Datar, I. and Betti, M. (2010). Possibilities for an in vitro meat production system. *Innovative Food Science and Emerging Technologies*. **11**, 13-22.

Delgado, C., Rosegrant, M., Steinfeld, H., Ethui, S. and Courbois, C. (1999). *Livestock 2020: the next food revolution*. IFPRI. May. Brief 61.

Dickie, G. (2014) Q&A: Inside the World's Largest Indoor Farm. *National Geographic.* July 19. http://news.nationalgeographic.com/news/2014/07/140717-japan-largest-indoor-plant-factory-food/. Accessed 25/07/2016

Feng, S. (2013). 'Office farming' greens Tokyo's urban jungle. http://www.wilderutopia.com/sustainability/japan-office-farming-greens-tokyos-urban-jungle/. Accessed 22/07/2016.

Galusky, W. (2014). Technology as responsibility: failure, food animals and cultured meat. *Journal of Environmental Ethics.* **27**, 931- 948.

Garnett, T., Appleby, M.C., Balmford, A., Bateman, I.J., Benton, T.G., Bloomer, P., Burlingame, B., Dawkins, M., Dolan, L., Fraser, D. and Herrero, M. (2013). Sustainable intensification in agriculture: premises and policies. *Science,* **341**(6141), 33-34.

Garfield, L. (2016). The world's first robot-run farm will harvest 30,000 heads of lettuce daily. http://www.techinsider.io/spreads-robot-farm-will-open-soon-2016-1. Accessed 28/07/2016.

Gibbons, G. (2000). Turning a farm art into science-an overview of precision farming. http://www. precisionfarming.com. Accessed 25/01/2017

Goodwin, J.N. and Shoulders, C.W. (2013). The future of meat: a qualitative analysis of cultured meat media coverage. *Meat Science.* **95**, 445- 450.

Gotham Greens Local Produce (2016) Our story. http://gothamgreens.com/our-story/. Accessed 17/07/2016.

Griffin, T.W., Lowenberg-DeBoer, J. (2005). Worldwide adoption and profitability of precision agriculture: implications for Brazil. *Revista de Politica Agricola* **14** (4), 20–38.

GrowUp Urban Farms (2014). Aquaponics and vertical farming. http://growup.org.uk/aquaponicsverticalfarming/. Accessed 27/07/2016.

Harrison,R., Carson, R., Dawkins, M. S., Webster, J., Rollin, B. E., Fraser, D. and Broom, D.M. (2013). *Animal Machines*, Cabi, Wallingford.

Hocquette, A., Lambert, C., Sinquin, C., Peterolfi, L., Wagner, Z., Bonny, S.P.F., Lebert, A. and Hocquette, J-F. (2015). Educated consumers don't believe artificial meat is the solution to the problems with the meat industry. *Journal of Integrative Agriculture.* **14** (2), 273 – 284.

Jones, N. (2010). A taste of things to come. *Nature,* **468**(7325), 752-753.

Laestadius, L. I. and Caldwell, M. A. (2015). Is the future of meat palatable? Perceptions of in vitro meat as evidenced by online news comments. *Public Health and Nutrition.* **18**(13), 2457-67

Langelaan, M. L. P., Boonen, K. J. M., Polak, R. B., Baaijens, F. P. T., Post, M. J. and Van der Schaft, D. W. J. (2010). Meet the new meat: tissue engineered skeletal muscle. *Trends in Food Science and Technology.* **21**, 59- 66.

Li Sun Exotic Mushrooms (2014). Tunnel History. http://www.li-sunexoticmushrooms.com.au/history. Accessed 28/07/2016.

Lufa Farms (2014) Our Story. https://lufa.com/en/our-story.html. Accessed 27/07/2016.

8

Mattick, C. S., Landis, A. E. and Allenby, B. R. (2015). A case for systemic environmental analysis of cultured meat. *Journal of Integrative Agriculture*. **14** (2), 249 – 254.

Mok, H.F., Williamson, V.G., Grove, J.R., Burry, K., Barker, S.F. and Hamilton, A.J. (2014). Strawberry fields forever? Urban agriculture in developed countries: a review. *Agronomy for S ustainable Development*, **34**(1), 21-43.

Moritz, M.S.; Verbruggen, S.E.L. and Post, M.J. (2015). Alternatives for large-scale production of cultured beef: a review. *Journal of Integrative Agriculture*. 14(2), 208-216

Morris, C. and Potter, C. (1995). Recruiting the new conservationists: farmers' adoption of agri-environmental schemes in the UK. *Journal of Rural Studies*, **11**(1), 51-63.

Nesta, (2015) The future in UK agriculture. http://www.nesta.org.uk/blog/precision-agriculture-almost-20-increase-income-possible-smart-farming. Accessed 25/01/2017

Orsini, F., Gasperi, D., Marchetti, L., Piovene, C., Draghetti, S., Ramazzotti, S., Bazzocchi, G. and Gianquinto, G., (2014). Exploring the production capacity of rooftop gardens (RTGs) in urban agriculture: the potential impact on food and nutrition security, biodiversity and other ecosystem services in the city of Bologna. *Food Security*, **6**(6), 781-792.

Orsini, F., Kahane, R., Nono-Womdim, R. and Gianquinto, G., (2013). Urban agriculture in the developing world: a review. *Agronomy for Sustainable Development*, **33**(4), 695-720.

Prager, K. and Posthumus, H. (2010). Socio-economic factors influencing farmers' adoption of soil conservation practices in Europe, In Napier, T. (ed.)*Human Dimensions of Soil and Water Conservation. A Global Perspective*. Nova Science Publishers

Polland, M. (2006). *The Omnivore's Dilemma: A natural history of four meals*. Penguin Press.

Sanyé-Mengual, E., Anguelovski, I., Oliver-Solà, J., Montero, J. and Rieradevall, J. (2016). Resolving differing stakeholder perceptions of urban rooftop farming in Mediterranean cities: promoting food production as a driver for innovative forms of urban agriculture. *Agriculture and Human Values*, **33**(1), 101-120.

Schaefer, G. O. and Savulescu, J. (2014). The ethics of producing in vitro meat. *Journal of Applied Philosophy*. **31** (2), 188-202.

Serizawa, R., Shitara, M., Gong Jin, Makino, M., Kabir, M.H. and Furukawa, H. (2014). 3D jet printer of edible gels for food creation Proc. SPIE 9058, *Behavior and Mechanics of Multifunctional Materials and Composites*, 90580A (March 9); doi:10.1117/12.2045082 Conference Volume 9058.

Sher, D. and Tuto, X. (2015). Review of 3D food printing, *ELISAVA Temes de disseny*, **31**, 104-117.

Sky Greens. (2014) About Sky Greens. http://www.skygreens.com/about-skygreens/. Accessed 16 July 2016.

Smil, V. (2013). *Should We Eat Meat? Evolution and consequences of modern carnivory*. John Wiley & Sons.

Snook, R. (2014) Battery urban farm: A real working farm in downtown Manhattan with pick-your-own veggies & educational programs for kids. https://mommypoppins.com/content/battery-urban-farm-a-real-working-farm-in-downtown-manhattan-with-pick-your-own-veggies. Accessed 28/07/2016.

Southerland, D., Walters, P. and Huson, D. (2011). Edible 3D Printing. In conference proceedings of NIP & Digital Fabrication Conference, International Conference on Digital Printing Technologies. pp. 418-826.

Stanford, C.B. (1999). *The Hunting Apes: Meat eating and the origins of human behaviour.* Princeton University Press.

Sun, J., Zhou, W., Huang, D., Fuh, J. Y. and Hong, G.S. (2015). An overview of 3D printing technologies for food fabrication. *Food and Bioprocess Technology*, **8**(8), 1605–1615. doi:10.1007/s11947-015-1528-6).

Surnar, S.R., Sharma, O.P. and Saini, V.P., (2015). Aquaponics: Innovative farming. *International Journal of Fisheries and Aquatic Studies*, **2**(4), 261-263

Tey, Y. S. and Brindal, M. (2012). Factors influencing the adoption of precision agricultural technologies: a review for policy implications. *Precision Agriculture*, **13**(6), 713-730.

Thomaier, S., Specht, K., Henckel, D., Dierich, A., Siebert, R., Freisinger, U. B. and Sawicka, M. (2015). Farming in and on urban buildings: Present practice and specific novelties of Zero-Acreage Farming (ZFarming). *Renewable Agriculture and Food Systems*, **30**(01), 43-54.

Touliatos, D., Dodd, I.C. and McAinsh, M. (2016). Vertical farming increases lettuce yield per unit area compared to conventional horizontal hydroponics. *Food and Energy Security*, **5**(3), 184-191.

Tong, Z., Whitlow, T.H., Landers, A., Flanner, B. (2016). A case study of air quality above an urban roof top vegetable farm. *Environmental Pollution*, **208**, 256-260.

United Nations (2012). *World Urbanization Prospects: The 2014 Revision.* New York: UN, Dept of Economic and Social Affairs, (ST/ESA/SER.A/366). https://esa.un.org/unpd/wup/Publications/Files/WUP2014-Report.pdf. Accessed 27/07/2016.

Tropea F and Morvan, (2014) Precision Agriculture: an opportunity for EU farmers – potential support with the CAP, 2014-2020, European Parliament http://www.europarl.europa.eu/RegData/etudes/note/join/2014/529049/IPOL-AGRI_NT(2014)529049_EN.pdf

Urban Organics (n.d.) Urban Organics. http://www.urbanorganics.com/home/. Accessed 23/07/2016.

Vermeiren, K., Adiyia, B., Loopmans, M., Tumwine, F. R. and Van Rompaey, A. (2013). Will urban farming survive the growth of African cities: A case-study in Kampala (Uganda)?. *Land Use Policy*, **35**, 40-49.

Wojciechowska, R., Długosz-Grochowska, O., Kołton, A., Żupnik, M. (2015). Effects of LED supplemental lighting on yield and some quality parameters of lamb's lettuce grown in two winter cycles. *Scientia Horticulturae*, **187**, 80-86.

8

Yang, Y., Zheng, Y., Cao, W., Titov, A., Hyvonen, J., Manders, J.R., Xue, J., Holloway, P.H. and Qian, L., (2015). High-efficiency light-emitting devices based on quantum dots with tailored nanostructures. *Nature Photonics*, **9**(4), pp.259-266.

Yeh, N. and Chung, J. P. (2009). High-brightness LEDs – Energy efficient lighting sources and their potential in indoor plant cultivation. *Renewable and Sustainable Energy Reviews*, **13**(8), 2175-2180.

Zarco-Tejada, P., Hubbard, N. and Loudjani, P. (2014) *Precision Agriculture, an opportunity for EU farmers. Potential support with the CAP, 2014-2002*. Brussels, European Commission.

Zero Carbon Food (2016). Zero Carbon Food. http://www.zerocarbonfood.co.uk/. Accessed 25/07/2016.

Zhang, N., Wang, M. and Wang, N. (2002). Precision agriculture – a worldwide overview. *Computers and Electronics in Agriculture*, **36**(2), 113-132.

9 Alternative Food Production: Nanotechnology in Agri-food Applications

Frank Vriesekoop, Yongqin Wei, Renato Grillo and Hao Liang

Introduction

As indicated in the previous chapter, technological solutions have tended to be promoted as ways in which the issue of food security may be addressed. Another technological advance that affects the complete supply chain is that of nanotechnology. Nanotechnology can be explained as the science and technology used to design and build apparatuses in which almost every atom and chemical interaction is precisely known (Mukhopadhyay, 2014). Nanotechnology is not necessarily a specific set of techniques, devices or products, but rather the set of capabilities that can be utilized to achieve improvement in yields and exploitation beyond what can be achieved by traditional means. Nanoscience and nanotechnology have found applications in a wide range of fields, which include energy production (e.g. solar panels), medicine, electronics, communications, and agriculture and food (Sozer and Kokinin, 2009; Handford *et al.*, 2015; Azzawi, *et al.*, 2016; Hanaei *et al.*, 2016). Some nano-applications are based on nanodevices that mimic naturally occurring molecules such as proteins, DNA, and membranes; while other nano-applications work specifically on the premise that tiny particles are produced that have a markedly increased surface area per unit mass. In almost all instances, equivalents to nano particles can be found in nature. For instance, proteins from the planet's most abundant bacterium (*Pseudomonas syringae*) are present on all decaying plant material in autumn, and get carried into the atmosphere where the proteins act as nucleation sites for snowflakes (Davies, 2014). The equivalent nano-biotechnological application is the use of *P. syringae* derived biological ice nuclei for the production of artificial snow (Hara *et al.*, 2016). While the applications of nanotechnology are quite wide and diverse, this text will focus on some of the applications of nanotechnology as they apply to the agricultural and food supply chain in its broadest form.

Agricultural applications of nanotechnology

The search for sustainable agriculture through the development of new technologies or the improvement of existing farming practices has been one of the main goals to enhance food availability and to reduce the environmental impacts caused by traditional intensive agricultural practices such as agrochemicals (Anderson *et al.*, 2016). The use of nanotechnology in conjunction with biotechnology has proved to be a promising tool to combat such problems, promising higher yields in the field and lower production costs (Das *et al.*, 2015). In this way, several engineered nanomaterials (ENMs) with different compositions and morphologies are being synthesized with the aim of increasing the quality and production yields of crops, improving the physical-chemical stability of pesticides and fertilizers, minimizing nutrient losses during the application of fertilizers, reducing applications of plant protection products, and increasing yields through optimized nutrient management (Khot *et al.*, 2012; Campos *et al.*, 2014; Parisi *et al.*, 2014). Engineered nanomaterials present different properties compared to their more traditional counterparts, since ENMs have a greater surface area to volume ratio, and therefore they are more biologically available. Such ENMs are often employed in the form of lipids, polymers or emulsions, titanium dioxide nanoparticles (TiO2-NPs), silver nanoparticles (Ag-NPs) or silica nanoparticles (Si-NPs) (Gogos *et al.*, 2012; Martirosyan and Schneider, 2014). The United States and China are the pioneers in the development of ENMs, however many other countries, including Japan, Russia, South Korea, Brazil, Canada, Singapore, India, Germany and some other European countries, are increasing their studies and investments in the agricultural sector (Gogos *et al.*, 2012; Donga *et al.*, 2016).

Recently, a wide range of review articles have been described addressing the potential use of nanotechnology in agriculture (Nair *et al.*, 2010; Gogos *et al.*, 2012; Khot *et al.*, 2012; Kah and Hofmann, 2014; Cicek and Nadaroglu, 2015; Das *et al.*, 2015; Dasgupta *et al.*, 2015; Parisi *et al.*, 2015; Fraceto *et al.*, 2016; Grillo *et al.*, 2016; Rizwan *et al.*, 2017). Among these we can highlight: nanocarriers, the fabrication of nano and biosensors, synthesis of nanostructures, and the exploitation/development of catalytic properties of nanoparticles.

The development of nanocarriers can be associated with pesticides (de Oliveira *et al.*, 2014; Kashyap *et al.*, 2015; Grillo *et al.*, 2016), genes (Torney *et al.*, 2007) and fertilizers (Corradini *et al.*, 2010), whose main purpose is promoting a controlled release of these active ingredients in order to reduce their toxicity and improve the physical-chemical stability and specificity for target sites (Kah and Hofmann, 2014; Grillo *et al.*, 2016). The fabrication of nano- and biosensors can be used for enhancing the sensitivity and speed of detection of various active ingredients used in agriculture (Valdes *et al.*, 2009; Rai *et al.*, 2012; Duran and Marcato, 2013). Alternatively, nano- and biosensors can be employed to predict environmental changes that could compromise a crop, as well as assist in the diagnosis of pathogens (Valdes *et al.*, 2009; Gibson *et al.*, 2016). The synthesis of nanostructures can aid in facilitating enhanced seed germination and plant growth, for example, by treating it with carbon nanotubes (Haghighi and da Silva, 2014), or through soil management, using nanoclays or nanozeolites (Fraceto *et al.*, 2016). Finally, nanotechnology can be used in agriculture, through the synthesis or enhancement of catalytic properties of nanoparticles (e.g. TiO_2, silver, gold, platinum, SnO_2, ZnO), nanofilters, nanoadsorbents, and nanomembranes, for remediation of pesticides, dyes or metals in soils and water (Zheng *et al.*, 2008; Shan *et al.*, 2009; Patil *et al.*, 2016). In addition to these examples, the development of advanced hybrid systems, consisting of organic and inorganic materials with capacity to combine multiple applications on a single system, is rapidly becoming a hot research topic in nanoagriculture, as it is already established in nanomedicine (Nguyen and Zhao, 2015). Moreover, agriculture can be enhanced by applying nanotechnology in other economic sectors, such as energy efficiency, through the creation of new solar cells, fuel cells and batteries (Baxter *et al.*, 2009; Das *et al.*, 2015). Thus, it is possible to reduce irrigation costs (Alnaimi *et al.*, 2014) and to promote the development of more efficient electric drives and machines for agriculture (Karner *et al.*, 2014). Furthermore, it is also possible to produce nanotech-based tools and equipment with greater functionality and lifespan to be used by rural workers.

Food applications of nanotechnology

The food industry is directing new product development towards the area of functional foods, due to consumers' demand for healthier foods, containing lower concentrations of synthetic additives and a greater presence of compounds that facilitate biological functions that are perceived to be of benefit to maintaining a healthy lifestyle. Among the explorational nanotechnological studies that have been carried out in recent decades, there have been many functional components that have been rapidly and efficiently applied to the development of functional and improved foods. Many functional components, especially active ingredients in plants such as flavonoids, isoflavones, and anthocyanins, have preventive and therapeutic potential in the treatment and prevention of diseases. However, many of these components have low levels of solubility, stability and bioavailability in the human body, which makes their inclusion in (functional) foods at their effective levels in the target tissues somewhat unrealistic (Wang *et al.*, 2014). Formulation improvement into highly stable, water-soluble and orally bioavailable forms is regarded as a prerequisite for the nutritional or clinical application of those functional components (Shakeri and Sahebkar, 2016). Various nanotechnologies can be applied to compensate for their insolubility and consequent slow dissolution rate, which commonly includes nanoemulsions, solid lipid nanoparticles, micelles, nanoliposomes, and poly lactic-co-glycolic acid (PLGA) nanoparticles.

■ Nanoemulsions

Nanoemulsions are kinetically stable liquid-in-liquid dispersions with droplet sizes in the order of 100 nm. A typical (nano)emulsion contains oil, water, surfactant and possibly a co-surfactant (Figure 9.1) (Gupta *et al.*, 2016).

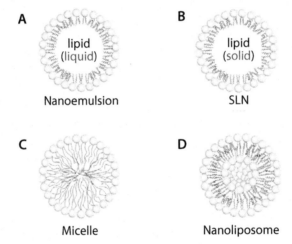

Figure 9.1: Schematic structure of nanoemulsion (A), solid lipid nanoparticle (B), micelle (C) and nanoliposome (D).

Emulsions may be of the oil-in-water (O/W) type, or water-in-oil (W/O) type; depending on whether the oil is dispersed as droplets in water (O/W), or as water droplets dispersed in oil as the continuous phase (W/O) (McClements, 2012). With regards to nanoemulsions, their nano size leads to advantageous properties such as: lasting stability, high surface area per unit volume, optically crystal clear appearance, and tunable rheology (Gupta *et al.*, 2016). Over the past decade or more, much research has focused on preparing nanoemulsions through various methods, broadly classified into two primary categories: high-energy and low-energy methods (Fryd and Mason, 2012; Solans *et al.*, 2005; Tadros *et al.*, 2004).

High-energy methods include the application of high-pressure homogenization and ultrasonication; while low-energy methods include phase inversion where an emulsion might start off as a W/O emulsion, but with the application of carefully selected (co)-surfactant and temperature conditions.

The various advantageous properties of nanoemulsions which have provided numerous applications in pharmacy as drug delivery systems (McClements, 2012), will find application in food in the future too. Due to the long-term stability issues, many proposed formulations are self-emulsifying systems in which the nanoemulsions are produced just before their application. In relation to food based applications, Zahi *et al.* (2014) proposed an approach for producing D-limonene organogel-based nanoemulsion by high-pressure homogenization technology to improve the hydrophobic and oxidative nature of this poorly water-soluble functional monoterpene. The organogel-based nanoemulsion application was then further explored in order to improve the antimicrobial activity of D-limonene (Zahi *et al.*, 2015). The concept of organogel-based nanoemulsions has also been explored in order to achieve greater antioxidant potential of the water-soluble tea polyphenols in oil-based applications (Shi *et al.*, 2014). Instead of just the application of a single active compound, the employment of multiple active compounds to achieve a multitude of beneficial characteristics has been successfully achieved (Zhang *et al.*, 2014, Bei *et al.*, 2015).

Both Bei *et al.* (2015) and Zhang *et al.* (2014) reported that organogel-nanoemulsion containing with D-limonene and nisin may be an effective antimicrobial system for the production and preservation of foods.

■ Solid lipid nanoparticles

Solid lipid nanoparticles (SLNs) (Figure 9.1 B), are an alternative novel carrier system to traditional nanocarriers such as polymeric nanoparticles and nanoemulsions. SLNs have a similar structure to the O/W nanoemulsion, including a hydrophilic shell and a hydrophobic lipid core, however, the lipid core is solid at room temperature (Puri *et al.*, 2009). Functional hydrophobic compounds can be encapsulated into the solid lipid core, resulting in an increased stability, reduced degradation, and sustained prolonged release (Müller *et al.*, 2000). SLNs are often favored because of their high biocompatibility, avoidance of organic solvent, excellent reproducibility, even using different preparation methods, and their easily scaled-up synthesis processes (Harde *et al.*, 2011). Li *et al.* (2016) prepared astaxanthin solid lipid nanoparticles with stearic acid. Astaxanthin is a keto-caroteroid with great antioxidative potential, found naturally in many foods. However, astaxanthin is poorly absorbed in the human digestive tract. The inclusion of astaxanthin in solid lipid nanoparticles significantly enhanced its chemical stability and SLNs could provide prolonged release of ASTA in simulated gastric and intestinal juices (Li *et al.*, 2016).

■ Micelles

Micelles are self-assembling nanosized colloidal particles with a hydrophobic core and hydrophilic shell that are currently successfully used as pharmaceutical carriers for water-insoluble drugs, and demonstrate a series of attractive properties as drug carriers. (Kwon *et al.*, 1995). The traditional micelles are lipid based (Figure 9.1 C), and usually have a diameter between 20 and 80 nm. When amphiphilic phospholipid concentrations reach the critical micelle concentration and temperatures reach the critical micellization temperature, micelles are formed (Lim *et al.*, 2012). Benzaria *et al.* (2013) prepared phosphocaseins micelles containing curcumin. The phosphocaseins micelles were found to be resistant to pepsin but were degraded by pancreatin, providing the possibility of a spatiotemporally controlled release and protection of bound biomolecules.

■ Nanoliposomes

Liposomes are spherical vesicles composed of one or more phospholipid bilayers (Figure 9.1 D). Lipophilic functional compounds can be incorporated into the lipid bilayers while hydrophilic compounds can be solubilized in the inner aqueous core (Gregoriadis and Florence, 1993). Nevertheless, nanoliposomes having the same chemical, structural and thermodynamic properties as micro liposomes, could yield larger interfacial areas of encapsulated compounds with biological tissues and thus provide higher potential to increase the bioavailability of encapsulated compounds (Mozafari *et al.*, 2009). Zou *et al.* (2014) successfully prepared tea polyphenol nanoliposomes and found that their nanoliposome encapsulated tea polyphenols achieved equivalent antioxidant activities compared with unencapsulated tea polyphenol solution. However, the nanoliposome encapsulated tea polyphenols had a marked improved stability in alkaline conditions.

■ Inclusion complexes

Other than the nanoemulsified applications, there are also other technologies used for functional components, such as solid dispersions, inclusion technology, etc. Inclusion complexes, which are comprised of a host molecule and a guest molecule, have been widely used in pharmaceutical applications (Loftsson and Duchêne, 2007; Lakkakula and Krause, 2014; Jambhekar and Breen, 2016). The most commonly used host materials for complexation are cyclodextrin, cholic acid, starch, cellulose, and proteins. Among all potential host materials, the cyclodextrins seem to be the most utilised ones, due to their versatile characteristics which make them suitable for applications in analytical chemistry, agriculture, the pharmaceutical field, in food and cosmetic articles (Szejtli, 1998).

Cyclodextrins are cyclic (α-1,4)-linked oligosaccharides of α-D-glucopyranose having a toroid-shaped molecular structure (Figure 9.2 A), containing a relatively hydrophobic central cavity and a more hydrophilic outer surface (Loftsson and Brewester, 1996). Depending on the number of glucopyranose units included in their cyclic structure, they are either be referred to as α-CD, β-CD, and γ -CD for 6, 7, or 8 units respectively. The greater the number of glucopyranose units, the larger the inner toroid space to carry guest compounds in. The most notable feature of cyclodextrins is their ability to form inclusion complexes (host-guest complexes, Figure 9.2 B) with a wide variety of hydrophobic molecules by a molecular complexation. This can lead to advantageous changes in the chemical and physical properties of the guest molecules (Del Valle, 2004). Cyclodextrins have no reported innate antimicrobial properties, and they can be considered to be nutritionally inert with no adverse effects on human health (Szente, 2004).

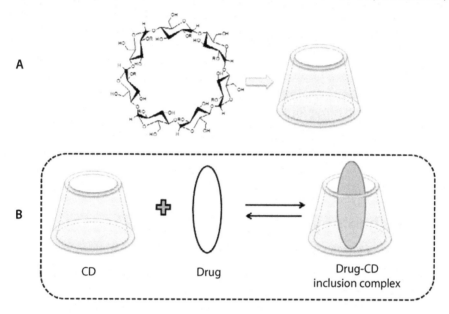

Figure 9.2: Chemical structure of the β-cyclodextrin molecule (a) and the schematic illustration of drug-CD inclusion complex (1:1).

There are numerous applications associated with functional components benefiting from cyclodextrin inclusion complexes. The physical stability of sulforaphane (a potent anticancer and antioxidant compound) could be enhanced by forming an inclusion complex with HP-β-cyclodextrins, while the anticancer and antioxidant function of sulforaphane was still maintained (Wu *et al.*, 2010). Furthermore, a range of cyclodextrins were shown to enhance the antimicrobial potency of essential oils against both bacteria and yeasts (Liang *et al.*, 2012); while Inagaki *et al.* (2016) reported that α-cyclodextrins could enhance the solubility of piceatannol (a naturally occurring antiviral compound) in both neutral and acidic solutions and improve the piceatannol absorption in the small intestine.

Nanotechnology in food packaging

Apart from the direct applications of nanotechnology in agricultural production and food products; nanotechnology plays an increasing important role in food packaging. The key functions of food packaging systems include:

- to simply contain the product;
- to facilitate transportation and distribution;
- to protect and preserve the quality of the product;
- to present and identify the product;
- to provide various types of information (i.e. use-by-date, nutritional information. etc.).

The potential benefits of nanotechnology in food packaging fit a number of the key functions of packaging. For instance, nano applications are developed and used to achieve improved packaging which overlaps with simple containment and maintaining quality through: temperature and moisture stability; mechanical strength; and durability and stability. On the other hand, there are nanotechnological applications that can be characterized as either: active packaging (scavengers, emitters, and blockers); intelligent packaging (quality indicators, data devices, holograms, etc.); and smart packaging (self-cleaning, self-healing, self-cooling, and self-heating) (Mlalila *et al.*, 2016).

■ Nanotechnology and improved food packaging

Containment longevity of packing materials is of great importance. It might well be sufficient to place a food product in a container so that the product will be held within that container; however, many foods are stored in warehouses for very long periods of time and the packaging material have to be able to withstand varying temperature and moisture conditions. This means maintaining the integrity of the packaging material itself and the integrity of the food materials stored within the packaging material. Clay nanoparticles and nanocrystals can be included into standard packing materials (paper, cardboard, plastics, etc.) as nanoreinforcement components in such a manner that temperature or moisture progression through the materials is markedly delayed (de Azeredo, 2009; Kuswandi, 2016). Furthermore, the inclusion of nanocomposites can enhance the packaging material's thermal degradation temperature, which has been employed in the packaging in boil-in-bag foods (Arora and Padua, 2010; Kuswandi, 2016). These nanoreinforcements present benefits both in terms of quality retainment of the products stored in the packaging materials, and the strength and durability of the packaging material itself.

Nanotechnology and active food packaging

In the application of active packaging, nanomaterials are employed to enhance the protection of the product by either interaction with the food on the inside of the packaging or with the environment on the outside of the packaging material. For instance, silver-based nanomaterials can be incorporated into the packaging material as an extrinsic antimicrobial barrier to limit the microbial ingress after the food has already been packaged (Llorens *et al.*, 2012). Nanotechnology applications that delay the ripening of climacteric foods have been successfully implemented by scavenging the gaseous, ripening-promoting plant hormone ethylene through the inclusion of nano-palladium, nano-titanium or nano-silver in packaging materials (Fujimoto *et al.*, 1974; Fernandez *et al.*, 2010; Llorenz *et al.*, 2012).

TiO$_2$ nanoparticles provide many protective attributes to food packaging, including protecting food from the photodegradative influence of UV irradiation while maintaining efficient optical clarity of transparent packaging material (Duncan, 2011).

Nanotechnology and intelligent food packaging

Intelligent food packaging is not a stand-alone application, instead it is part of a systematic approach which provides the ability to monitor the conditions and quality of food products in the supply chain, particularly during distribution and storage of the packaged food (Bastarrachea *et al.*, 2011). Intelligent food packaging can inform distributors and consumers about the status of the food while still in the unopened package (Biji *et al.*, 2015). For instance, time-temperature indicators with nano-inclusions on strips have been used successfully for nearly two decades to confirm that foods have been kept at the appropriate temperatures during storage and distribution (Taoukis and Labuza, 1989). Similarly, gas indicators have been employed that could inform the user of the packaged food whether the packaging or its content were exposed to conditions not conducive to good product quality, such as oxygen indicators in vacuum packed foods. These applications also extend to gas sensors that can be used detect the presence of specific micro-organisms based on their characteristic gas emissions (Biji *et al.*, 2015).

Intelligent food packaging also includes the use of freshness indicators, which can provide a signal output that indicates functions of product quality. The freshness indicators typically display an output based on a reaction between the microbial growth-related metabolites and the integrated nano-indicators within the package. For instance, colourimetric indicator labels that react to volatile amines have been used to indicate the relative freshness of fish and seafood products (Hogan and Kerry 2008). Similarly, biobased pH nano-indicators that can be incorporated into food packaging material were developed by Yoshida *et al.* (2014) in order to detect common metabolites associated with microbial growth.

9

An elevated presence of microbial metabolites is then taken as an indication of storage beyond freshness.

Another application of nanotechnology in food packaging is the inclusion of data capturing devices. The most common application involves the use of radio-frequency identification (RFID), which is an automatic identification technology that uses wireless sensors to identify items and gather data without human intervention. In order to facilitate the communication between the package-associated nanodevice and the user, the data on the device is read by an external reader Hong *et al.*, 2011). In many instances these nanodevices are powered by a reader. When radio waves from the reader are encountered by a RFID nanodevice, a component within the nanodevice will establish a magnetic field that fuels the energy requirement of the nanodevice in order to transmit its stored data (Biji *et al.*, 2015). A very visual presence of applications of nanotechnology associated with food packaging is the use of holograms to assure product authenticity, and in the battle to combat counterfeiting and tax evasion (Li, 2013; Shah *et al.*, 2010; Dobrucka and Ryszard, 2014).

Nanotechnology and smart food packaging

Smart packaging applications involve the packaging of ready meals which have the ability to facilitate the self-heating of food without external heat sources or power. Self-heating packaging employs calcium or magnesium oxide and water to generate an exothermic reaction (e.g. Bommaraju, 2007). It has been used for plastic coffee cans, military rations, and on-the-go meal platters (Brody *et al.*, 2008). Traditional self-heating devices occupy a significant amount of volume within the package; nano-applications will be able to reduce the overall volume required to accommodate the self-heating system. Self-cooling packaging, on the other hand, incorporates the evaporation of an externally applied compound (e.g. water), where the heat of evaporation draws heat from the contents contained within the packaging material (Brody *et al.*, 2008).

Apart from the thermal smart nano-applications, self-healing and self-cleaning are also nano-application in food packaging. Self-healing (or self-repairing) applications involve dynamic swelling and electrostatic repairing of polyelectrolyte multilayers and pre-embedded healing agents distributed throughout the packaging materials (Zhu *et al.*, 2015). With these nano-inclusions, various minor fractures, tears and even corrosion induced wear-and-tear can be repaired in-situ, providing improved storage capabilities of packaging material. Self-cleaning packaging materials often involve the inclusion of nanocomposites that impose superhydrophobicity and reduced contact angle (Mlalila *et al.*, 2016). Much of the underpinning success of any self-cleaning application is to attempt to decrease the wettability of the packaging material, which is supposed to result in a poor contact of any dirt with the packaging material (Youngblood and Sottos, 2008).

Concluding remarks

Given the low levels of solubility, stability and bioavailability of active ingredients in foods of functional components in the body, nanotechnologies are a promising tool for increasing bioavailability and bioactivities. While there is a need for continued researches in many other relatively unexplored potential uses, such as the cost-effectiveness and the safety of long-term using for those nanoparticles.

Although there is much potential of nanotechnology in agricultural and food applications, we know that the real applications of these ENMs are only marginally implemented in commercial application, with the greatest interest in ENMs still in R&D stage (Das *et al.*, 2015; Dasgupta *et al.*, 2015). One of the main reasons for the lack of commercial uptake of the technology is the lack of regulation for ENMs, since little is known about equipment and analytical methodologies capable of identifying the potential interactions and toxic effects of ENMs in the environment and with regards to human health (Amenta *et al.*, 2015; Fraceto *et al.*, 2016; Patil *et al.*, 2016). It is well established that properties, such as: size, shape, chemical composition, physiochemical stability, crystal structure, surface area and surface roughness, all influence the toxicity effects of the ENMs in different organisms (Gatoo *et al.*, 2014), which further increase the difficulties of standardizing the toxicity protocols (Wang *et al.*, 2016). In addition, most of the toxicity studies conducted are not be able to reach the potential risks of ENMs for sensitive receptors such as humans, plants and animals (Patil *et al.*, 2016; Servin and White, 2016). In this context, new studies must be undertaken or improved in order to better understand the risks and benefits of nanomaterials, addressing themes such as, impacts in nutritional quality, trans generational studies, trophic transfer, low doses exposures, effects in plants and co-contaminant, as well described by Servin and White (2016).

In conclusion, nanotechnology has been shown as a potential sustainability tool throughout the agri-food sector, which may increase production and quality of agricultural products, better utilization of active components within foods, and smarter packaging materials, bringing numerous socio-economic and quality benefits for the planet.

9

References

Alnaimi, F.B.I., Chu, Y.C., and Sahari, K.S.M. (2014). Hybrid renewable power system for agriculture irrigation system. System Integration (SII), 2014 IEEE/SICE International Symposium, 736 - 742.

Amenta, V., Aschberger, K., Arena, M., Bouwmeester, H., Moniz, F.B., Brandhoff, P., Gottardo, S., Marvin, H.J.P., Mech, A., Pesudo, L.Q., Rauscher, H., Schoonjans, R., Vettori, M.V., Weigel, S. and Peters, R.J. (2015). Regulatory aspects of nanotechnology in the agri/feed/food sector in EU and non-EU countries. *Regulatory Toxicology and Pharmacology*, **73**, 463-476.

Anderson, J.A., Gipmans, M., Hurst, S., Layton, R., Nehra, N., Pickett, J., Shah, D.M., Souza, T.L.P.O. and Tripathi, L. (2016). Emerging agricultural biotechnologies for sustainable agriculture and food security. *Journal of Agricultural and Food Chemistry*, **64**(2), 383-393.

Arora, A. and Padua, G.W. (2010). Review: nanocomposites in food packaging. *Journal of Food Science*, **75**(1), R43–R49.

Azzawi, M., Seifalian, A. and Ahmed, W. (2016). Nanotechnology for the diagnosis and treatment of diseases. *Nanomedicine*, **11**(16),2025-2027.

Bastarrachea, L., Dhawan, S. anf Sablani, S. S. (2011). Engineering properties of polymeric-based antimicrobial films for food packaging: a review. *Food Engineering Reviews*, **3**(2), 79-93.

Baxter, J., Bian, Z.X., Chen, G., Danielson, D., Dresselhaus, M.S., Fedorov, A.G., Fisher, T.S., Jones, C.W., Maginn, E., Kortshagen, U., Manthiram, A., Nozik, A., Rolison, D.R., Sands, T., Shi, L., Sholl, D. and Wu, Y.Y. (2009). Nanoscale design to enable the revolution in renewable energy. *Energy & Environmental Science*, **2**(6), 559-588.

Bei, W., Zhou, Y., Xing, X., Zahi, Z. M. R., Li, Y., Yuan, Q., & Liang, H. (2015). Organogel-nanoemulsion containing nisin and D-limonene and its antimicrobial activity. *Frontiers in Microbiology*, **6**. https://www.ncbi.nlm.nih.gov/pmc/articles/PMC4585035/

Benzaria, A., Maresca, M., Taieb, N. and Dumay, E. (2013). Interaction of curcumin with phosphocasein micelles processed or not by dynamic high-pressure. *Food Chemistry*, **138**(4), 2327-2337.

Biji, K.B., Ravishankar, C.N., Mohan, C.O. and Gopal, T.S. (2015). Smart packaging systems for food applications: a review. *Journal of Food Science and Technology*, **52**(10),6125-6135.

Bommaraju, T.V. (2007). Hydrogen mitigation and energy generation with water-activated chemical heaters. U.S. Patent Application 11/657,852.

Brody, A.L., Bugusu, B., Han, J.H., Sand, C.K. and McHugh, T.H., (2008). Innovative food packaging solutions. *Journal of Food Science*, **73**(8), R107-R116.

Campos, E.V.R., de Oliveira, J.L. and Fraceto, L.F. (2014). Applications of controlled release systems for fungicides, herbicides, acaricides, nutrients, and plant growth hormones: A review. *Advanced Science, Engineering and Medicine*, **6**(4), 373-387..

Cicek, S. and Nadaroglu, H. (2015). The use of nanotechnology in the agriculture. *Advances in Nano Research*, **3**(4), 207-223.

Corradini, E., de Moura, M.R. and Mattoso, L.H.C. (2010). A preliminary study of the incorparation of NPK fertilizer into chitosan nanoparticles. *Express Polymer Letters*, **4**(8), 509-515.

Das, S., Sen, B. and Debnath, N. (2015). Recent trends in nanomaterials applications in environmental monitoring and remediation. *Environmental Science and Pollution Research*, **22**(23), 18333-18344.

Dasgupta, N., Ranjan, S., Mundekkad, D., Ramalingam, C., Shanker, R. and Kumar, A. (2015). Nanotechnology in agro-food: From field to plate. *Food Research International*, **69**, 381-400.

Davies, P.L. (2014). Ice-binding proteins: a remarkable diversity of structures for stopping and starting ice growth. *Trends in Biochemical Sciences*, **39**(11),548-555.

de Azeredo, H.M. (2009). Nanocomposites for food packaging applications. *Food Research International*, **42**(9),1240-1253.

de Oliveira, J.L., Campos, E.V.R., Bakshi, M., Abhilash, P.C., and Fraceto, L.F. (2014). Application of nanotechnology for the encapsulation of botanical insecticides for sustainable agriculture: Prospects and promises. *Biotechnology Advances*, **32**(8), 1550-1561.

Del Valle, E. M. M. (2004). Cyclodextrins and their uses: a review. *Process Biochemistry*, **39**(9), 1033-1046.

Dobrucka, R. and Cierpiszewski, R. (2014). Active and intelligent packaging food-research and development–a review. *Polish Journal of Food and Nutrition Sciences*, **64**(1), 7–15.

Donga, H., Gao, Y., Sinkob, P.J., Wu, Z., Xua, J. and Jia, L. (2016). The nanotechnology race between China and the United States. *Nano Today*, **11**(1), 7-12.

Duncan, T.V.(2011). Applications of nanotechnology in food packaging and food safety: barrier materials, antimicrobials and sensors. *Journal of Colloid and Interface Science*, **363**(1), 1-24.

Duran, N. and Marcato, P.D. (2013). Nanobiotechnology perspectives. Role of nanotechnology in the food industry: a review. *International Journal of Food Science and Technology*, **48**(6), 1127-1134.

Fernandez, A., Picouet, P. and Lloret, E. (2010). Cellulose-silver nanoparticle hybrid materials to control spoilage-related microflora in absorbent pads located in trays of fresh-cut melon. *International Journal of Food Microbiology*, **142**(1), 222-228.

Fraceto, L.F., Grillo, R., de Medeiros, G.A., Scognamiglio,V., Rea, G. and Bartolucci, C. (2016). Nanotechnology in agriculture: Which innovation potential does it have? *Frontiers Environmental Science*, **4**, art. 20.

9

Fryd, M.M. and Mason, T.G. (2012). Advanced nanoemulsions. *Annual Review of Physical Chemistry*, **63**, 493-518.

Fujimoto, K., Takeda, H. and Kunugi, T. (1974). Catalytic oxidation of ethylene to acetaldehyde. Palladium chloride-active charcoal catalyst. *Industrial Engineering Chemistry*, **13**(4), 237-242.

Gatoo, M.A., Naseem, S., Arfat, M.Y., Dar, A.M., Qasim, K. and Zubair, S. (2014). Physicochemical properties of nanomaterials: implication in associated toxic manifestations. *Biomedical Research International*, art. 498420.

Gibson, T. (2016). Use of VOC analysers in non-laboratory settings for early detection of disease, *Sensors in Food and Agriculture Conference*, Cambridge, United Kingdom.

Gogos, A., Knauer, K. and Bucheli, T.D. (2012). Nanomaterials in plant protection and fertilization: Current state, foreseen applications, and research priorities. *Journal of Agricultural and Food Chemistry*, **60**(39), 9781-9792.

Gregoriadis, G. and Florence, A. T. (1993). Liposomes in drug delivery. *Drugs*, **45**(1), 15-28.

Grillo, R., Abhilash, P.C. and Fraceto, L.F. (2016). Nanotechnology applied to bio-encapsulation of pesticides. *Journal of Nanoscience and Nanotechnology*, **16**(1), 1231-1234.

Guptaa, A., Eralbc, H. B., Hattona, T. A. and Doyle, P. S. (2016). Nanoemulsions: formation, properties and applications. *Soft Matter*, **12**(11), 2826-2841.

Haghighi, M., and da Silva, J.A.T. (2014). The effect of carbon nanotubes on the seed germination and seedling growth of four vegetable species. *Journal of Crop Science and Biotechnology*, **17**(4), 201-208.

Hanaei, H., Assadi, M.K. and Saidur, R. (2016). Highly efficient antireflective and self-cleaning coatings that incorporate carbon nanotubes (CNTs) into solar cells: A review. *Renewable and Sustainable Energy Reviews*, **59**, 620-635.

Handford, C. E., Dean, M., Spence, M., Henchion, M., Elliott, C. T. and Campbell, K. (2015). Awareness and attitudes towards the emerging use of nanotechnology in the agri-food sector. *Food Control*, **57**, 24-34.

Hara, K., Maki, T., Kakikawa, M., Kobayashi, F. and Matsuki, A. (2016). Effects of different temperature treatments on biological ice nuclei in snow samples. *Atmospheric Environment*, **140**, 415-419.

Harde, H., Das, M. and Jain, S. (2011). Solid lipid nanoparticles: an oral bioavailability enhancer vehicle. *Expert Opinion on Drug Delivery*, **8**(11), 1407-1424.

Hogan, S.A. and Kerry, J.P., (2008) Smart packaging of meat and poultry products. In: Kerry, J., Butler, P. (eds), *Smart Packaging Technologies for Fast Moving Consumer Goods*. Chichester: John Wiley & Sons, pp. 33–59

Hong, H., Dang, J., Tsai, Y., Liu, C., Lee, W. and Chen, P. (2011). An RFID application in the food supply chain: A case study of convenience stores in Taiwan. *Journal of Food Engineering*, **106**(2), 119–126

Inagaki, H., Ito, R., Setoguchi, Y., Oritani, Y. and Ito, T. (2016). Administration of piceatannol complexed with alpha-cyclodextrin improves its absorption in rats. *Journal of Agricultural and Food Chemistry*, **64**(18), 3557-3563.

Jambhekar, S.S. and Breen, P. (2016). Cyclodextrins in pharmaceutical formulations I: structure and physicochemical properties, formation of complexes, and types of complex. *Drug Discovery Today*, **21**(2),356-362.

Kah, M. and Hofmann, T. (2014). Nanopesticides research: State of knowledge, current trends, and future priorities. *Abstracts of Papers of the American Chemical Society*, **248**.

Karner, J., Baldinger, M. and Reichl, B. (2014). Prospects of hybrid systems on agricultural machinery. *Journal on Agricultural Engineering*, **1**(1), 33-37.

Kashyap, P.L., Xiang, X. and Heiden, P. (2015). Chitosan nanoparticle based delivery systems for sustainable agriculture. *International Journal of Biological Macromolecules*, **77**, 36-51.

Khot, L.R., Sankaran, S., Maja, J.M., Ehsani, R. and Schuster, E.W. (2012). Applications of nanomaterials in agricultural production and crop protection: A review. *Crop Protection*, **35**, 64-70.

Kuswandi, B. (2016). Nanotechnology in food packaging. In Ranjan, S., Dasgupta, N., Lichtfouse, E. (eds.), *Nanoscience in Food and Agriculture* (1), pp. 151-183. Springer International Publishing, Cham, Switzerland.

Kwon, G. S., Naito, M., Yokoyama, M., Okano, T., Sakurai, Y. and Kataoka, K. (1995). Physical entrapment of adriamycin in AB block copolymer micelles. *Pharmaceutical Research*, **12**(2), 192-195.

Lakkakula, J.R. and Krause, R.W.M. (2014). A vision for cyclodextrin nanoparticles in drug delivery systems and pharmaceutical applications. *Nanomedicine*, **9**(6),877-894.

Li, L. (2013). Technology designed to combat fakes in the global supply chain. *Business Horizons*, **56**(2),167-177.

Li, M., Zahi, M. R., Yuan, Q., Tian, F. and Liang, H. (2016). Preparation and stability of astaxanthin solid lipid nanoparticles based on stearic acid. *European Journal of Lipid Science and Technology*, **118**(4), 592-602.

Liang, H., Yuan, Q., Vriesekoop, F. and Lv, F. (2012). Effects of cyclodextrins on the antimicrobial activity of plant-derived essential oil compounds. *Food Chemistry*, **135**(3), 1020-1027.

Lim, S. B., Banerjee, A. and Önyüksel, H. (2012). Improvement of drug safety by the use of lipid-based nanocarriers. *Journal of Controlled Release*, **163**(1), 34-45.

Llorens, A., Lloret, E., Picouet, P.A., Trbojevich, R. and Fernandez, A., 2012. Metallic-based micro and nanocomposites in food contact materials and active food packaging. *Trends in Food Science & Technology*, **24**(1),19-29.

Loftsson, T. and Duchêne, D. (2007). Cyclodextrins and their pharmaceutical applications. *International Journal of Pharmaceutics*, **329**(1),1-11.

Loftsson, T. and Brewester, M. (1996). Pharmaceutical applications of cyclodextrins (1). Drug solubilization and stabilization. *Journal of Pharmacetical Sciences*, **85**(10), 1017-1025.

Martirosyan, A. and Schneider, Y.J. (2014). Engineered nanomaterials in food: implications for food safety and consumer health. *International Journal of Environmental Research and Public Health*, **11**(6),5720-5750.

McClements, D. J. (2012). Nanoemulsions versus microemulsions: terminology, differences, and similarities. *Soft Matter*, **8**(6), 1719-1729.

Mlalila, N., Kadam, D.M., Swai, H. and Hilonga, A. (2016). Transformation of food packaging from passive to innovative via nanotechnology: concepts and critiques. *Journal of Food Science and Technology*, **53**(9),3395-3407.

Mozafari, M. R., Pardakhtyb, A., Azarmic, S., Jazayerid, J. A., Nokhodchie, A. and Omrif, A. (2009). Role of nanocarrier systems in cancer nanotherapy. *Journal of Liposome Research*, **19**(4), 310-321.

Mukhopadhyay, S.S. (2014). Nanotechnology in agriculture: prospects and constraints. *Nanotechnology, Science and Applications*, 7,63-71.

Müller, R.H., Mäder, K. and Gohla, S. (2000). Solid lipid nanoparticles (SLN) for controlled drug delivery - a review of the state of the art. *European Journal of Pharmaceutics and Biopharmaceutics*, **50**(1), 161-177.

Nair, R., Varghese, S.H., Nair, B.G., Maekawa, T., Yoshida, Y. and Kumar, D.S. (2010). Nanoparticulate material delivery to plants. *Plant Science*, **179**(3), 154-163.

Nguyen, K.T. and Zhao, Y.L. (2015). Engineered hybrid nanoparticles for on-demand diagnostics and therapeutics. *Accounts of Chemical Research*, **48**(12), 3016-3025.

Parisi, C., Vigani, M. and Rodriguez-Cerezo, E. (2015). Agricultural nanotechnologies: What are the current possibilities? *Nano Today*, **10**(2), 124-127.

Parisi, C., Vigani, M. and Rodríguez-Cerezo, M. (2014). *Proceedings of a workshop on 'Nanotechnology for the agricultural sector: from research to the field'*. Luxembourg: Publications Office of the European Union.

Patil, S.S., Shedbalkar, U.U., Truskewyczc, A., Chopaded, B.A. and Ball, A.S. (2016). Nanoparticles for environmental clean-up: A review of potential risks and emerging solutions. *Environmental Technology & Innovation*, **5**, 10-21.

Puri, A., Loomis, K., Smith, B., Lee, J.-H., Yavlovich, A., Heldman, E. and Blumenthal, R. (2009). Lipid-based nanoparticles as pharmaceutical drug carriers: from concepts to clinic. *Critical Reviews in Therapeutic Drug Carrier Systems*, **26**(6), 523.

Rai, V., Acharya, S. and Dey, N. (2012). Implications of nanobiosensors in agriculture. *Journal of Biomaterials and Nanobiotechnology*, **3**, 315-324.

Rizwan, M., Ali, S., Qayyum, M.F., Ok, Y.S., Adrees, M., Ibrahim, M., Zia-ur-Rehman, M., Farid, M. and Abbas, F. 92017). Effect of metal and metal oxide nanoparticles on growth and physiology of globally important food crops: a critical review. *Journal of Hazardous Materials*, **322**, 2-16.

Servin, A.L., and White, J.C. (2016). Nanotechnology in agriculture: Next steps for understanding engineered nanoparticle exposure and risk. *NanoImpact*, **1**, 9-12.

Shah, R.Y., Prajapati, P.N. and Agrawal, Y.K. (2010). Anticounterfeit packaging technologies. *Journal of Advanced Pharmaceutical Technology and Research*, **1**(4), 368-373.

Shakeri, A. and Sahebkar, A. (2016). Opinion paper: Nanotechnology: A successful approach to improve oral bioavailability of phytochemicals. *Recent Patents on Drug Delivery & Formulation*, **10**(1), 4-6.

Shan, G.B., Surampalli, R.Y., Tyagi, R.D. and Zhang, T.C. (2009). Nanomaterials for environmental burden reduction, waste treatment, and nonpoint source pollution control: a review. *Frontiers of Environmental Science & Engineering in China*, **3**, 249-264.

Shi, R., Zhang, Q., Vriesekoop, F., Yuan, Q. and Liang, H. (2014). Preparation of organogel with tea polyphenols complex for enhancing the antioxidation properties of edible oil. *Journal of Agricultural and Food Chemistry*, **62**(33), 8379-8384.

Solans, C., Izquierdo, P., Nolla, J., Azemar, N. and Garcia-Celma, M. J. (2005). Nano-emulsions. *Current Opinion in Colloid and Interface Science*, **10**(3), 102-110.

Sozer, N. and Kokini, J. L. (2009). Nanotechnology and its applications in the food sector. *Trends in Biotechnology*, **27**(2), 82-89.

Szejtli, J. (1998). Introduction and general overview of cyclodextrin chemistry. *Chemical Reviews*, **98**(5), 1743-1753.

Szente, L. (2004). Cyclodextrins as food ingredients. *Trends in Food Science and Technology*, **15**(3), 137–142.

Tadros, T., Izquierdo, P., Esquena, J. and Solans, C. (2004). Formation and stability of nano-emulsions. *Advances in Colloid and Interface Science*, **108**, 303-318.

Taoukis, P.S. and Labuza, T.P. (1989). Applicability of time-temperature indicators as shelf life monitors of food products. *Journal of Food Science*, **54**(4),783-788.

Torney, F., Trewyn, B.G., Lin, V.S.Y. and Wang, K. (2007). Mesoporous silica nanoparticles deliver DNA and chemicals into plants. *Nature Nanotechnology*, **2**(5), 295-300.

Valdes, M.G., Gonzalez, A.C.V., Calzon, J.A.G. and Diaz-Garcia, M.E. (2009). Analytical nanotechnology for food analysis. *Microchimica Acta*, **166**(1-2), 1-19.

Wang, P., Lombi, Z., Zhao, F. and Kopittke, P.M. (2016). Nanotechnology:A new opportunity in plant sciences. *Trends in Plant Science*, **21**(8),699-712.

Wang, S., Su, R., Nie, S., Sun, M., Zhang, J., Wu, D. and Moustaid-Moussa, N. (2014). Application of nanotechnology in improving bioavailability and bioactivity of diet-derived phytochemicals. *Journal of Nutritional Biochemistry*, **25**(4), 363-376.

Wu, H., Liang, H., Yuan, Q., Wang, T. and Yan, X. (2010). Preparation and stability investigation of the inclusion complex of sulforaphane with hydroxypropyl-β-cyclodextrin. *Carbohydrate Polymers*, **82**(3), 613-617.

Yoshida, C.M., Maciel, V.B.V., Mendonça, M.E.D. and Franco, T.T. (2014). Chitosan biobased and intelligent films: Monitoring pH variations. *LWT-Food Science and Technology*, **55**(1),83-89.

9

Youngblood, J.P. and Sottos, N.R., 2008. Bioinspired materials for self-cleaning and self-healing. *Material Research Society Bulletin*, 33(8),732-741.

Zahi, M. R., Wan, P., Liang, H. and Yuan, Q. (2014). Formation and stability of d-limonene organogel-based nanoemulsion prepared by a high-pressure homogenizer. *Journal of Agricultural and Food Chemistry*, 62(52), 12563-12569.

Zahi, M.R., Liang, H. and Yuan, Q.(2015). Improving the antimicrobial activity of d-limonene using a novel organogel-based nanoemulsion. *Food Control*, **50**, 554-559.

Zhang, Z., Vriesekoop, F., Yuan, Q. and Liang, H. (2014). Effects of nisin on the antimicrobial activity of D-limonene and its nanoemulsion. *Food Chemistry*, **150**, 307-312.

Zheng, F., Li, C., Yuan, Q. and Vriesekoop, F. (2008). Influence of molecular shape on the retention of small molecules by solvent resistant nanofiltration (SRNF) membranes: A suitable molecular size parameter. *Journal of Membrane Science*, **318**(1), 114-122.

Zhu, D.Y., Rong, M.Z. and Zhang, M.Q. (2015). Self-healing polymeric materials based on microencapsulated healing agents: From design to preparation. *Progress in Polymer Science*, **49**,175-220.

Zou, L.-Q., Liu, W., Liu, W.-L., Liang, R.-H., Li, T., Liu, C.-M., Cao, Y.-L., Niu, J. and Liu, Z. (2014). Characterization and bioavailability of tea polyphenol nanoliposome prepared by combining an ethanol injection method with dynamic high-pressure microfluidization. *Journal of Agricultural and Food Chemistry*, **62**(4), 934-941.

10 The Role of Urban and Peri-urban Agriculture in Food Security and Resilience

Luís Kluwe Aguiar and Jane Eastham

Introduction

In Chapter 8, it has been suggested that urban agriculture is a potential means by which to address the issue of food security. Utilising any available space within urban areas would not only increase the land available for production but would also produce food in the locale in which is predominantly consumed. In this next chapter, the issue is examined in more depth and places a question of the extent to which the solution is realistic.

The Anthropocene period, a term used to define the epoch in which human activities have started to have an impact on the Earth's geology and ecosystems, has been deemed to have begun at the start of the Industrial Revolution (Rockstrom, 2009). It is now seen to have reached a point beyond the 'safe operating space' threshold, a term which refers to a point at which certain natural systems have become irreversibly destroyed and lost. These events have placed increasing pressure on the resilience of the food system, particularly where there is increasing competition for resources, such as land.

Urban agriculture is defined as the production of crop and livestock goods within cities and towns, and has been one of the ways in which policy makers have sought to address these problems. Indeed, it is suggested that the sector is growing rapidly with some 200 million people employed within the sector, contributing food to around 800 million urban dwellers.

Rigorous empirical research into the reality of benefits generated by urban agriculture is sparse, yet intuitively it makes sense to put into food production otherwise waste land that is in close proximity to populations to increase the availability, when we are faced with issues of population growth and land constraints and the ecological impact of feeding people. Yet, it is important to note that there is limited existing literature that examines in any depth the impact of urban agriculture on food poverty. There is little research into the volume of production, the impact of seasonality and the implications of periods of glut and of fallow. This chapter examines these issues in the context of developing and developed countries and further suggests that without training, practitioners may misuse pesticides and other chemicals and adopt poor sanitary practices, contributing to phytosanitary risks. It is possible that urban agriculture may throw up more problems than it solves.

Defining the problem

It is widely accepted that in the current epoch, the Anthropocene period, human activity has placed many ecologies in a position of potential near-destruction. Until the advent of the Industrial Revolution, the boundaries between where food was produced and where it was consumed (Rockstrom, 2009) were not clearly delineated. Food production has always taken place in a gradient of geographical land use from urban/peri-urban, to farmland on the edge of the urban area, remote rural areas either indigenous or in international spaces. In certain regions, urban areas are expanding, taking over valuable agricultural land, in line with population growth and the continuation of the exodus of rural populations to urban areas. In many regions, the boundaries between rural and urban are blurred as the growing population competes with agriculture for land resources.

These events present challenges for the distribution of sufficient accessible food. Food is supplied from outside the urban sprawl to be distributed through various marketing channels, such as street markets, grocers, corner stores and supermarkets. In such circumstances, as the urban landscape spreads, food production is not only pushed further away but, in a globalised world, food is also being sourced from thousands of miles away.

Furthermore, highly populated urban areas, where often the landscape is dominated by buildings and other infrastructure, have in many cases little vegetation. Inhabitants are frequently subject to high pollution levels, which are injurious to health. In addition, the high intensity of living conditions may lead to social problems, including substance abuse, which can also be linked to poor diets and health.

It is within this context that authorities, pressure groups and society in general have started rethinking some of the dynamics of the exploitation of the natural world, especially regarding the production and consumption of food. These dynamics are changing because of complex issues such as global warming, population growth and an over-reliance on global food networks (FAO, 2009). Indeed, these problems are expected to place ecological systems under even greater stress over the next decades.

On the other hand, in many cases, farmland also does not represent a healthy space. The over-utilisation of land has caused problems in the soil such as compaction, erosion and destruction of the natural balance within it, further heightened by pollution from excessive use of artificial fertilisers (phosphate and nitrogen) not to mention the cumulative effect of heavy metals and agrochemical residues.

Human use of land and other natural resources has wrought intense changes to the planet's climate, which has highlighted the fragility of some food production systems. Climatic change is evidenced from a rise in temperature, at a greater extent than in normal temperature fluctuations found in interglacial periods. Such climatic changes have in turn caused more land to be less suitable for agriculture (FAO, 2009). Furthermore, rising sea levels will also cause loss of agricultural land as saline water is likely to flood coastal plains, which, added to the projected population growth by 2050, will put a lot of stress on existing food production systems (FAO, 2009). Urban dwellers are more and more distanced from the source of food production and might be at risk of not having enough food at affordable prices, as it was the case in the food crisis of 2008 and 2009.

The recent food inflation crisis has led policy makers, activists and researchers to pay more attention to ways of building food resilience. As a result, alternative food production activities have surfaced as solutions to reduce vulnerability in the most needed communities, which also are felt to deliver sustainable food supply systems and offer food with a higher nutritional value to consumers, thereby meeting the challenge of addressing food security.

The shift in the emphasis of food production systems away from distanced and global towards more local supply chains has gained prominence in many policy and industry forums. For many the focus is on initiatives promoting fair, healthy and sustainable local food systems through a network of local, mainly organic, produce sold through farm shops, farmers' markets and pick-your-own farms, which have all grown in popularity in more economically developed countries (MEDCs). Such alternative food marketing channels also offer a social value and the support of strong local communities in the quest of accessing fresh healthy food (Food Links UK, 2015). On the other hand, in less economically developed countries (LEDC), local food production solutions have also been fostered to improve both nutrition and economic resilience.

10

The issue to be addressed is whether the production of food in an urban/peri-urban area offers greater food resilience within MEDCs and LEDCs, and whether urban/peri-urban agriculture has the capacity to safely and sustainably feed an urban population. An analysis of existing research in this area suggests that there is limited objective analysis of the benefits and drawbacks of urban production and its ability to deliver.

With the reputed 200 million city dwellers supplied through urban farms, it is notable that in African countries 40% of urban dwellers are said to be engaged in some sort of agricultural activity and this percentage rises to 50% in Latin America. If these numbers are accurate (and they may well not be), urban agriculture may have a role to play in addressing urban food insecurity problems in developing regions. The estimate is that about a quarter of the developing world's poor live in urban areas (Ravallion *et al.*, 2007). Numbers of urban poor are increasing in line with the expansion of urban areas (Gomez and Barton, 2013) resulting in the appropriation of vast areas of ecosystems and the elimination of productive land from cultivation (Gerster-Bentaya, 2013).

Although by no means a new phenomenon (Rockstrom *et al.*, 2009), the expansion of urban areas creates a conflict of interest between rural areas and cities for economic and political rights and privileges (Graue, 1929). In urban agriculture, an activity that infringes upon the traditional activity of rural areas and thereby in itself presents a source of conflict, there is a particular need to understand its role in urban planning, particularly whether urban agriculture might act as a vector for rejuvenation – environmental, economic and social.

Impact on the ecology

In the MEDCs the emphasis is placed on preserving a healthy environment, a verdant landscape and a habitat for birds and other species (Pollans and Roberts, 2014). The role of urban agriculture in MEDCs is to enable more of an intrinsic connection or reconnection of consumers to the land and access to pleasant recreational areas (Morrison, 2006), offering residents more greater access to open spaces as well as beautiful and pleasant landscapes for recreation or leisure (Gerster-Bentaya, 2013).

Such access to open spaces has the added benefit of food cultivation, thus allowing for more food security, resilience and promoting healthy and tasty eating, and it also enables good social behaviour. This is in line with the ecological public health model proposed by Lang and Rayner (2012), who consider ecological public health in context of four aspects namely: material, biological, cultural and social or institutional. It is suggested that urban agriculture delivers a structural element for leisure activities and engagement of communities (Flores, 2007), as well as empowerment of people and communities. It needs to be noted though, that since the food crisis, food poverty is a growing issue in some MEDCs.

In MEDC urban societies, it is thus not simply one of climate change and ecological crisis, as suggested by Montiel and Renting (2013) but of growing disparities in wealth, and the need in the face of food poverty for policy makers to consider alternative ways to feed the urban population. This has created more impetus towards better management of the urban ecosystem for the production of food. It is in times of crisis that urban agriculture grows in popularity for urban dwellers, local authorities and activists. This was true during war time in Europe, especially the 'Dig For Victory' campaign in Britain, and in times of economic crisis as experienced in recent years in many countries.

■ Ecology and food poverty

Yet, whilst the movement in the MEDCs now has attained a greater focus on redressing the issue of food poverty, in LEDCs the issue is not the environment, but the increasing numbers of urban poor. The exodus to urban areas contributes to the urban poor in LEDCs, with around 12.6 % of the urban population (32.7% of the whole) living in slums, and more than half living below the poverty line, particularly in countries in the South Americas and Africa such as Angola, Bolivia, Chad, Colombia, Guatemala, Haiti, Madagascar, Malawi, Mozambique, Niger, Sierra Leone and Zambia. Here populations risk not only food insecurity but also violence and criminality. Food is found in local markets, but its costs are exclude many slum dwellers.

Table 10.1: Undernourishment around the world, 1990-2 to 2012-4. Number of undernourished and prevalence (%) of undernourishment

	1990-2		2014-6	
	No.	%	No.	%
World	1,010.6	18	794.6	10.9
Developed regions	20.0	<5	14.7	<5
Developing regions	990.7	23.3	779.9	12.9
Africa	181.7	27.6	232.5	20.0
Sub-Saharan Africa	175.7	33.2	220.0	23.2
Asia	741.9	23.6	511.7	12.1
Eastern Asia	295.4	23.2	145.1	9.6
South-Eastern Asia	137.5	30.6	60.5	9.6
Southern Asia	291.2	23.9	281.4	15.7
Latin America & Carib.	66.1	14.7	34.3	5.5
Oceana	1.0	15.7	1.4	14.2

10

In peri-urban and rural areas of the tropics, human health issues are frequently related to malnourishment of the population, and evidence suggests that whilst the total figures have declined since the 1990s, they still represent a significant proportion of the population – as much as 20% in Africa. As such it is of arguably greater importance to convert new lands to agriculture; urban agriculture in LEDCs allows this without losses to the ecosystem of forests, grasslands and other areas of important biodiversity.

The land resource and owner

It is important to bear in mind the value of the land asset. Land is valued according to a ranking of economic benefits it might deliver, which reveal a hierarchy in land use motivations (Brinkley, 2012) and value dimension (Gomez and Barton, 2013). It is in urban areas that the value of land is the greatest. Large open spaces are at a premium and a cost-benefit analysis of producing food from these spaces requires some careful consideration. Nonetheless, it is in less economically developed countries (LEDC) that urban agriculture has a more significant bearing on the question of food security, food resilience, cash generation and gender roles.

However, in MEDC issues of land ownership and tenure tend to hinder the more widespread take up of urban agriculture (Grewal and Grewal, 2012). Similarly, in LEDCs the lack of title deeds to the land has been highlighted as being the single most important problem for urban agriculture production (May and Rogerson, 1995). The pressures imposed by land value (Brinkley, 2012) have also been highlighted in the African case of the Tembisa women who farmed land, which was left vacant because it was earmarked for future housing. In cultivating the land, Tembisa farmers were viewed as squatters and were fined (May and Rogerson, 1995). Some caution is also needed in understanding the context of many of the success stories and experiences reported in the literature.

Much of the initiatives reported in forums such as the food studies conference in Urbana-Champaign in 2012 were unpinned more by crusadic principles than academic research. Specific research foci emerging in the last century, Memon (1993) suggests that the examination of urban agriculture should be taken more from the perspective of human relations and informal economies than rural agriculture. In addition, there is a question as to the type of ownership and governance of initiatives. It is questionable whether in capitalist societies, there is evidence that the private model of plot ownership is of greater benefit and more sustainable than the communal one (Atkinson, 1995).

In the case of the Cuban small urban gardens experience, which has been much fêted by the enthusiasts of urban agriculture who claim that up to 60% of the country's total vegetable production came from small vegetable gardens

(Morrison, 2006), when the crisis was over, it was evident that there had been a progressive decline of small garden vegetable production in favour of larger pseudo-commercial operations. This was attributable not simply to economic recovery but the perennial desire for convenience by city dwellers as similarly evidenced in MEDCs during periods of economic recovery (Morrison, 2006).

■ Can urban agriculture really bring benefits and are there limitations?

Despite this, can urban agriculture reduce food insecurity in both MEDCs and LEDCs in times of crisis by building resilience (FAO, 2008)? In many LEDCs urban agriculture is a vibrant part of the local, usually informal, economic activity as it supplements households with nutrition and cash. Atkinson (1995) pointed out that the main advantage of urban agriculture is its potential to produce food cheaply for the urban poor, using marginal waste land and skills of recent migrants from rural areas. According to Flores (2007), urban and peri-urban agriculture has become a key element in food security strategies. However, its relevance, and impact on nutrition, food security and health varies tremendously from case to case. Much of the literature focuses on very poignant examples but which are lacking rigorous research. The real value of the urban agriculture as a sustainable solution and a step towards 'hunger proof cities' needs to be urgently explored (Koc *et al.*, 1999).

Food availability

Zezza and Tasciotti (2010) mentioned the difficulty in attempting to understand the real contribution of urban agriculture to food security, its importance and nature. One question is whether there could be sufficient produce grown, i.e. could sufficient food to feed the cities be supplied by urban agriculturalists. It is broadly assumed that by simply encouraging the production of food in urban areas, the volume produced will go some way to meeting urban demand. The issue to be faced by those who promote urban agriculture is twofold. On the one hand, fresh produce, particularly vegetable matter, is traditionally seasonal. Genetic innovations of seeds have allowed an extended growing period, but even were such seeds available to a largely domestic market, the ability of urban producers to generate fresh produce throughout the year in many areas of the world could problematic.

There are initiatives such as the underground farm which is growing herbs in disused Second World War bunker in London beneath the Northern line at Clapham, and technological developments such as horizontal horticultural production, but these at present are fairly rare and (Knapton, 2015).

However, it is evident that both levels of venture capital funds and working capital required for means to ensure heat and light would be prohibitive in such initiatives to many urban producers.

The circumstances are marginally different for livestock and milk production, in that their production does not need to vary quite as much in relation to seasonal climatic conditions, where stock may be kept indoors, however again indoor feeding will normally quite high investments of working capital for feedstuffs.

This suggests that for many MEDCs and LEDCs yearlong availability may be problematic and, of course, reduce the contribution of food production to the urban producer's household income. As a corollary to this, during harvesting months there will normally be considerable over-production, particularly in the case of fresh produce. In certain cases, there may be an opportunity to preserve excess produce for personal consumption, where producer has access to appropriate storage facilities and processes. Principles of supply and demand mean that the condition of oversupply will have a negative effect on the prices received by the householders for their produce and potentially create a level of food wastage.

Again, the situation is marginally ameliorated for livestock farmers, where product flows can be more evenly managed, e.g. in pork and milk production, but it must be noted that there has been limited consideration of implications of the nature of the food production process on poverty and hunger. (Cofie, 2003),

■ Potential for reducing poverty and ill health

There is also potentially a lack of quality data on the benefits generated through the use of "underutilised factors of production such as derelict spaces, recycled sewage water and unemployed labour" (Zezza and Tasciotti, 2010). Despite the recognition of urban agriculture's potential for reducing poverty, improving food security, resilience and the general public's health, especially of the more vulnerable groups (Flores, 2007), limited investigations have been undertaken into the potential risks associated with the activity (Gerster-Bentaya, 2013).

The production of food from heavy metal-polluted brownfield soils (Lacroix, 2013), vacant land (Pollans and Roberts, 2014) and water littered with refuse and contaminants as well as other toxic residues, is a major threat to human health. Moreover, city air can carry a lot of pollution containing noxious gases such as SO_2, NO_2 and O_3, which not only cause a reduction in yields but are detrimental to health owing to their cumulative presence (Gerster-Bentaya, 2013). In countries, especially LEDCs, where public sanitation is not widespread, food-borne diseases are a constant threat to public health when untreated water is used for irrigation in vegetable production. Urban food production which enters the informal economy and reaches consumers might actually represent a localised hazard. Similarly, when the surplus of urban agriculture enters more formal marketing chains, as reported in many African success stories (Flynn, 2001), the potential risk of contamination should not be overlooked.

These risks are not isolated to LEDCs. Misuse of pesticides and the potential for bacterial and other pathogenic contamination of food stuffs, including *E.coli*, *Campylobacter*, *Salmonella* and Swine flu amongst many others, are prevalent in both MEDC's livestock and soils as in LED countries. In MEDCs food hygiene legislation and assurance schemes should theoretically protect the consumer, but the inspection and control of urban producers would represent a mammoth task for the regulatory bodies, particularly as there is increasing consumer pressure on the food chain to divulge information on and control of quality and safety and source of food products. According to Morrison (2006) by 2001, some 60% of all the vegetables and most of the eggs and poultry produced in Cuba came from vegetable gardens. In Cleveland (USA), Grewal and Grewal (2012) mentioned that in disadvantaged neighbourhoods urban agriculture has allowed for the poor to have access to healthy food, reduce hunger and obesity. Yet, little is undertaken or indeed considered within the literature with respect to food safety.

Indeed it is often in MEDCs that the responsibility for the inspection of foods produced from villages, towns and cities falls under the remit of local authorities and municipalities, who have faced increasing financial constraints since the financial crisis of 2008. The constraints placed on public spending have not been ameliorated where there are increasing problems of public health.

The planning and organisation of urban agriculture

10

Financial constraints, it is posited, (Gerster-Bentaya, 2013) have consequences for not only food safety but also land use and town planners. Urban productive open spaces for agriculture are not fully addressed by land use plans and town planning schemes and thus the management and control of urban agricultural land use tends to be disjointed.

Gupta and Gangopadhyay (2014) noted this and proposed that urban agriculture should become an inherent component of urban planning. However, until this happens, urban agriculture remains a 'poor cousin' in urban planning (Gerster-Bentaya, 2013). As such, securing land tenure for food production needs to be protected by regulation, zoning, agreements and demarcation, which are vital for the likely future role the activity might have in feeding the cities in earnest. Zezza and Tasciotti (2010) proposed that a good starting point would be mapping the available unused areas in towns to really identify the total potential of food production and the local needs. As mentioned before, land title is the main problem relating to the marginal nature of the economic activity generated by urban agriculture. Thus, enhancing initiatives by facilitating temporary use of waste land in the city might help.

It is in the nature of policy making that it created a reliance on grants to support urban agriculture initiatives. When these are removed, without community legitimacy, common gardens fail (Atkinson, 1995). Yet, the Ohio Land Reutilization Program, which enables municipalities to purchase unproductive lands via tax incentives, could be a good model. It was intended to enable a more proactive re-utilization of unproductive lands. In Cleveland (USA), according to Grewal and Grewal (2012), new policies and bylaws have enabled the utilisation of available areas for production.

Were more land to become available, it would allow for the scaling up of urban agricultural production (Pollands and Roberts, 2014), were there not considerable number of alternative demands on this limited resource (Pollans and Roberts, 2014). Hence, it could be argued that the whole understanding of urban agriculture as being a major saviour of food insecurity should be treated with caution. Caution on the basis of undermining commercial and industrial enterprises located within an urban area, as well as failing to deliver safe, sufficient food.

Policy makers might be seduced by ideas that may sound idyllic "the return to the natural world" but these could represent more of an economic, social threat than a saviour.

Concluding remarks

As a result, in the face of simple calculations, it is clear that, despite the recognition of the importance of urban agriculture in food security strategies that have been adopted by many policy makers (FAO, 2008). This chapter suggests that whilst interesting, the idea is perhaps idealistic given that population growth is taken place particularly in cities. Caution is needed when planning and developing strategies of food resilience for the future, if we are to deal effectively with the future food crisis.

The fact that urban agriculture has become more prominent in recent years and its popularity has increased might be related to its capacity to rejuvenate towns and deprived inner cities, to involve vulnerable people and communities as well as promoting change in eating habits. However, the actions are localised, the successes are transient and good data to support a strong argument non-existent.

Yet, the divide between urban and rural spaces is expected to intensify. Food production which has the capacity to safely sustain large swathes of the population would still be dependent on the capitalist commercial agriculture model.

Conversely, urban agriculture interventions depend on public funding from local authorities and are rarely self-sustained. It is clear that the cities' greenbelts need to be looked after for their functionality in supplying a variety of locally produced fruit and vegetables to supplement or complement the dietary needs of a population. Eating fresh produce is vital for good nutrition as they provide main sources of vitamins and minerals. Promoting urban agriculture as an instrument for an ecological public health policy could actually be a distraction, though it is undeniable that urban agriculture has a role in times of food crisis, which causes social stress.

The role of urban agriculture varies from those more economically developed to those less economically developed countries. As a system, it is vulnerable with respect to access permanent access to land and the use of clean/unpolluted spaces, not to mention the informality inherent to the system. This is particularly a problem with respect to food safety risk, and it is possible that with respect to health, urban agriculture may cause more harm than good. It might provide some food resilience, but as a system it is very vulnerable. In the quest to feed a growing population, commercial agriculture will also have to change and adapt to more or less intensification, sustainability and preservation of natural resources.

References

Atkinson, S. J. (1995) Approaches and actors in urban food security in developing countries. *Habitat International*, **19** (2): 151-163. http://www.sciencedirect.com/science/article/pii/0197397594000638. Accessed: 23/02/2015.

Brinkley, C. (2012). Evaluating the benefits of peri-urban agriculture. *Journal of Planning Literature*, **27**(3), 259-269.

Cofie, O.O., Van Veenhuizen, R. and Drechsel, P., 2003. Contribution of urban and peri-urban agriculture to food security in sub-Saharan Africa. Africa Day of the 3rd WWF in Kyoto, pp.17-3.

FAO (2008) Urban agriculture for sustainable poverty alleviation and food security. http://www.fao.org/fileadmin/templates/FCIT/PDF/UPA_-WBpaper-Final_October_2008.pdf. Accessed 17/02/2015.

FAO. 2009. How to feed the world in 2050. http://www.fao.org/fileadmin/templates/wsfs/docs/expert_paper/How_to_Feed_the_World_in_2050.pdf. Accessed 10/11/2015.

Food Links UK. (2015). http://www.localfoodlinks.org.uk/2015/10/ Accessed: 15/11/2015.

Flores, M.O. (2007) Agricultura urbana: nuevas estrategias de integración social y recuperación ambiental en la ciudad. *Revista Electrónica DU&P Diseño Urbano y Paisaje*. **4** (11). Centro de Estudios Arquitectónicos, Urbanísticos y del Paisaje. Universidad Central de Chile.

10

Flynn, K.C. (2001) Urban agriculture in Mwanza,Tanzania. *Africa*, **71** (4): 666-691.

Gerster-Bentaya, M. (2013). Nutrition-sensitive urban agriculture. *Food Science*. **5**, 723–737.

Gómez-Baggethun, E. and Barton, D.N. (2013). Classifying and valuing ecosystem services for urban planning. *Ecological Economics*. **86**, 235–245.

Graue, E. (1929) Agriculture versus urban enterprise. *Journal of Farm Economics*, **11** (4), 609-622.

Grewal, S.S. and Grewal, P.S. (2012) Can cities become self-reliant in food? *Cities*, **29** (1): 1-11.

Gupta, R. and Gangopadhyay, S.G. (2014). Urban agriculture, planning and food price control. *Economic & Political Weekly*, **69** (21)

Knapton, (2015) London's first underground farm opens in WW2 air raid shelter, the *Telegraph* 29 Jun. http://www.telegraph.co.uk/news/earth/agriculture/farming/11706406/Londons-first-underground-farm-opens-in-WW2-air-raid-shelter.html. Accessed 1/12/2016.

Koc, M., MacRae, R., Mougeot, L.J.A. and Welsh, J. (1999). For Hunger-Proof Cities: Sustainable urban food systems. IDRC.

LaCroix, C. J. (2014) Urban agriculture and the environment (contaminated land and water pollution issues). *Urban Lawyer*, **46** (2), 227-248.

Lang, T. and Rayner, G. (2012) Ecological public health: the 21st century's big idea? *British Medical Journal*. **345** (7872), 17-20.

May, J. and Rogerson, C.M. (1995). Poverty and sustainable cities in South Africa: the role of urban cultivation. *Habitat International*. **19** (2), 165–181.

Memon, P. A. (1993) Urban agriculture in Kenya. *Canadian Journal of African Studies/ Revue Canadienne Des Études Africaines*, **27** (1): 25.

Montiel, M. S. and Renting, H. (2013) Agricultura urbana: practicas emergentes para un Nuevo urbanismo. *Hábitat y Sociedad*. **6**: 3-8.

Morrison, M.J. (2006) Book review on Mougeot, L.J.A. (Ed.). 2005. *Agropolis: The social, political and environmental dimensions of urban agriculture*. Earthscan and the International Development Research Centre: 286.

Pollans, M. and Roberts, M. (2014) Setting the table for urban agriculture. *Urban Lawyer*. **46**(2): 199-225..

Ravallion, M., Chen, S. and Sangraula, P. (2007). New evidence on the urbanization of global poverty. *Population and Development Review*, 33(4), 667-701.

Zezza, A. and Tasciotti, L. (2010). Urban agriculture, poverty, and food security: Empirical evidence from a sample of developing countries. *Food Policy*, **35** (4): 265-273.

Part 3
Case studies and new areas of research

11 Rural Land Use in Conflict? Energy and Food in the UK

Jonathan C. Cooper

Introduction

In recent years global sustainability challenges have often been characterised in terms of the water–energy–food nexus, or sometimes the water–energy–food–climate nexus, and such conceptualisations have been used to emphasise the interlinkages between these natural resources, especially in the context of rising population and increased demand for them (Dodds, 2016). Other examples of nexus thinking have also been used to describe agricultural land use change such as the nexus between population growth and changing diets in the face of increased demand for bioenergy (Alexander *et al.*, 2015). This short chapter focusses on one of the sticking points within the water–energy–food nexus; it considers in general terms the land use conflicts associated with two renewable resources, bioenergy (including biomass, biogas and biofuels) and solar energy (principally ground-mounted photovoltaic arrays), in 21st century Britain. Installations developed in order to exploit these resources are sometimes characterised as being at odds with the food supply chain. This paper does not include a consideration of other renewable technologies, which could also lead to land use conflicts between energy and food production, such as wind turbines and hydroelectric projects. Wind energy developments have a limited impact on land use as crops can be grown and livestock can be grazed in their immediate vicinity, although such farming activities could be disrupted during the relatively brief construction phase. Large-scale hydroelectric schemes could certainly have a significant impact on food production as the damming of watercourses necessarily floods land and removes it from agricultural production. However, in Britain most recent hydroelectric schemes are small in scale and tend to divert streams over short distances and so do not result in the flooding of land (although a small number of exceptions apply). This paper will not discuss the land use conflicts caused by non-renewable energy resources such as fossil fuels and nuclear power as such large developments are relatively few in number.

The use of renewable energy resources in the UK has increased rapidly during the twenty-first century due to technological advances, policy drivers to reduce greenhouse gas emissions from fossil fuel combustion and economic incentives for landholders to install renewable technologies, amongst other factors. The technologies used for the exploitation of bioenergy resources will be introduced alongside the technology used for the generation of electricity from solar resources. The land use conflicts arising from such developments will be discussed with particular reference to the UK, although the principles will be applicable in other territories, especially in developed economies. This paper will conclude with a brief exploration of likely land use conflicts between energy and food in the future.

Policy drivers for renewable energy in the UK

In spite of the results of the referendum in June 2016, European policy drivers continue, for the time being, to influence energy futures in the UK. For example, the EU Renewable Energy Directive (2009) requires that 20% of energy consumed across the European Union should be generated from renewable resources by the year 2020; the specific national target for the UK is 15%. Although the UK technically remains committed to such a target, it is widely anticipated that it will not be met and the importance of such European drivers is likely to diminish in the near future. Recent domestic policy drivers such as the Climate Change Act (2008) and the Energy Act (2008) remain forceful. The former requires an 80% reduction in carbon dioxide emissions (compared to 1990 levels) by the year 2050 and the latter brought in economic incentives for renewable energy developments in the form of Feed-in Tariffs and the Renewable Heat Incentive. Such measures result in monetary payments for the generation of energy, depending upon such factors as the technology that is deployed, the energetic output of the system and the date of its installation. Further payments are made when electricity generated by such schemes is fed onto the National Grid. These incentive schemes have been a major factor in the recent de-carbonisation of the energy system in the United Kingdom. This has been further enhanced by the Energy Act (2013) which aims to reform the electricity market through carbon price support and other mechanisms such as 'contracts for difference', which seek to give additional investor confidence, and the introduction of capacity markets to ensure that short-term energy

11

demand is met. However, more recently reviews of the system of Feed-in Tariffs have resulted in payment rates being dramatically reduced. Such changes have resulted in criticism from a range of stakeholders. It is worth considering that such measures were not intended to be permanent but, rather, to stimulate the emerging renewable energy industry at the time. Controversy remains, especially surrounding the timing of drastic tariff reduction.

Bioenergy

Due in large part to the introduction of measures such as the Renewable Heat Incentive (see above), there has been a proliferation of bioenergy developments in the United Kingdom in recent years. Bioenergy is a general term which refers to the production of electricity and/or heat from organic matter, that is to say living organisms. Bioenergy can be sub-divided into categories such as biomass, biogas and biofuels. Biomass refers to the production of heat through the combustion of materials such as woodfuel, timber waste and residues or crops such as woody coppice or miscanthus as well as various agricultural wastes; biogas refers to the production of heat and/or electricity from crops, wastes and other materials through the process of anaerobic digestion; and biofuels refer to fuels such biodiesel which are derived from plant matter, rather than from conventional fossil fuel sources, and used as alternatives for transportation and other uses (Prag, 2013; Twidell and Weir, 2015). This is not an exhaustive list of everything encompassed within the term bioenergy but is intended to give an overview of the varied land use required to grow the feedstocks necessary for such processes. Aside from land use conflict, the production of bioenergy crops also raises questions about impacts on biodiversity and the cycling of nutrients.

Bioenergy is sometimes regarded as being in conflict with 'traditional' agricultural land use, i.e. for the production of food, but the usefulness of such a characterisation has also been questioned (Karp and Richter, 2011). Notions of 'crop displacement' whereby food production is given up in favour of energy crop production have influenced perceptions of bioenergy as necessarily resulting in land use conflict. However, although such displacement does sometimes arise, it is an over-simplification of an issue which is not necessarily insoluble. Increasing intensification, for example, results in increased demand on fuels for vehicles and the production of biofuels on agricultural land is one way in which demand for expensive and environmentally damaging fossil fuels can be managed. Reviews of energy crop policy in the UK over the past few decades have been critical and it has been indicated that their introduction has been largely unplanned (Adams and Lindegard, 2016). Studies of stakeholder perceptions of anaerobic digestion (specifically, as one form of bioenergy) have indicated that there is a low risk of a shift in agricultural practice towards giving over large areas of land to grow energy crops in the UK (Röder, 2016). The introduction 'flex crops' which can be used either for food or for energy production, as immediate demand dictates, is one practice through which this issue might be resolved; the multi-functionality of land is another (Tomei and Helliwell, 2016). It has also been suggested that marginal land, not particularly suitable for the economically viable production of food crops, could be used for the production of some energy crops (Shortall, 2013). It seems clear, however, that the large-scale expansion of the cultivation of energy crops is likely to affect the value of commodities such as food and energy as well as having an impact on water availability in some regions; the integration of energy, land use and water management policies is, therefore, imperative (Popp *et al.*, 2014).

Solar energy

Due in large part to the introduction of Feed-in Tariffs (see above), there has also been a proliferation of solar energy developments in the United Kingdom in recent years. Solar energy is exploited using two main technological categories: solar thermal (for the production of heat from solar radiation) and solar photovoltaic (for the generation of electricity from sunlight) (Prag, 2013; Twidell and Weir, 2015). We will concern ourselves with the latter category as it is being used in large-scale developments covering agricultural land whereas the former is used on a relatively small scale, mostly on the roofs of individual buildings for water heating purposes, and so does not have a large impact upon land use conflicts.

When such technology is arrayed in a large ground-mounted grouping it is commonly referred to as a 'solar farm', analogous with the term 'wind farm' used to describe a cluster of turbines. Criteria for the development of solar farms have been identified and include the availability for lease for at least 20 years of at least 10–20 ha of low grade, flat or gently sloping land ideally with a south facing aspect; such land should not be prone to flooding neither should it be overlooked nor have shadows cast upon it by trees or buildings and it should have access for construction and maintenance vehicles; it should also be free of rights of way, underlying pipes and overhead powerlines and it should not be in an environmentally or archaeologically sensitive landscape (Jones *et al.*, 2014). In Britain, southern regions are more favourable than northern regions for the siting of such developments due to increased insolation and therefore energy output. However, solar developments in other regions can also be profitable and examples are to be found in northern Scotland. The impact of such technology on land use conflicts with food production, therefore, is not limited to particular regions but is a nationwide phenomenon.

11

Solar farms can result in conflict on land used for arable production due to crop displacement (see above). In this case, however, the land is not used for energy crops but for the ground-mounting of solar arrays; the shading and obstruction caused by such installation makes land unsuitable for most cropping. This technology can also cause land use conflicts with pasture as well as with arable farming. However, such conflicts are not necessarily irresolvable. The grazing of large ungulates such as cattle is not generally advisable in the immediate vicinity of a solar array as panels can be damaged by these animals. As well as this practical consideration, it is often difficult to obtain insurance cover for a solar development on land which will continue to be used for grazing purposes. However, it is sometimes possible to graze smaller animals, such as sheep and geese, among solar arrays as these are less likely to cause damage to an installation. Remaining potential damage can be minimised by covering wiring with robust protection to prevent chewing, for example. That is not to say that any land use conflict is therefore entirely resolved. The shade cast by solar installations reduces the yield of fodder crops such as grass and clover. As such, animals grazed on the same land after a solar installation will likely show reduced growth or will require a greater land area for grazing or increased dietary supplements. If animals are not grazed on land on which a solar array is sited, it could still be possible to grow fodder crops for silage around the installation but mowing would prove difficult due to the typical arrangement of the panels in tightly spaced rows.

Concluding remarks

Various projections about future land use in the UK to the mid-twenty-first century have been made and the identification of energy as an increasingly important factor over this period has been consistent (Burgess and Morris, 2009; Dwyer, 2011; Howard et al., 2009; Konadu et al., 2015). The nexus approach to the study of land use conflicts between the production of food and energy may become increasingly pertinent as the effects of climate change, increasing global population and the necessary further intensification of global agriculture are felt more strongly over the coming decades (Harvey and Pilgrim, 2011; Sharmina, 2016). Renewable energy developments do not necessarily have a significant impact on the sustainability of food supply in every instance. However, there are some cases where land use conflicts have arisen and it is likely that further cases of this nature will continue to arise in the future.

References

Adams, P. W. R. and Lindegard, K. (2016). A critical appraisal of the effectiveness of UK perennial energy crops policy since 1990, *Renewable and Sustainable Energy Reviews*, **55**, 188-202.

Alexander, P., Rounsevell, M.D.A., Dislich, C., Dodson, J.R., Engström, K. and Moran, D. (2015). Drivers for global agricultural land use change: The nexus of diet, population, yield and bioenergy, *Global Environmental Change*, **35**, 138-147.

Burgess, P. J. and Morris, J. (2009). Agricultural technology and land use futures: The UK case, *Land Use Policy*, **26S**, S222-S229.

Dodds, F. and Bartram, J. (eds) (2016). *The Water, Food, Energy and Climate Nexus*, Abingdon: Routledge.

Dwyer, J. (2011). UK Land Use Futures: Policy influence and challenges for the coming decades, *Land Use Policy*, **28**, 674-683.

Harvey, M. and Pilgrim, S. (2011). The new competition for land: Food, energy, and climate change, *Food Policy*, **36**, S40-S51.

Howard, D.C., Wadsworth, R.A., Whitaker, J.W., Hughes, N., Bunce, R.G.H. (2009). The impact of sustainable energy production on land use in Britain through to 2050, *Land Use Policy*, **26S**, S284-S292.

Jones, P. Hillier, D. and Comfort D. (2014) (2014). Solar farm development in the United Kingdom, *Property Management*, **32** (2), 176-184.

Karp, A. and Richter, G. M. (2011). Meeting the challenge of food and energy security, *Journal of Experimental Botany*, **62** (10), 3263-3271.

Konadu, D. D., Mourão, Z.S., Allwood, J.M., Richards, K.S., Kopec, G., McMahon, R. and Fenner, R. (2015). Land use implications of future energy system trajectories – The case of the UK2050 Carbon Plan, *Energy Policy*, **86**, 328-337.

Popp, J., Lakner, Z., Harangi-Rákos, M. and Fári, M. (2014). The effect of bioenergy expansion: Food, energy, and environment, *Renewable and Sustainable Energy Reviews*, **32**, 559-578.

Prag, P. (2013). *Renewable Energy in the Countryside*, 3rd edn, Abingdon: Routledge.

Röder, M. (2016). More than food or fuel. Stakeholder perceptions of anaerobic digestion and land use; a case study from the United Kingdom, *Energy Policy*, **97**, 73-81.

Sharmina, M., Hoolohan, C., Bows-Larkin, A., Burgess, P.J., Colwill, J., Gilbert, P., Howard, D., Knox, J. and Anderson, K. (2016). A nexus perspective on competing land demands: Wider lessons from a UK policy case study, *Environmental Science & Policy*, 59, 74-84.

Shortall, O. K. (2013). 'Marginal land' for energy crops: Exploring definitions and embedded assumptions, *Energy Policy*, **62**, 19-27.

Tomei, J. and Helliwell, R. (2016). Food versus fuel? Going beyond biofuels, *Land Use Policy*, **56**, 320-326.

Twidell, J. and Weir, T. (2015). *Renewable Energy Resources*, 3rd ed, Abingdon: Routledge.

11

12 Food Miles versus Lifecycle analysis: GHG – way to go!!!

Jane Eastham and Simon Thelwell

Introduction

The debate over food miles versus lifecycle analysis and carbon footprint, has been one of interest to many over at least the last decade, driven by different weightings placed on ecological, economic, and perceptions of food quality and local food agendas. Different measures provide different determinations of the relative impacts on the environment of particular courses of action by businesses, supply chains and individuals.

Food miles, have for a long time been used to depict the distance travelled by a product, the perception being that the greater the mileage the greater the carbon emissions and impact on the environment. There is also a concept of 'enhanced food miles' which augments the concept of miles to consider different efficiencies and relative impacts of different transport modes and their emissions on the environment. Thirdly there is the concept of carbon footprint and full lifecycle analysis which are concerned more with the total emissions from parts or indeed the entirety of the supply chain including beyond the consumer.

At one level the shifts in conceptualisation of food miles over lifecycle analysis represent an advance in our ability to effectively measure carbon emissions as a means of eliminating or at least neutralising the impact of human activity on the environment, at another it represents alternative agendas and self -interests.

Saunders *et al.* (2006) for instance, use lifecycle analysis to compare the relative damage to the environment of equivalent products produced in New Zealand versus those produced in the UK. Their findings show that produce supplied from New Zealand to the UK consumer has fewer externalities than those supplied from the UK. The research was driven by fears that the food mile agenda was a threat to New Zealand exports, where 50% of all exports were food.

Yet the food miles agenda was in the first instance, at least in part, driven by the need to reconnect the British consumer with the sources of food in the local food movement, and came to the forefront following the foot and mouth outbreak in 2001. The agenda served both to underpin drivers of rural regeneration through endogenous economic growth and shorter chains, as well as to protect food integrity through improved traceability.

This paper explores these issues with respect to the Brundtland definition of sustainable development and argues that matching the conflicting needs of the present could be more complex than usually declared.

The problem stated

The concept of sustainability is often seen to be based on three key pillars, that of environmental, economic and social sustainability. Environmental relates to the ability to maintain rates of renewable resource harvest, minimise pollution creation, and non-renewable resource depletion. Economic sustainability is the ability to support a defined level of economic production. Social sustainability is the ability of a social system, such as a country, to function at a defined level of social wellbeing over time. The achievement of the sustainability agenda focuses thus, not simply on the environmental issue but the continued and future wellbeing of economies and people.As stated by the Brundtland report: "Sustainable development is development that meets the needs of the present without compromising the ability of future generations to meet their own needs". This has a particular focus on the World's poor and the constraints placed on the delivery of past and future needs by both technology and society.

In the context of sustainable agriculture and supply chains, carbon emissions across regions can be seen to vary quite considerably, yet so too does food poverty and the extent to which a country relies upon food as a source of GDP. Some countries are heavily reliant on food as an export, for example the FAO/UNCTAD suggest the food exports of New Zealand are at 9.2% of GDP, across the globe only the Ivory Coast is higher at 12.9%, and this is hugely important as a means of balancing trade or developing the economy.

Agriculture can also be seen to be critical in the maintenance of the social and economic fabric of communities, and, particularly in developed countries, it plays a crucial role in the health, as the maintenance of land through agriculture presents urban populations with access to green spaces for the purpose of recreation.

12

Whilst the Brundtland report suggests that the conflict of interest is between the present and the future, perhaps there are greater tensions between the diverse needs in different regions and stakeholders. The questions become: Where do we draw the line? How do we need prioritise? And do we need to determine who should be the winners and who the losers?

Food miles

The concept of food miles was first coined in the mid 1990s (Paxton, 1994), with concerns that the distance food travels from farm to consumer had increased significantly since the Second World War. In the UK, studies were commissioned in 1992, 1997 and 2002 that formed part of the UK government's sustainable farming and food strategy, although it was found that simple vehicle miles was insufficient a measure and the relative CO_2 emissions from modes of transport were taken into consideration, the so called 'enhanced food miles' (Van Passel, 2013).

The concepts of local food and food miles have been sometimes seen to be polemic, where calculations have shown that miles travelled by consumers to farm shops, and markets exceed those of the same products to major retailers (Coley et al., 2009). Others implicitly and explicitly see greater parallels between the two concepts (Curry, 2002; Brown and Geldard, 2008), and have deployed the term 'food miles' to promote such initiatives such as slow food, farmers' markets and other alternative markets and social movements.

Therefore the concept of food miles became increasingly associated with the concept of local food and its focus on the re-territorialisation or re-spatialisation of food production, emergence of localised food supply systems and the promotion of local economies and ecologies, terroirs and social conditions.

This was particularly evident in the UK and in the publication of the food and farming report, which called for shorter alternative food supply chains, and distribution strategies and channels which valorise local areas and ensure greater traceability (e.g. Curry, 2002; Coley et al.,2009).

Carbon footprint and lifecycle analysis

Carbon footprint is a more holistic concept than that of food miles, in that it looks at the total emissions associated with production and distribution. Carbon footprints measure not simply the impact of the delivery of the product from the farm gate to the consumer but the amount of carbon dioxide released into the atmosphere as a result of the activities of a particular individual, organization, or community. The measure of greenhouse gases, (GHG) as emitted through transport, land clearance, food production and consumption, is expressed in terms of CO_2 or its equivalent to other GHG, such as methane (Wright *et al.*, 2011). In effect, the measure looks at one specific activity or organisation within a supply chain. The term lifecycle offers a more longitudinal analysis of the supply chain activities and looks to manage what is sometimes called the carbon profile, of a product from end to end of its supply-chain, including use and end-of-life recovery and disposal.

Lifecycle analysis is covered under ISO 14040 and ISO 14044 and evaluates the environmental impacts and resources consumed along the lifecycle of products; from the extraction of raw materials, the manufacture of goods, their use by final consumers or for the provision of a service, to recycling, energy recovery, and disposal of remaining waste, which represents an extended profile of carbon footprints. The determination and elimination of CO_2 emissions is of growing importance within the EU.

Food miles versus lifecycle analysis

The distinction between food miles and lifecycle analysis (LCA) is in the emphasis placed on transport versus all emissions. In the emphasis on transport emissions, even in the consideration of 'enhanced food miles', there is a priority for shorter supply chains, rural area as an amenity and knowing the producer. There is no such consideration in LCA. In food miles, the issue is as much about the stewardship of the rural environment and the value of the countryside, as a means to both support human health and counterbalance carbon emissions through green space, as it is about economic viability of rural areas and agriculture.

The 'Eat the View' initiative in the late 1990s certainly supported this notion and was clearly interested in re-embedding societies and supply chains, as indeed was the concept of reconnecting supply chains as found within the Curry report post foot and mouth (Curry, 2002). Furthermore they were intent on the idea that there was a need to rethink the nature of food production and delivery, but at the extreme, what might be the implications of countries reliant on food as an export?

For New Zealand for instance, food represents 50% of its exports, an issue which was of particular significance when the rhetoric of food miles emerged. Saunders *et al.*, (2006) used LCA to undertake a comparison of GHG emissions generated from New Zealand apples, lamb, onions and dairy exported to the UK with those which were UK grown. In each case they found that emissions were lower for New Zealand produce than UK alternatives.

The issue of food miles, i.e. the number of food miles clocked up by transport within the UK and imports into the UK, has proved problematic for New Zealand.

12

The geographical location of New Zealand, results in many food miles and the UK represents an important market for the New Zealand producers. Products produced by New Zealand are similar and thus substitutable with those from the UK. If the concept of food miles were to prevail, this would potentially allow for the loss of the UK market to NZ with a significant impact on farm income. The lifecycle assessment strategy allows for the inclusion of characteristics of New Zealand farming, which uses less fertiliser, yearlong outside grazing for cattle with few concentrate feeds, again a source of GHG, as well as more environmentally friendly shipping transportation to the UK. Their lifecycle analysis concluded that New Zealand produce sent to the UK displays lower emissions than the UK equivalent.

Similar studies have demonstrated that utilising the carbon footprint framework showed that countries such as Kenya again emit lower GHG from a similar products than their European equivalents. In the production of cut flowers, for instance, it appears that the Kenyan operation uses substantially less primary and fossil energy and emits smaller quantities of GHG than from the Dutch horticulturalist (Williams, 2007). Suggestions were made that 10 times more emissions were generated from the production of flowers in Holland as opposed to Kenya, with 70% higher yields per acre in Kenya. The global warming potential (GWP) of Dutch over Kenyan rose production, for instance, was 5.8% higher. With 42% of its 44 million population reported to live below the poverty line, the exports of fresh flowers may bring much needed GDP to the region, although it might be argued that flowers reduce the potential for food production within the region.

Concerns and ethics

In research in New Zealand and Kenyan examples, the discussions have particularly favoured lifecycle analysis, which now must be thought to have become the dominant discourse. A discourse has been defined as an institutionalized way of portraying reality, determining what can be said or not said about the world (Foucault, 1991; 1998). Foucault also suggests that what is seen to be the knowledge that underpins the discourse is always an exercise of power. In the current example the suggestion here is that the emergent discourse is that of lifecycle analysis and the longitudinal measurement of supply chain emissions as is evident from the plethora of academic research and policy initiatives (Guinee *et al.*, 2010).

This is particularly a concern in the context of agriculture, where, in the EU, it has been established that agriculture contributes some 40% of emissions in the food supply chain. These are particularly from N_2O from nitrogen fertilisers, and methane from livestock production, as well as CO_2 from machinery. Considerable research has been undertaken into new technologies and techniques to mitigate climate change by better management of production. Such technologies are designed to reduce their impact on climate change either though sequestering CO_2 into terrestrial biosphere, thereby reducing the emissions of CO_2 into the atmosphere caused by soil degradation and erosion, or by increasing the efficiency in the use of inputs, which in farming means reducing inputs in the form of water, fertiliser, pesticides, fuel and labour. Farm inputs can be minimalised with aid of careful monitoring of crops, using robotics, drones and GPS in a practice known as precision farming, or by implementing better farming practices that reduce or eliminate tillage and the disruption of soil structure.

However, the concern in the context of sustainability, is not simply one of ecology and the longer term view taken by LCA but also, as suggested by the Brundtland report, the health, economic and social sustainability of current generations. Claims are that international trade of food will become a necessity as climate temperature rises and inhibits the production of sufficient food in certain areas (Nelson *et al.*,2010), but perhaps there is value in safeguarding existing agricultural areas for the meantime. Global trade and greater levels of cheaper imports place pressure on farm gate prices in the UK, and offer greater opportunity for food adulteration and other threats to food integrity. Whilst there may remain higher GHG even where better management of production should emerge, greater localisation of food would result in greater valorisation of rural areas, and their maintenance as a societal resource and 'common good'.

Outside the UK, if we consider how the LCA discourse justifies the extension of the production of green beans and flowers and other cash crops for the export markets in Kenya, it is notable that not only are there resource conflicts, inhibiting the growth of crops which form the Kenyan staple diet, but also a risk of augmented food poverty in the indigenous population.

■ The Sustainable Development Goals

On 25 September 2015, the 193 countries of the UN General Assembly adopted the Sustainable Development Goals, officially known as *Transforming our world: the 2030 Agenda for Sustainable Development* which is made up of seventeen aspirational 'Global Goals' with 169 targets between them. The measures came into effect in January, 2017. These Global Goals make a universal call to establish a sustainable approach, including protecting the planet, and ending poverty. The 17 goals, as illustrated in Figure 12.1, are designed to build upon the previous Millennium goals but add additional goals associated with climate action, life below water, life on earth, peace and justice, with a strong emphasis on partnership. The UNDP indicate that they offer clear guidelines and targets for all countries and suggest that these goals can only be achieved through a strong commitment to global

12

partnership and cooperation, particularly along the North-South, South-South divide. They suggest that there should be the continued delivery of aid and official development assistance to encourage growth of international trade, with a "universal rules based and equitable trading system, fair and open and" that "benefits all"

Figure 12.1: The Global Goals. http://www.undp.org/content/undp/en/home/sustainable-development-goals.html

Initiatives which have stemmed from these measures could have a radical impact on costs of production in developing countries, and could swing the issue of food security more comprehensively towards measuring impact on the premise of carbon footprint and lifecycle analysis. Africa is now re-determining its relationship to the multi-trillion dollar energy industry. The development of alternative power sources, the emergence of mini-grids, smart metering and mobile money have begun to transform the energy landscape for Africa. Whilst these are similarly being adopted across nation states, their impact on Africa, and the potential availability of energy sources could transform its energy landscape, fuelling first generation modern energy users both to the benefit of domestic and commercial sectors. The use of off-grid energy has had a beneficial impact on health through the reduction of pollution. Such initiatives have emerged in Ethiopia, Kenya, Morocco, and Rwanda, as such the ready availability of energy could further advantage and extend production for such countries; but at what cost to local production in western local areas? It is potentially correct that initiatives addressing other Global Goals could offset, at a global competitive level, those advantages gained for Africa, but here perhaps is the ethical dilemma and the crux of the problem.

Concluding remarks

We are faced with dilemmas. Sustainable food systems are currently challenged by complex interrelated and often incongruous factors. Food production, in the quantities and food forms demanded by developed and newly developing countries where populations are growing, places pressure on the ecology of the planet. This calls for a holistic, co-ordinated, approach that allows for the disparate interests of the multiple stakeholders within global economies.

References

Brown, H. and Geldard, J. (2008). Supplying local food to mainstream customers. Market Drayton, UK, Westley Consulting. http://www.westleyconsulting.co.uk Accessed April 16, 2010.

Coley, D., Howard, M. and Winter, M.(2009). Local food, food miles and carbon emissions: A comparison of farm shop and mass distribution approaches. *Food Policy*, **34**(2), 150-155.

Curry, D. (2002). *Farming and food, a sustainable future*, Policy Commission on Future of Farming, London.

Foucault, M. (1991). *Discipline and Punish: The Birth of a Prison*. London, Penguin.

Foucault, Michel (1998). *The History of Sexuality: The Will to Knowledge*, London, Penguin.

Guinee, J.B., Heijungs, R., Huppes, G., Zamagni, A., Masoni, P., Buonamici, R., Ekvall, T. and Rydberg, T. (2010). Life cycle assessment: past, present, and future. *Environmental Science &Technology*, **45**(1), 90-96.

Nelson, G.C., Rosegrant, M.W., Palazzo, A., Gray, I., Ingersoll, C., Robertson, R., Tokgoz, S., Zhu, T., Sulser, T.B., Ringler, C. and Msangi, S. (2010). *Food security, farming, and climate change to 2050: Scenarios, results, policy options* (Vol. 172). International Food Policy Research Institute.

Paxton, A. (1994). *Food Miles Report*. Safe Alliance.

Saunders, C., Barber, A. and Taylor, G. (2006). *Food Miles - Comparative Energy/Emissions Performance of New Zealand's Agriculture Industry*. Research Report 295. Agribusiness and Economics Research Unit, Lincoln University

Van Passel, S. (2013). Food miles to assess sustainability: a revision. *Sustainable Development*, **21**(1), 1-17.

Williams, A. (2007). *Comparative Study of Cut Roses for the British Market Produced in Kenya and the Netherlands*. Cranfield University.

Wright, L., Kemp, S. and Williams, I. (2011). 'Carbon footprinting': towards a universally accepted definition. *Carbon Management*. **2** (1): 61–72.

12

13 Current Challenges for the Pick Your Own Market – Health and Prosperity

Gabriella Parkes and Lucy Gilbert

Introduction

Pick Your Own (PYO) farms hold nostalgic memories for many of us. In the 1980s there were thousands of them in the UK, but now there are only a few hundred (Sukhadwala, 2014). In their heyday they offered easy access to sources of soft fruit for urban communities and a reconnection of urbanised communities with sources of food. Pick Your Own allowed those disconnected with primary food production to reconnect, and in addition offered a cheaper source of essential nutrients. In recent years we can note their decline. This contribution explores, on the basis of primary research, the reasons behind the decline in PYO numbers, since the 1980s. The findings are interesting in that the work here suggests that increasing opportunism amongst consumers – the something for nothing ethos, has significantly impacted on the viability of such initiatives, playing into the hands of the more powerful players within supply chains. The work reviews the core product of PYO: fruit retailing or family day out, and suggests that whilst cultural and ethical changes challenges the nature of traditional Pick Your Own, those who have survived have developed mitigation strategies to ensure this.

Recent trends in the Pick Your Own market

In the 1980s there were over 4000 PYO farms in Britain, but by 2010 there were only 600.

Jemima Lewis (2009) of the *Telegraph* wrote:

"The closest I ever got to nature during my London childhood was harvesting fruit for my mother's jam. Those memories – …. the smell of warm earth and straw, and the startling sweetness of contraband berries whipped straight from plant to mouth – still linger on the palate... "

This quote, in praise of the PYO farm also contains the seeds of their decline, as eating and not paying for fruit is shown to be a major threat to their financial sustainability. PYO farmers face several challenges, which if not addressed could result in the closure of the PYO business – factors like weather, liability and risk assessment, pricing, promotion, waste and theft.

Under the Common Agricultural Policy, there is still encouragement for farmers to develop multi-functionality of their land, and hence multi-income streams. Commercial pressures caused by economic structural changes, changes in consumer spending habits, international competition, weather uncertainty, specialisation, price pressures and market instability all act as push factors to diversify incomes.

The growth of 'agri-tourism' – a secondary business on the farm and based on agricultural activities (Tew and Barbieri, 2012) – is a response to the need for alternative income streams. As income from farming has varied and in some sectors is not profitable without subsidies, agri-tourism (Forbord *et al.*, 2012) contributes more to the farming household income than mainstream agricultural activity. (NFU, 2016) PYO is such a diversification – on farm but non-farm and involving the welcoming of 'visitors' onto the farm, for a retail or a recreational activity. As agri-tourism has grown, the agri-tourist has had a greater choice of activities, and the nature of agri-tourists has evolved over time, in line with changes in mainstream tourists. Their age, cultural, educational and occupational profiles have not remained static.

13

Threats faced by PYO farms

■ Waste

PYO increases the wastage of fruit, due to careless picking and children playing amongst the fruit. Lefort (2010) quotes a PYO farmer bemoaning the fact that pickers sometime leave half full baskets of fruit in the field after eating their fill.

Additionally visitors will be deterred by the weather and fruit ready for picking will become over ripe if poor weather puts off pickers, who are looking for a day trip out and are unlikely to venture out in poor weather. In the UK a series of poor summers and increasingly unpredictable weather patterns has had this effect. Bill Forgie of Forgie's Fruit Farm, Lewisburg, writes that for a person that is easily stressed with customers in the orchard, Pick Your Own probably wouldn't be a good option. "Customers may not treat your trees with the same care you would, and they waste much more product."

■ Theft

When Lewis (2014) wrote of "the startling sweetness of contraband berries whipped straight from plant to mouth – still linger on the palate", she did not consider the losses to the PYO farmer of pickers eating the fruit. There is a dissonance between the views of the pickers and the farm owners on this issue. PYO farms are experiencing an increase in thefts, and this has caused some farms to go out of business, and others to go to the expense of paying for security personnel to deter pickers eating the fruit before paying. Pickers expect to enjoy a "free buffet" and rustlers sneak through fences and throw cherries over the hedge to avoid paying. One PYO farmer comments that the situation seems to be worsening, and there is a greater lack of understanding of the concept of PYO. This certainly seems to be a major threat to the future survival of PYO farms, not only from the point of view of business profits, but also from the irritation and frustration it causes the farm owners. This can be linked to Doxey's index of irritation (1975), as the views expressed demonstrate that some PYO owners are in the annoyance stage, and those who have left the industry could have done so because they had entered the antagonism stage.

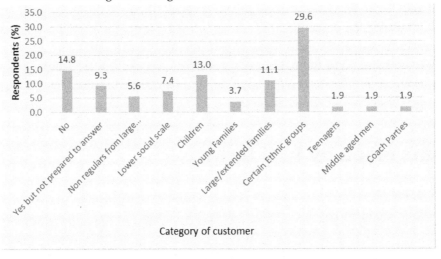

Figure 13.1: Which groups caused the most problems. Source: Gilbert (2016)

Mark Spight, the manager of Hacker's Fruit Farm in Dry Drayton, Cambridgeshire, closed his PYO business in 2015 after losing around £10,000 to 'greedy gorgers'. He claimed last year to have seen a family turn up with a bowl of cream to eat with strawberries that had not been paid for.

■ Public liability

The price of public liability insurance can be high and some PYO farms find it prohibitive. Boddingtons Berries closed for this reason. Following an accident on their premises and having to pay compensation, their insurance premiums rose significantly and they were required to install expensive safety measures. As litigation increases, all PYOs are gambling that they will not have a similar experience.

■ Weather

Most tourism organisations identify weather as a major determinant of tourism. Due to the reliance on weather for sales, few farmers rely solely on PYO operations to sell their produce

■ Location

Rural businesses are particularly vulnerable to exogenous challenges. The more rural their location, the greater this challenge is. The population in surrounding areas for customers and as a pool of labour, together with ease of access are all important factors related to location of a PYO operation. Studies in America have found that PYO customers travelled 20-25 miles to reach the farm, so the local population does not seem to be the core customer base in the USA for PYO (Leffew and Ernst, 2014.). But English PYOs still believe they have a core of locals who regularly visit their PYO.

As the market has changed to a 'farm experience' rather than fruit production, the proximity to the market is increasingly important. Parents bringing children to the PYO don't want long journeys with a car full of children.

■ Food quality

As more consumers live in cities, environmentally aware consumers like to know where their food comes from and are concerned about food miles. These consumers seek out local, seasonal produce believing it to be "packed with higher nutritional value', and to eat 5 a day. Increasingly consumers seek a sense of connection with their food. Customers are searching for interaction with nature, and welcome the seasonality of PYO. The experience of selecting and harvesting their own fresh produce is part of the attraction of PYO for these consumers.

13

■   A change in the core product

Using the only available listing of PYO farms in the UK, all listed farmers were asked what they thought the core product was that they were selling. 30% said they believed it to be the whole farm experience, while 50% believed it to be the fruit/vegetables and their freshness and traceability, and 20% thought visitors came to the farm for the shop and cafe.

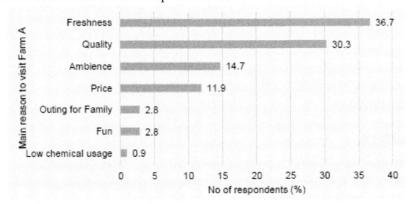

Figure 13.2: Reasons for visiting a Pick Your Own Farm. Source: Gilbert (2016)

PYO owners have different views of their market, and it seems that the survivors are the ones who have augmented the core fruit product with activities and recreational offerings, especially for children. A review of 10 PYO farms listed on the www.pyofarms.org.uk websites, showed that all 10 were offering a range of augmentations to the core product. Activities such as children's playgrounds, cafes, farm shops, farm tours, campsites, glamping, fishing, and all sorts of seasonal activities are advertised on the websites.

However a survey of 53 PYO visitors to a large PYO in Herefordshire found that 50% came for the fruit and only 37% for a whole farm experience. 67% of them came to the PYO for freshness and quality produce. This reveals a conflict with the views of the owners, and suggests that there are two market segments using PYOs now: day trippers and' jammers'. The group traditionally coming to PYOs, older women, possibly WI members, who pick large quantities of summer fruit to make jam.

■   Supermarkets

Supermarkets were responsible for reducing the numbers of customers to unsustainable levels. First, by stocking seasonal soft fruit and vegetables all year round, by sourcing from overseas, and second by charging lower prices. PYO farms who are not able, or maybe willing, to transform into a 'farm experience', have stopped offering PYO.

Survival strategies

In a survey done in 2016, surviving PYOs were found to be using the following strategies to cope with the changing market place and challenges:

■ Weather

To deal with the problem of more unpredictable weather PYOs have adopted the following strategies:

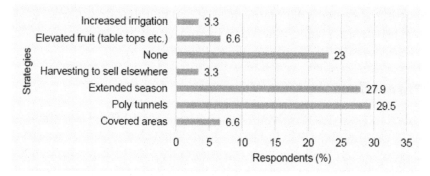

Figure 13.3: Strategies used to overcome impacts of poor weather by 60 PYO farms. Source: Gilbert (2016)

Clearly many take no mitigating actions, but 75% of PYO farmers have done something to try to counteract the effects of poor and unpredictable weather.

■ Theft (eating without paying)

Figure 13.4 identifies strategies PYO proprietors use to reduce the impact of people consuming the fruit and vegetables without paying. 23.4% of the respondents stated that they do not use any form of strategy to mitigate the impact of theft/ visitors consuming without paying, but most use one or more of those listed.

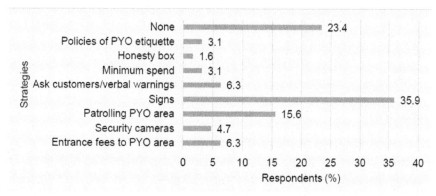

Figure 13.4: Strategies used to reduce impact of theft Source: Gilbert (2016)

13

■ Signage

Many farms use signage to deter visitors from consuming without paying. Trying to appeal to the better nature of the visitors, and use signs saying "we would like you to try our fruit but please do not abuse our trust and take advantage".

■ Security

Some PYO proprietors have people patrolling the PYO area and exit. They walk around the farm and speak to any visitors who are considered to be taking advantage of the system. Other farms have stated that they do not want the visitors to feel like they are being watched or monitored, so they prefer to explain the rules to customers before they enter the PYO areas.

■ Entrance fees

A few farms charge entrance fees to the PYO areas. One of the largest PYO farms in England, Court Farm in Hertfordshire tried charging entry fees to counteract the problem of theft, but after one season they decided to abandon the practice due to the loss of customer goodwill, and difficulties in enforcing the policy. They have diversified strategically and have chosen to absorb the losses to the PYO; their main income streams are now from outdoor recreational activities like mountain boarding and fishing instead.

■ Pricing

The majority of PYO proprietors base produce prices on competitor prices, and do increase prices to reflect rises in costs and inflation. Some PYOs aim to undercut supermarkets, which leaves them very low profit margins. The majority of proprietors do not take into account the 'PYO experience' in the prices and the majority do not charge higher prices to take into account the produce eaten.

Few customers visiting a major PYO farm said that price was the main reason for visiting, contradicting the findings of DEFRA (2014) who stated that price is the most important factor. As mentioned before, some PYOs have implemented strategies such as entrance fees or minimum charge to generate income and combat financial issues caused by PYO threats.

■ Location

Location can be a threat to PYO farms, but if the PYO is in a very rural location, visitors treat it as a visit to the country and increased use of advertising (in particular online) can be used to promote the enterprise to a large customer base. The success of a PYO is only partly dependent on a farm's location, but they do not need to be close to major population centres to be successful. Comparisons of websites revealed that 9 out of 10 PYOs have a website. However, only 20% were rated a sophistication level which requires an advanced interaction, attractive layout and extras such as enlisting subscriptions and online newsletters. Proximity to road networks is more important than being located close to the customer base. American PYOs have found that most visitors travel over 50+ miles and only visit once a year, with their whole family.

■ Changing market

In Gilbert's study of UK PYO farms in 2016, owners were asked which customer group posed particular problems, and results showed that there do seem to be groups who eat more than others. This could show a level of cultural naivety in these groups, who aren't familiar with the PYO business model. It also explains the change in attitudes of PYO owners located close to urban centres, who consequently experienced more theft and wastage issues than more remotely located PYO farms. These owners demonstrated a movement through Doxey's index to antagonism. These disillusioned and financially struggling owners have ceased doing PYO in large numbers since the 1980s.

PYO owners have recognised that the customer profile of their visitors has changed over the years. The most common visitor is now aged 31-40, travelling up to 20 miles and only visiting once a year, with their whole family. Large groups, however, do not often spend the most money and would appear to just enjoy the day out. This could lead to increased theft, damage and public liability claims, and appears to be a contributor as to why some PYOs are now struggling.

Concluding remarks

PYO farmers have faced falling profits due to downwards price pressure and falling sales due to competition from supermarkets; consumers have started to expect cheap food, which PYOs have not been able to provide. When faced with the decision between cheap food or low food miles and environmentally friendly produced food, not enough consumers are willing to pay the margins for sustainably produced food. These macro factors on top of the sector-specific challenges of theft, wastage, public liability and other challenges covered above have caused PYOs to close in large numbers over the 1990s and noughties.

In order to survive, PYO farmers have had to extend their offering into a range of recreational ventures. Visitors still seek fresh, high quality PYO produce, but, to protect their profit margins proprietors offer ancillary services such as a cafés and play/picnic areas. The websites of the successful PYO farms show a wide range of activities on offer – very few only do PYO anymore.

13

References

DEFRA (2014) *Farm Business Survey*, Department for Environment, Food & Rural Affairs

Doxey G.V. (1975). A causation theory of visitor-resident irritants: methodology and research inferences in the impact of tourism. In: Sixth Annual Conference Proceedings of the Travel Research Association. San Diego, CA, (Sept): 195.

Forbord, M., Schermer, M. and Grießmair, K. (2012). Stability and variety: Products, organization and institutionalization in farm tourism. *Tourism Management*, **33**(4), 895-909.

Gilbert. L. (2016). An investigation into the key issues causing a decline in PYO enterprises in the UK and strategies producers utilise to overcome these issues. Harper Adams unpublished dissertation.

Leffew, M. and Ernst, M. (2014). A farmer's guide to a pick-your-own operation. The University of Tennessee. https://extension.tennessee.edu/publications/documents/pb1802.pdf

Lefort, R. (2010). Farmers report rise in 'pick-your-own' thefts. *Telegraph*, 25 July.http://www.telegraph.co.uk/foodanddrink/foodanddrinknews/7908276/Farmers-report-rise-in-pick-your-own-thefts.html

Lewis, J. (2009) Pick your own: The last oases of the good life. *Telegraph*, 06 Jun. http://www.telegraph.co.uk/comment/columnists/jemima-lewis/5461426/Pick-your-own-The-last-oases-of-the-good-life.html

NFU (2016) How agriculture is changing: the importance of diversification. https://www.nfuonline.com/cross-sector/rural-affairs/planning-and-local-authorities/planning-news/how-agriculture-is-changing-the-importance-of-diversification. Accessed 02/03/2017

Sukhadwala, S. (2014). Nearest Pick your own farms. Londonist. http://londonist.com/2014/06/nearest-pick-your-own-farms-to-london?gallery=611070. Accessed 29/01/2017.

Tew, C. and Barbieri, C. (2012). The perceived benefits of agritourism: The provider's perspective. *Tourism Management*, **33**(1), 215-224

14 British Foods and the Emergence of Local Food Initiatives

Andy Swinscoe, Eddie Andrew and Jane Eastham

Introduction

The Food Programme on BBC Radio 4 was established in 1979 by Derek Cooper, and is now in its 38th year and presented by Sheila Dillon. Each year the programme hosts the annual Radio Food and Farming Awards, which celebrate specific entrepreneurial initiatives within the food supply chain. As we go to press, Sheila Dillon announced the launch of the 2017 awards, in which local food and small food businesses faced some of the greatest challenges ever. The award, and indeed *The Food Programme*, celebrates both the production of traditional foods and new creative ideas within food businesses. The programme and the awards have done much to promote local and authentic foods and raise the interest of the British consumer. This contribution introduces *The Food Programme* and two businesses which have received these awards in the dairy supply chain, a chain which has been much affected by the neoliberal agenda.

The nature of the Food and Farming Awards

The award celebrates entrepreneurs and innovators throughout the supply chain, including farmers, producers, retailers and foodservice; recognised through the range of awards delivered. These awards are offered under a number of different categories and celebrate farmers, producers, and retailers. These change each year but normally include categories of:

- Best Food Producer
- Best Drink Producer
- Future Food (open to all parties in supply chain)
- A farming award
- Best Food Retailer
- Best Market
- Best Takeaway or Street Food
- Derek Cooper award

Table 14.1: Categories for 2016 and 2017 food and farming awards

2017 categories	2016 categories	Winners of 2016
Best Food Producer	Best Food Producer	Charcutier Ltd
Best Drink Producer	Best Drink Producer	Hallet Real cider
You and Yours Best Takeaway and Street Food	Best Food Market	St Dogmaels local producers market
Future of food award	Future of Food Award	Our Cow Molly
Country File Young Farmers	Countryfile Farming Hero	Julia Evans
Best Food Retailer	Best Food Retailer	Almeley Food Market & Deli
The One Show Cook of the Year	Cook of the Year	Dee Woods
World Service Food Chain programme's award *	BBC Radio Bristol's Food Hero	Barry Haughton
Derek Cooper Outstanding Achievement Award	Derek Cooper Outstanding Achievement Award	Joan Morgan

* The first international award in 2017 for the person or organisation who's changed the global food system for the better.

As is evident – whilst there are some standard categories, other categories such as the World Service Food Chain and BBC Radio Bristol's Food Hero vary year on year.

The initiative is launched each year and listeners are called upon to put forward nominations for each category. A panel of judges make a long list from thousands of nominations, then a short list of three is chosen in each category. Everyone on the short list is then visited by two specialist judges. From this journalistic exercise the winners are chosen (except in the case of the *Derek Cooper* and the *World Service Awards*, which are researched and chosen by the judges themselves).

Such initiatives bring farmers, small producers, cooks, and other parties who are passionate about food and offer them the limelight to further develop their businesses and activities. Not all awards will be given to businesses. For instance the Derek Cooper Award for outstanding achievement was awarded in 2016 to Joan Morgan, who wrote *The Book of Pears* and *The Book of Apples*, based on her scholarly research at the National Fruit Collection at Brogdale in Kent. Many specialists believe her work helped the world-famous collection to survive commercial threats to its integrity.

The awards and indeed *The Food Programme* itself can be seen to be linked to the drive to promote local food initiatives and the development of sustainable and self-sufficient food supply chains. They have also coincided with the drive within rural policy over the last 20 or more years to encourage diversification and pluri-activity within agricultural communities. It is very much associated with promoting the very smallest initiative as well as the larger enterprises. A key element of their work, since the beginning, has been against the conformity that has at times been imposed on UK food chains by major multiple food buyers. Their impact is nowhere more remarkable than in the Dairy sector, where prices paid to farmers are often lower than the cost of production as a consequence of increased consolidation within the processing section, a function of the drive by retailers to force prices down and utilise milk as a loss leader. *The Food Programme* has actively promoted many different category initiatives, one of which is the dairy sector. In the following case studies we examine two such initiatives.

Case study: Courtyard Dairies

In the first case study, within the Dairy sector, a cheese shop, Courtyard Dairies, is a small business initiative that achieved acclaim from the food and farming awards. In this case it was a small retail outlet promoting niche traditional cheese producers. This case study looks at alternative marketing channels for dairy, but for specialist handmade cheeses.

The UK dairy industry has faced significant restructuring in the last few years. Liquid milk is now predominantly supplied to the major retailers through two key players, Muller and Arla; both are owned by companies based in other EU states. The takeover of the UK dairy processing sector by European competitors was made possible the dissolution of the four UK Milk Marketing Boards, which from the 1930s had protected UK farm gate prices. The decision to remove the boards was an attempt to make the dairy industry more competitive, following measures put in place the Uruguay round of GATT negotiations.

Since the removal of the MMBs, farmers have experienced low prices and as a consequence financial difficulties. Claims are that the cost of producing milk for farmers is greater than farm gate prices. Estimates are that the cost of production vary from 25-30 pence per litre, whereas average farm gate prices, including farm bonus payments, are around 25.57 ppl although those farmers who are on direct contracts within supplier groups are receiving higher prices at around 33 ppl. (Downing, 2016). The survival of dairy farmers, often based in more remote areas can be seen to be critical to the survival of rural communities. Initiatives such as Courtyard Dairies offer alternative solutions and in effect allow farmer to attain greater value from the production of milk.

14

The Courtyard Dairy

The Courtyard Dairy is located off the A65 near Settle in North Yorkshire, in a set of traditional farm-barns alongside six other independent shops and a cafe. From being a derelict barn, they are now an "inspiring, and upmarket rural shopping destination".

Since their opening, Andy and Kathy have attained a number of awards including the 'Cheesemonger of the Year' in 2013 in the World cheese awards and The Farm Shop & Deli Awards 2016. In 2014, they received the award of runner up for the BBC Food and Farming Awards for the Best Food Retailer category. Subsequently they have begun a thriving online business alongside their shop.

Their ethos is to "champion and support the handful of remaining independent British farmhouse cheese makers". And these are cheese makers, who make cheese by hand using milk produced from their own herds. Many of their suppliers are not widely known and the business is as much about educating the consumer as purveyance. Their website very much reflects this focus: https://www.thecourtyarddairy.co.uk.

One of their better known suppliers is Kirkham's Lancashire, but they also have lesser known British and continental cheeses, sometimes from very small holdings of fewer than 50-60 cows. The business does not only buy these cheeses, but in their maturing room, age them, as Andy says, " to perfection".

 Andy's interest in cheese was stimulated during his university studies in Culinary Arts and Wines. Following his placement year in fine-dining, he worked briefly for the oldest UK cheese-monger establishment, Paxton and Whitfield, before going on to be an apprentice with Hervé Mons – one of the most established and recognised "affineurs" in France. His studies were funded by the Queen Elizabeth Scholarship Trust. Following his apprenticeship he returned to the UK and gained experience at Bath's Fine Cheese Company before opening The Courtyard Dairy in 2012.

They were shortlisted for the BBC food and farming best retail award from over 5000 retailers as one of the final three, alongside butcher Edge & Son (in The Wirral) and fishmonger Veasey & Sons (in East Sussex), and the award of runner-up facilitated the growth of the business, after just 15 months of trading.

Before then they had already won awards (World Cheese, British Cheese Awards, Yorkshire Life Food Awards), which in turn had got them national and local press (this brought more business than the award itself); but coming runner up in the BBC Food and Farming Award catapulted them onto a new level. Attracting exactly the right type of clientele in their listening demographic (those interested in quality food and where it comes from), and presenting the shop in its true light with a detailed feature on primetime Radio 4 was a key part in helping increase the shop turnover by double over the following two years. The staff went from two full-time employees to four, almost overnight after their feature on Radio 4.

Not only did it attract the right clientele, but the award also helped by increasing the profile of the shop and its owners, Andy & Kathy, as experts in their field. This meant the press attention would continue to snowball as they were then turned to by other media outlets for information and quotes on British cheese for their articles and features.

Figure 14.1: Andy Swinscoe and his cheese

Interestingly since then the shop has gone onto to win and be runner up in numerous other awards but none have had quite the effect on business as did the BBC Food and Farming Awards.

An alternative way of facilitating the development of local food supply can be found in the next case study. Our Cow Molly is a family run Dairy farm, again in Yorkshire, which has over time developed a range of businesses and its own alternative marketing channels in addition to developing added value products. In effect it operatives as a complete supply chain.

Case study: Our Cow Molly

Cliffe House Farm, located at Dungworth on the outskirts of Sheffield was originally purchased in 1947 by Hector Andrews and is now managed by Graham Andrews and his two sons, Eddie and Dan. The farm operates under the brand name Our Cow Molly, and sells milk to local shops, a local university and the cooperative.

Our Cow Molly is a prime example of pluri-activity. In addition to being a dairy farm, the farm bottles milk to distribute to local shops, produces ice cream, offers short tours around their farm so as to raise awareness of the process of farming and the supply chain, as well as offering entertainment and events such as Bonfire night. The service they offer is a much about education as good quality local dairy products.

14

Hector originally started farming with just 10 cows, which has now grown to a herd of around 80. Originally Hector delivered 'loose milk', decanting it out of churns into tea pots or any vestal the homeowner had available. Later came glass bottles, first with cardboard lids and then foil. The farm bottling plant was also set up by Hector when he took over the farm. Sixty years later, on returning from University, his grandson Eddie saw an opportunity to diversify and use cream, a by-product from the process of skimming milk, to create ice cream. With home produced cream and flavourings from Italy, they entered into the ice cream market, selling to local shops. In 2009, the ice cream had taken 4th place in the national ice cream awards. The emphasis was very much focused on the idea of local, and the distances travelled. The supply of liquid milk to shops and universities has gone from strength to strength. The success of Our Cow Molly is down to the hard work and ingenuity of the Andrew family. They have established a firm business in the Sheffield Area supplying to over 100 businesses, including the Barista coffee bars for which the freshness of the milk and high protein levels are particularly important in the production of a stable foam, as well as all cafes and restaurants located in the University of Sheffield. The deal with the University requires milk for a period of 8-9 months and surplus during the summer is sold to Meadow foods for the ingredients market, a recent move when their previous buyer, a large scale dairy company, ceased to collect milk from the Yorkshire area.

Outside recognition of their achievements has done much promote their interests. In addition to the national ice cream award, Our Cow Molly has twice been a finalist in the Eat Sheffield awards, in 2011 and in 2015. In 2013 they were awarded the Countryside Alliance (Rural Oscars) Yorkshire Champion, and went on to be awarded UK Champion. In 2015, they also received an award in the Great Yorkshire show for their role in educating the public about the journey of food from farm to fork. Their success in becoming the winner of the Future of Farming in 2016 has raised their profile to the extent that more opportunities have come their way.

Having secured funds, from Nat West and the bank's asset finance partner Lombard, they were able to set up a £500,000 dairy, including pasteurising equipment, storage tanks, a milk filling line, cooling tanks and a generator. This has increased the weekly output from 8,000 to 40,000 litres. The establishment of the dairy has enabled the deal signed with the Sheffield Co-op to supply milk produced by Sheffield farmers direct to Sheffield Co-op Supermarket stores. Previously all the milk sourced for the Sheffield Co-op was produced in Yorkshire but needed to be transported to London to be pasteurised and bottled. Their ability to deliver 40,000 litres has been made possible through a collective agreement with two adjacent dairy farmers. In a recent Food Programme, the deal with Cooperative Supermarket has been linked by Eddie to their placement in the awards of 2016 (Food Programme, 2017)

The business continues to move forward, as might be suggested by the title of the award. Future developments include an initiative that stemmed out of a meeting of the Free

Range Dairy group (run by Neil Darwent) which was held at Cliffe House Farm. This stimulated discussions with TUCO, the professional membership and procurement arm of the Higher and Further Educational catering sector. The value for the Andrew family is that TUCO are committed to advancing ethical and sustainable sourcing.

Concluding remarks

The concept of local food has achieved greater prominence over the last two decades, particularly since the publication of the Curry report following the 2001 foot and mouth epidemic. Initiatives such as the Food Programme, the Food and Farming Awards and Eat the View have done much to encourage consumer interest, thereby offering opportunities to small entrepreneurs. Shortened supply chains facilitate the reconnection of consumers with their food, improve farm gate prices and offer a valuable income stream to rural communities and economies. Honouring food producers through awards, whether national cheese awards, recognising their efforts to educate the consumer, or in this case the Food and Farming awards, does much to stimulate the local food agenda, food integrity and indeed sustainable food supply chains. In the cases identified above, this is particular necessary as increasingly dairy farmers find it difficult to survive, given the price negotiated by retailers and dairies, and paid to farmers.

References

BBC Food Programme, http://www.bbc.co.uk/programmes/b006qnx3. Accessed 20/01/2017.

Downing, E. (2016) *The UK Dairy Sector*, House of Commons, CDP, 2016, 100089.

14

15 Brexit: An opportunity for the UK to give more priority to nutrition related health in agricultural policy?

Philippa Griffiths

Introduction

The Brexit vote could be said to be one of the most significant public votes of the 21st century. The effect on agricultural policy could be immense, with the impact reverberating further than the farm gate. This is at a time when global food systems are under intense pressure from the challenges of population increase, demographic change, resource scarcity, food inequality, diet related disease and climate change. These challenges have spawned concerns relating to food security and sustainability (Lang and Barling, 2012). Consequently, post-Brexit it is essential that the United Kingdom (UK) develops a strong agricultural policy that can ensure sustainable food security. Garnett (2013) highlights that the food system is a complex multi-stakeholder field and so the development of post-Brexit policy is likely to be fraught with difficulty. The most powerful policy influencers will be reluctant to alter the established and ingrained political agenda, but they must be persuaded that in the interests of achieving sustainable food security, nutrition related health problems should be given more priority in agricultural policy (Hawkesworth *et al.*, 2010; Sonnino *et al.*, 2014; Lang and Heasman, 2016).

The following section begins by giving a brief contextual history of the European Common Agricultural Policy (EU CAP), followed by a summary of the latest 2013 reforms. It is then argued that whilst environmental considerations have been integrated into the CAP, human nutritional priorities have been neglected and must be considered. This is because diet related health problems continue to escalate, impacting on the security of food systems. We can but speculate on the outcome of the UK break from the EU, nonetheless, it it could be argued that it is an opportunity for the UK to deliver an improved agricultural policy package that will consider a nutrition related health agenda.

Agricultural policy in a historical context

In 1957, the European Common Agricultural Policy was created to form a cooperative alliance in order to support farmers and ensure sufficient food supply for health following the food shortages of the war era (Lang *et al.*, 2009). However, the UK chose to opt out of this alliance, continuing commitment to their own post War agricultural policy that focused on increasing production through state subsidies and industrialisation. This regime dominated the world agricultural market in the 1960s, and has been referred to as the productionist paradigm (Lang and Heasman, 2016). In the midst of world food crisis, the UK joined the CAP in 1975 (Lang *et al.*, 2009). The 1970s was a period of neo-liberalisation in the food sector (sometimes referred to as post productivism), which focused on free enterprise while minimizing as much as possible the role of the state (Oosterveer and Sonnenfeld, 2012). Agricultural policy became less about ensuring health and more about increasing the flexibility and diversity of food products available on the market through an increasingly globalized and complex agri-food supply chain (Oosterveer and Sonnenfeld, 2012). This neo-liberalised political agenda continues to dominate global agriculture in the 21st century.

■ CAP Reform 2013: an opportunity to give more priority to nutrition related health?

Since the introduction of EU CAP there has been a number of reforms to improve policy (Lang *et al.*, 2009). The latest reform in 2013 was a new package for the period 2014-2020. This retained the two pillars of support for farmers and aimed to offer a more holistic and integrated approach that can ensure sustainable food security. Pillar 1 covers direct payments to farmers; this includes a basic payment scheme, which replaces the pre-2013 single farm payment. This reform also included the introduction of a greening component, giving additional payments to farms for environmental friendly farming practices. The introduction of greening in Pillar 1 aimed to achieve more connection with Pillar 2, which focuses on rural development including financial payments for agri-environment schemes (European Commission, 2016).

15

Agri-environment schemes were first integrated into the CAP in the 1980s, due to increasing concerns for environmental sustainability as a result of intensive farming. Marston and Morley (2014) argue that in the 1980s nutritional sustainability was not developed in the same way as environmental sustainability. This is despite evidence emerging at this time against a regime that focused on quantity over quality (Robbins, 1979). A direct and indirect consequence of such policy was that diseases related to overconsumption began to escalate (Lang *et al.*, 2009). In the 21st century, diet is the foremost cause of global obesity and other conditions such as cardiovascular disease (WHO, 2000). As a result of these health problems the World Health Organisation (WHO) produced a Global Strategy on Diet, Physical Activity and Health (WHO, 2004) and recommended that agricultural policy should integrate nutritional health concerns. The inherent assumption of this measure was that policy has the power to influence food price and availability (Dangour *et al.*, 2013). However, the 2013 CAP reform failed to address any of the concerns raised by the WHO report with respect to the relationship between agricultural activity and human nutrition, beyond actuating a focus on ensuring sufficient production.

CAP and public health

The priorities of CAP are mainly focused on ensuring economic sustainability, a facet which presents certain difficulties for the integration in policy of nutrition related health concerns (Kirwan and Maye, 2013). Agricultural policy focuses on progress and wealth creation through economic growth and liberalised agricultural trade, as driven by a commitment to sustainable intensification (Tomlinson (2013). Sustainable intensification, defined as increasing yields without adverse environmental impact or increasing the area of land under cultivation (Baulcombe *et al.*, 2009), applies technology, such as precision agriculture, to increase efficiency whilst decreasing environment damage. It is argued that sustainable intensification overly focuses on delivering sufficient calories rather than nutritional quality (Hawkesworth *et al.*, 2010).

CAP, it is suggested, overly focuses on ensuring that there is adequate food production, a feature which stems from the initial motive for the introduction of CAP, which, as already stated, was to prevent malnutrition after the War era (Lang and Heasman, 2016). With rising issues of national health, the EU CAP policy now needs to adapt to problems of overconsumption of diets high in fat, sugar and salt, and low in fruit, vegetables and whole grains.

This has proved difficult for a number of reasons. One reason is that CAP stakeholders (largely agri-business) believe that nutrition related health is not a mandate for agricultural policy, and that diet related health problems should be continued to be dealt with through demand side interventions such as educational campaigns, health promotion and better food labelling (Walls *et al.*, 2016). It has been suggested that in this way the consumer's ability to select a healthy diet, will not be impeded by the dynamics of the market – the neo-liberal political agenda (Garnett, 2013).

Similarly it is argued that the EU CAP serves the interests of many stakeholders, with a variety of interests and perspectives which give issues other than nutrition greater political clout. Such stakeholders include retailers, food manufacturers, farming organisations, government and non-government agencies, who have various priorities associated with markets and resource efficiencies (Griffiths, 2016).

Despite these difficulties, Walls *et al.* (2016) suggest that with better communication between different stakeholders and a clearer EU mandate it would be possible to achieve greater priority for nutrition and health in EU CAP. In a UK context, it is concluded that if stakeholder's values are fully understood and effectively communicated it is possible to find some common ground (Griffiths, 2016). However, both these studies highlight that policy will not be changed without strong engagement from public health experts and civil society organisations. The Brexit vote should be seen by these groups as an opportunity to campaign to construct a new UK agriculture policy that integrates nutrition related health concerns.

Referendum 2016 speculation

In the referendum, nutrition related health held little or no ground in the debates on agriculture. Discussion was engulfed by uncertain and controversial speculation mainly focused on economic issues. Supporters of Brexit, such as the organisation Farmers for Britain, focused on benefits such as the reduction of red tape and regulation, with suggestion that a vote out of Europe would encourage European countries to negotiate new more desirable trade deals (Farmers for Britain, 2016). The Brexit camp argued that greater political sovereignty would enable the UK to increase food production and become more food secure. In polarisation, Bremain supporters stressed that by remaining in the EU the UK would have negotiating power to improve CAP (Swinbank, 2016). The National Farmers Union (NFU) openly supported the Bremain position after their commissioned report concluded a vote to leave Europe would have a significant negative impact on farm incomes. The potential damage to UK sheep farmers was particularly highlighted, as this industry relies heavily on CAP subsidies (Van Berkum *et al.*, 2016). In agreement the DEFRA secretary Liz Truss voiced concerns that the Brexit vote would risk the EU trading mutton and lamb with New Zealand and Australia rather than

15

the UK (Case, 2016). Similarly to sheep farming, the dairy industry is heavily subsidised by the EU, with the NFU report warning that a vote to leave could be fatal for small family farms struggling with milk prices (Van Berkum *et al.*, 2016). In contrast, farming minster George Eustice insisted that Brexit would benefit the industry, with political sovereignty enabling better action on issues such as milk regulations (Driver, 2016). Behind the main political arguments a report commissioned by the Food Research Collaboration (Lang and Schoen, 2016) warned that a Brexit decision could threaten UK consumption of fruit and vegetables, as the country is 40% reliant on EU imports. At the same time UK fruit farms would be put under pressure due to the lack of availability of migrant workers. The British consumer's average intake is below the recommended intake of 5 a day, but even at these consumption levels, it is stated a Brexit vote could have considerable impact on diet. This statement stresses the importance that nutrition related health is considered now the vote to leave Europe has been decided.

Post-Brexit: What is the way forward?

At the current date (September 2016) speculation continues over how UK agriculture will be effected by Brexit, with the full effect not likely to be revealed for some years (Swinbank, 2016). The NFU are wary that the government will marginalise agricultural concerns and have stated that the organisation is committed to ensuring that farmers get a fair deal (Raymond, 2016). At present it is known that the government Treasury will retain the current level of agricultural funding under CAP Pillar 1 until 2020. As part of Pillar 2, agri-environment schemes signed and agreed before the autumn statement 2016 will be fully funded, but funding past 2020 is uncertain. The political uncertainty is causing schemes financed by Pillar 2 to be stalled, including diversification projects that can be integral to the survival of smaller farms (Midgley *et al.*, 2016). These initial announcements suggest that the government is continuing to equate increasing food production with food security, as retaining subsidies within Pillar 1 has been prioritised over Pillar 2. The lack of assurance given over agri-environmental schemes is an indication that environmental sustainability may be put at risk. It is worrying that these early announcements suggest that the UK government will create a policy "that clings to the architecture and infrastructures of the productionist and post production-ist agri-food regimes" (Marston and Morley, 2014), becoming what DeShutter (2011) calls a neo-productionist paradigm. If this speculation proves correct, the integration of nutritional concerns into agricultural policy will be low priority, consequently it will be essential that public health experts and civil society organisations work in collaboration to push forward the nutritional agenda.

Concluding remarks

Food system challenges will not be tackled by an interpretation of sustainable food security that influences agricultural policy to overly focus on increasing food production within a neo-liberal agenda. The public health crisis calls for more response than just demand side interventions. The Brexit vote is an opportunity to give more priority to nutrition related health concerns in agricultural policy. However, considering the current climate of uncertainty and fear this seems unlikely, but it is hoped that at the least some progress will be made, with stronger engagement in the agricultural policy debate from public health experts and civil society organisations.

References

Baulcombe, D., Crute, I., Davies, B., Dunwell, J. G., M., Jones, J., Pretty, J. and Sutherland, W. T. C. (2009). *Reaping the benefits: Science and the sustainable intensification of global agriculture*. London: The Royal Society.

Case, P. (2016). Truss: Brexit could risk livelihoods of 10,000 sheep farmers. *Farmers Weekly*. http://www.fwi.co.uk/truss-brexit-could-risk-livelihoods-of-10,000-sheep-farmers.htm. Accessed 11/09/2016.

Dangour, A., Hawkesworth, S., Shankar, B., Srinivasan, C., Morgan, E., Watson, L., Mehrotra, S., Haddad, L. and Waage, J. (2013). Can nutrition be promoted through agriculture-led food price policy? *British Medical Journal* Open 3, e002937.

De Schutter, O. (2011). The right of everyone to enjoy the benefits of scientific progress and the right to food: From conflict to complementarity. *Human Rights Quarterly*, **33** 304-305.

Driver, A. (2016). Brexit vote - what are the implications for UK farming? *Farmers Guardian*. https://www.fginsight.com/vip/vip/brexit-vote---what-are-the-implications-for-uk-farming-13146. Accessed 15/09/2016.

European Commission, (2016). The Common Agricultural Policy After 2013. http://www.ec.europa.eu/agriculture/cap-post-2013/. Accessed 3/09/2016.

Farmers for Britain, (2016). Brexit offers great opportunity, http://www.farmersforbritain.co.uk/blog-1/date/2016-04. Accessed 12/12/2016]

Garnett, T. (2013). Food sustainability: Problems, perspectives and solutions. *Proceedings of Nutrition Society*, **72** (1), pp. 29-39.

Griffiths, P. O. (2016). UK public health in crisis: Understanding stakeholder values regarding sustainable food security and its relationship with public health. MRes thesis (Agri food systems and health). Newport: Harper Adams University.

Hawkesworth, S., Dangour, D.A, Johnson, D., Lock, K., Poole, N., Ruston, J., Uauy, R. and Waage, J. (2010). Feeding the world healthily: the challenge of measuring the

15

effects of agriculture on health. *Philosophical Transactions of the Royal Society*, **365**, 3083-3097.

Kirwan, J. and Maye, D. (2013). Food security framings within the UK and the integration of local food systems. *Journal of Rural Studies*, **29**, 91-100.

Lang, T., Barling, D. and Caraher, M. (2009). *Food Policy: Integrating health, environment and society*. Oxford: Oxford University Press.

Lang, T and Barling, D. (2012). Food security and food sustainability: Reformulating the debate. *Geographical Journal*, **178** (4), 313-320.

Lang, T. and Heasman, M. (2016). *Food Wars. The global battle for minds, mouths and markets*. London: Earthscan.

Lang, T and Schoen, V. (2016). *Food, the UK and the EU: Brexit or Bremain?* UK: Food Research Collaboration.

Oosterveer, P. and Sonnenfeld, D.A. (2012). *Food, Globalization and Sustainability*. Routledge.

Marsden, T. and Morley, A. (2014). *Sustainable Food Systems: Building a new paradigm*. Abingdon: Routledge.

Midgley, O., Kidd, M. and Singleton, A. (2016). Plunged into the unknown. *Farmers Guardian*, 19th August, pp.2-3.

Raymond, M. (2016). EU Referendum Result: NFU statement. National Farmers Union. http://www.nfuonline.com/news/latest-news/eu-referendum-result-nfu-statement. Accessed on 12/09/2016.

Robbins, C.J. (1979). *National Food Policy for the UK*. Reading: University of Reading centre for Agricultural Strategy.

Sonnino, R., Morgagues, F. and Maggio, A. (2014). Sustainable food security: An emerging research policy agenda. *International Journal of the Sociology of Agricultural and Food*, **21** (1), 173-188.

Swinbank, A. (2016). Brexit or Bremain? Future options for agricultural policy and the CAP. *Eurochoices*, **15** (2) 5-10.

Tomlinson, I. (2013). Doubling food production to feed 9 billon: A critical perspective on a key discourse of food security in the UK. *Journal of Rural Studies*, **29**, 81-90.

Van Berkum, S. Jongenel, R.A., Van Leeuwen, M.G.A., and Jager, J.H. (2016). *Implications of a UK exit from the EU for British agriculture; Study for the National Farmers Union* (NFU), Warwickshire, UK. LEI Wageningen UR (University and Research centre).

Walls, H.L., Cornelsen, L., Lock, K. and Smith, R.D., (2016). How much priority is given to nutrition and health in the EU Common Agricultural Policy? *Food Policy*, **59**,12-23

WHO (2000). *Obesity: Preventing and Managing the Global Epidemic*. World Health Organ Technical Report Series 894. Geneva, World Health Organization.

WHO, (2004). *Global Strategy on Diet, Physical Activity and Health*. Geneva, World Health Organization.

Index

Printed in the United States
By Bookmasters